My Parent the Peacock

My Parent the Peacock

Discovery and Recovery from
Narcissistic Parenting

KATHLEEN SAXTON, DIP. PSYCH

sheldon PRESS

First published by Sheldon Press in 2025
An imprint of John Murray Press

1

A CIP catalogue record for this title is available from the British Library

Trade Paperback ISBN 978 1 39982 259 6
ebook ISBN 978 1 39982 260 2

Typeset by KnowledgeWorks Global Ltd.

Printed and bound in Great Britain by Clays Ltd, Elcograf S.p.A.

John Murray Press policy is to use papers that are natural, renewable and recyclable products and made from wood grown in sustainable forests. The logging and manufacturing processes are expected to conform to the environmental regulations of the country of origin.

John Murray Press
Carmelite House
50 Victoria Embankment
London EC4Y 0DZ

Sheldon Press
Hachette Book Group
123 South Broad Street
Ste 2750
Philadelphia, PA 19109, USA

www.sheldonpress.co.uk

John Murray Press, part of Hodder & Stoughton Limited
An Hachette UK company

The authorised representative in the EEA is Hachette Ireland, 8 Castlecourt Centre, Dublin 15, D15 XTP3, Ireland (email: info@hbgi.ie)

To my beloved children, Ned and Nancy – you are the greatest treasures of my lifetime. Your boundless love, mischievous humour and unswerving empathy blow my mind. Watching you independently soar, in your own light, is beyond human privilege. To the extraordinary children I've also been blessed to love and nurture along life's path, know that in my heart you will always find a loving home.

Contents

Acknowledgements

To the three remarkable Victorias who breathed life into this book: Victoria Roddam, my incredible publisher, who had the insight and courage to ignite this journey. Victoria Hobbs, my worldclass literary agent, who has guided my raw determination into something meaningful. And Victoria Zimmerman, who gifted me the courage to believe I could write at all – thank you for standing by my side with unwavering faith and kindness.

My professional thanks to Ella Dolphin for the fundamental genesis, Kyriaki Plyta for her unswerving patience and to Gaby Hollis for designing the images.

My personal thanks to: Kendall, Suki, Alia, Jesse, Laura, Kristina, Shula, Lehvashnee, Katalin, Rebecca, Rick, Dan G, Alexandra, Brad, Sandra, Andrew, Tom, Gaylin, Seth, Moon, David L, Carly, Claire, Maria, and Elaine. Thank you for being my urban family.

Finally, and most profoundly, to all the children of narcissistic parents and the courageous souls who sit with me in therapy rooms – this book is for you. My sincere hope is within these pages you will discover a pathway to finally acknowledging and validating the pain you carry, encouragement to ignite your curiosity, and meaningful guidance towards understanding. May you close its cover with inner strength, meaningful hope, and a renewed belief in the power of your own recovery and freedom.

Introduction

We are all somebody's child.

No matter how historic that date is on our birth certificate, we all came into this world with the innocent hope our parents and caregivers would forever offer a place of acceptance, encouragement, and love. A secure harbour to which we could bring our true selves with our triumphant hopes and ambitions, along with the defeats and wounds that every life can dispense, and know, unconditionally, that we would always be safe.

In our critical formative years, how we experience the world provides a template and a model for us to observe and potentially follow behaviourally and emotionally. Our interactions with our parents and the associated experiences, therefore, also provide the informative grounding for our intimate and critical relationships later in life. Our parents, and those who choose to bring us into and up in the world, hence have a duty of care to us as their children. Once just tiny, fragile, and developing humans, our need to be nurtured and cared for in ways that allow us to flourish, as independent people, is critical. Safe in the knowledge that those around us are only acting in our best interests. Their honouring of that unique position of trust has proven to be a fundamental indicator of the success of any child, with the ambition that one day we become a psychologically healthy adult, who can feel grateful and thankful for the care that our parents lovingly ensured we experienced.

When that duty of care is psychologically fractured, abused, distorted, or manipulated, it can do incredible and long-lasting harm to a child, no matter their age. As research continually seeks further to understand and appreciate the emotional and societal outcomes any distortions or harm imposed on any child may have, we further uncover the potential lifetime impact and consequences that child may need to realize and ultimately address.

Much has been written and understood about the devastation of both physical and sexual abuse towards a child at the hands of a parent or caregiver, especially across the last four decades. It has rightfully been met with the horror and condemnation it so searingly deserves. Thanks to legislations such as the 1989 and subsequent 2004 Children's Act, to the profile of organizations such as the National Society for the Prevention of Cruelty to Children (NSPCC), ChildLine, and many others, awareness and additional prevention strategies and protections, while not perfect, are now better in place. We are increasingly able, in a growing number of cases, to offer the critical helplines, emotional and physical protections, support, and the psychological therapies and treatments required to provide some level of acknowledgement and hope of healing for the children impacted by their abusive caregivers.

However, as we entered the twenty-first century there emerged a new level of harm we now identify as psychological abuse, ranging from coercive control to verbal bullying, physical to emotional neglect, emotional incest and enmeshment, parental alienation, and psychological manipulation as well as neglect by omission. Each, in their own right, abuse – but often in varied combinations. While this can sadly occur in any class, culture, religion, or nationality, it is often hidden within families, something we will discuss in depth in this book, and there appears to be a growing correlation between this abusive behaviour and when a parent is either diagnosed with or shows deep traits of a narcissistic personality.

The phenomenon of narcissistic parenting has been documented for decades, and its effects are both pervasive and damaging. The signs of narcissistic parents can be difficult to detect, but the emotional impact they have on their children and grandchildren is profound. Yet since 2020, the noise, discussion, column inches, and social media frenzy around narcissism has reached a crescendo. The term 'narcissistic' has entered the vernacular of everyday life around the world, and yet so much about the condition and its impact is still misunderstood.

Research continues to reveal the long-lasting harm caused by narcissistic parents and grandparents, with studies highlighting the emotional and psychological challenges faced by their children. Understanding and recognizing these patterns is the first step in breaking the cycle of narcissistic abuse, ensuring that future generations can grow up in healthier, more supportive environments.

While in many ways the increase of awareness opened up the chamber of intrigue, there is equally a dramatic level of misinformation that has arisen around the term 'narcissism'. This has unfortunately threatened to dilute the true impact of this mental health condition and personality disorder with false, amateur, and unqualified accusations and utilizations of the word employed merely as verbal weaponry. In this way, we risk diminishing the tremendous damage those with narcissistic personalities, or those diagnosed with Narcissistic Personality Disorder (NPD), inflict on the individuals around them. With the word 'narcissism' increasingly used as a mere side swipe or slight when someone is simply being a little self-centred, we need to work hard to bring clinical understanding to the fallout from this condition and allow those who have to suffer the lived experience and consequences at the hands of a narcissist to be heard and respected.

My Parent the Peacock has been written for anyone who suspects, knows, or wonders if they have grown up with or around a narcissistic parent and has witnessed, experienced, and suffered under the challenging and deeply wounding impact they can have. Recognizing the growing number of people – aged from 12 to 86 – who have begun to enter my therapy rooms since 2015, to enquire and quietly question whether indeed their mother or father is or was in fact a narcissist, has felt like the tip of an iceberg. In undertaking extensive research groups and interviews over the past year, in preparation for publishing this book, I have uncovered a depth of evidence in the adult children who have experienced decades of pain at the hands of parental narcissism which indicated to me a need to highlight this growing phenomenon more overtly, and offer understanding and healing to all those who have suffered or still suffer.

As you explore and further educate yourself through the early chapters, I very much hope the research, real-life case studies, and expert opinions will validate your experiences and allow you, and those you might share this book with, to understand the experiences and difficulties you have grown up dealing with. Later, progressively offering you new ideas, approaches, and pathways might help you accept, protect, and encourage you to find a more liberated, healthy, and optimistic way forward. A journey from understanding and acknowledgement towards healing – for the adult you are now and the inner splintered little parts that grew up dealing with your parent the peacock.

Living with the suspicion, question, or knowledge that you have a parent who is a narcissist may have been an isolating and lonely position to be in. Our friends who have experienced regulated, safe, and loving parents may struggle to fathom, from the outside, why we hurt so deeply and avoid, suppress, and struggle to maintain a positive family dynamic. They too may have been enthralled by our seemingly charismatic, demure, or charming peacock parent and, with good intentions, are eager for us to mend or heal parental discord, little knowing how much their actions in fact only further invalidate our truth. Yet they have no concept of the quantum of battle wounds and weeping scars we quietly nurse just to get through another birthday, another Christmas, or another family wedding.

I hope these pages will encourage you to recognize and trust your experience and know that you are understood and believed – by me and so many more.

There may even be some brave parents themselves who have been challenged or accused of narcissism who are willing to explore whether they indeed demonstrate elements of narcissistic traits. Perhaps they might be willing to seek support and help in order to facilitate change, with a hope of salvaging a relationship with their children, grandchildren or wider family while they remain on this beautiful planet.

So, while not strictly an academic, I offer you, as a qualified and practising psychotherapist, fellow human, daughter, mother, stepmother – and brave and embattled survivor of narcissistic abuse – my clinical knowledge, lived experience, and ongoing deep study into this devastating personality type. I hope by illuminating the frightening, the silent, the engulfing, the aggressive, the inconsistent, the cold, the overwhelming and simply bizarre upbringing you may have endured and may still be living, we can, together, come to terms with and navigate how to manage the situation in whichever way feels right for you from this moment on. From grieving for the relationship you did not have, before or after your parents' death; to seeking resolution if viable; to simply creating firm boundaries; to finally cutting off the parent completely; or indeed tackling the parent in the present day and accepting the situation with or without a diagnosis, I welcome all children who have been emotionally and psychologically hurt – you are so absolutely no longer alone, and this book is here to offer you a place of recognition and hope after all you have endured.

In a defiant act on behalf of all of you who have been belittled or demeaned for even introducing the notion of narcissism into the family, I have purposefully commenced this book with an avalanche of facts, statistics, and published research to set the ground for the more emotive and therapeutic chapters later on. It is important as we tackle this phenomenon in the world that we are equipped with empirical evidence to allow us truly to believe and understand what we are experiencing and to stand our ground when the narcissists and their enablers attempt to invalidate our experiences and resultant feelings. I invite and encourage you to endure and absorb the opening chapter before you move into the emotional and human elements, to ensure you stand firm on a solid foundation of proof, fact, and knowledge as you emerge into a world of deeper awareness and answers.

Most of all, I hope with every good fibre in my body that these pages will enlighten, embolden, and equip you to stride forward. You have suffered and endured your narcissistic parent for long enough in your lifetime, so I offer you fortitude to reach a new place of freedom, for the rest of your lifetime.

You are believed and, most importantly, in being seen you will heal.

Kathleen

1

Narcissism today

An introduction to the history and psychological advances in understanding narcissism

Narcissistic Personality Disorder is the only mental condition where the patient is left alone while everyone else needs treatment.

Narcissism has become the epidemic of the twenty-first century. Through the acceleration of developmental research by clinical psychologists, the breakthrough into societal awareness by expert academics, and a better understanding of the spectrum of symptoms and behaviours at the diagnostic stage, we are now highly conversant, certainly at the topline, as to what Narcissistic Personality Disorder may look and feel like when we are in its presence and with it the challenges both gaining diagnosis and any subsequent support can bring.

There is a clinical joke that goes: 'Narcissists are the only people in their family not in therapy or on anxiety medication.' For this is a condition which, while internally challenging to those who suffer with it, can create even greater psychological and emotional trauma to those close enough to be impacted by a parent, partner, or boss afflicted with it.

The concept of a duplex of pain vividly illustrates the intricate and often devastating emotional experiences associated with both being a narcissist and living with one. This dual-layered pain encompasses the internal struggles of the narcissist themselves, grappling with their own emotional vulnerabilities, and the external suffering endured by those in close relationships with them. This creates a complex psychological landscape marked by profound distress, manipulation, and emotional turmoil. In their desperate attempts to defend, cover, and mask their inner wounds, narcissists can bestow such crippling psychological and emotional damage behind closed doors on those closest to them, in an attempt to remain unchallenged or undetected, that some of their partners even suffer irreversible breakdowns.

For me, it is a condition so often hidden in plain sight that the secondary impact on those most acutely affected is not fully believed or understood when they reach for help or support from friends or family members around them – because that circle has (at a slight distance) already been successfully hoodwinked or manipulated by these, often charming, individuals. This increases further the devastation this condition causes to the partners and children most impacted in finding support and recovery.

What does the word 'narcissism' *really* mean?

'Narcissism' is no longer simply a diagnostic term reserved for psychiatrists and researchers, but a common term now equally in the vernacular of everyday relationships, corporate offices, and even playgrounds. Yet while the topic of narcissism has become ubiquitous in modern discourse, it has a deep, often misunderstood, and complex history. A wealth of misinformation around the word has infiltrated pop psychology, social media, and dinner-party conversations and with it has grown an elevated risk of cynicism and a dilution, away from offering help and support to those who suffer and, in fact, a growing resentfulness and comic dismissal of those brave enough to enquire or explain what they might be battling. This can lead to an individual's suffering being further diminished and overlooked while they try to cope with someone in their lives, often someone they love, who is psychologically destroying them whilst no one is looking.

The roots of the word, as we all know, can be traced back to the Greek myth of Narcissus, a youth who fell in love with his reflection in a pool of water, ultimately leading to his demise. However, the clinical understanding of narcissism emerged much later, largely through the work of pioneering psychoanalysts and psychologists, professors, practitioners, and academic researchers who continue to produce a wealth of theories on narcissism and their own translations of the expanding data. I have listed towards the end of the book some of the seminal papers and research now cited as we begin further to understand the difficulty and challenge of narcissism, ranging from theoretical discussions to empirical studies, all of which I offer to those of you who seek to study a little further. Knowledge brings consciousness, and once we are conscious, we are afforded the power of choice. This research has contributed to our growing awareness and understanding of how narcissistic traits in parents in particular can affect their children's psychological and emotional development, so we owe a great deal of gratitude to those who have uncovered and continue to explore this destructive condition, ranging from Freud all the way through to current-day academics such as Professor Sam Vaknin and the well-known Dr Ramani.

Freud and narcissism

It was not until the late nineteenth and early twentieth centuries that narcissism began to gain traction as an actual psychological diagnosis. The early exploration of narcissism began with *On Narcissism: An Introduction* by Sigmund Freud, who expanded the term beyond its mythical roots to describe a critical stage of early childhood development. Freud posited that all individuals go through a phase of primary narcissism, where the libido is focused on the self. This self-love is considered normal in early development, where the child is rather omnipotent, unaware of the difference between itself and others, but issues arise when the child never outgrows this stage, leading to what Freud called 'secondary narcissism', where the individual becomes fixated on themselves to the detriment of relationships with others.

Freud's theory laid the groundwork for understanding narcissism as a personality trait that could exist on a spectrum, ranging from normal self-esteem to pathological self-absorption. He also linked narcissism to other psychological conditions, such as schizophrenia, where an individual's withdrawal from reality reflects the self-centred nature of pathological narcissism.

Formal recognition of narcissism as a personality disorder began much later, with the publication of the third edition of the *Diagnostic and Statistical Manual of Mental Disorders* (DSM-III) by the American Psychiatric Association in 1980. This is the manual all psychiatrists and psychotherapists are trained with to aid them in identifying and diagnosing mental illnesses when required. Certainly, the DSM has many detractors, but the fact remains that, along with the International

Classification of Diseases (10th edition), it is used today by the mental health profession and health insurers alike to support diagnosis and offer coding and treatment plans across many mental health presentations.

As our understanding of narcissism evolved, so too did the way in which we make a distinction between narcissistic traits (traits we most probably all have under certain conditions), narcissistic personality (a consistent and pervasive sense of self-importance and lack of empathy for others), and Narcissistic Personality Disorder, a specific diagnosis that now resides within the broader category of what we clinically term personality disorders.

Personality disorders are a category characterized by enduring patterns of behaviour, cognition, and inner experience that deviate markedly from the expectations of an individual's culture. These patterns are inflexible, pervasive, and lead to distress or impairment in various aspects of life, such as relationships, work, or social functioning.

The DSM groups personality disorders into three clusters based on descriptive similarities. Narcissism now sits in what we call 'Cluster B'. This cluster includes three other personality disorders: Borderline Personality Disorder (BPD), Antisocial Personality Disorder (ASPD), and Histrionic Personality Disorder (HPD). Cluster B is referred to as the 'dramatic, emotional, or erratic' cluster and shares common features, such as emotional dysregulation, impulsivity, and difficulties in maintaining stable relationships. Individuals with these disorders often experience intense emotions, have difficulty controlling their impulses, and engage in behaviours that can be harmful to themselves or others. However, as the longer-term effects of childhood trauma, Post-Traumatic Stress Disorder (PTSD), and parental neglect become better understood, the therapeutic world is awakening to the potential that there lies a risk of misdiagnoses. Symptoms and behaviours of individuals who have suffered in their early life can sometimes mimic those of people with Cluster B behaviours and so further study and work are being undertaken to explore how we can better identify those who are simply responding to challenging and traumatic childhood experiences versus those who may truly be diagnosable within this cluster.

Like other B cluster disorders, NPD can lead to tumultuous relationships, impulsive behaviours, and challenges in maintaining a stable sense of self. It is classified as a personality disorder because it meets these criteria:

- **Enduring patterns:** NPD involves long-standing and persistent behaviours and thought patterns that are consistent over time and across different situations.
- **Deviance from norms:** Individuals with NPD exhibit behaviours and attitudes that deviate significantly from cultural norms, particularly in terms of how they relate to others.
- **Inflexibility:** The traits associated with NPD are rigid and resistant to change, even in the face of negative consequences.
- **Impairment and distress:** NPD leads to significant impairment in relationships, work, and other areas of life. It can also cause distress to the individual or those around them.

Narcissistic Personality Disorder was at that point in 1980 (and to a large degree still in 2025) defined by a pervasive pattern of grandiosity, need for admiration, and lack of empathy, beginning in early adulthood and present in a variety of contexts. The inclusion of NPD in the DSM marked a shift in our understanding of narcissism as a mere personality trait to a diagnosable mental health condition, but was simply recognized as a one-size-fits-all descriptor.

The spectrum of narcissistic presentations

The debate over the number of distinct types of narcissism reflects the complexity and evolving understanding of Narcissistic Personality Disorder. Professor Sam Vaknin, a well-known figure in the field of narcissism, posits in his work in 2003 that there are essentially two primary types of narcissism: grandiose and vulnerable. Vaknin argues that these types encompass the core manifestations of narcissism, with grandiose narcissism characterized by overt arrogance and a sense of entitlement, while vulnerable narcissism includes more covert forms of self-absorption and sensitivity. According to Vaknin, these two types cover the spectrum of narcissistic traits, and additional subtypes are variations or extensions of these core categories.

However, many psychologists and researchers contend that the diversity within narcissistic behaviours and traits necessitates a more nuanced classification. Theories and frameworks developed by various experts propose that narcissism can manifest in several distinct forms beyond just grandiose and vulnerable. For example, the classification includes malignant narcissism, which combines elements of grandiosity with antisocial and sadistic tendencies, and communal narcissism, where individuals exhibit narcissistic traits through a façade of altruism and moral superiority. These distinctions highlight the multifaceted nature of narcissism and suggest that a more granular approach is needed to understand its various manifestations and impacts.

The ongoing dispute over the number of narcissistic types underscores the broader challenge of categorizing complex psychological conditions. While Vaknin's binary model provides a streamlined perspective, the diversity of narcissistic behaviours observed in clinical practice and research supports the argument for a broader typology. By recognizing and differentiating between multiple forms of narcissism, researchers and clinicians can better address the unique needs and challenges associated with each type, leading to more effective treatment and support strategies. This debate reflects the dynamic nature of psychological research, as our understanding of narcissism continues to evolve with ongoing study and clinical experience.

As the decades have passed, many psychoanalysts and psychologists have agreed with the expansion of our understanding of differing presentations and roots of the disorder. Interestingly (and I believe importantly), in 2022 there was an alternative addition offered into the manual which included a more broadly psychopathological construct of 'vulnerable' narcissism (including manipulativeness, callousness, and deceitfulness). 'Vulnerable' narcissism is often masked behind a victim position, the narcissist displaying a quiet, humble charm, showing what we as clinicians call 'performative emotions' – displayed purely to misdirect the crowd or to pretend they care about others, when in fact they only pretend to do so, as a route towards gaining further recognition or acceptance. So, while we looked for grandiosity as the clue, many were going under the radar with their seemingly introverted personalities while their subverted narcissism was running wild. It was these 'vulnerable' narcissists (you may know them better as 'covert') who brought the greatest psychological damage to relationships and families, as their wider social circle simply could not reconcile the pleasant and performative individual they themselves encountered versus the palpable cruelty and abusive regime the victim later described.

Key to much of the progress over the last 50 years have been a number of brilliant individuals, each with their own theories and approaches. I have summarized some of them in the Further Reading section of this book for those of you keen to understand the impact and advancements we have made in uncovering critical aspects of this condition, which have allowed us better to understand the complexity and often explain our lived experiences.

- Otto Kernberg distinguished between normal and pathological narcissism.
- Heinz Kohut proposed the 'Self-Psychology' model, introducing the idea of lack of emotional attunement from parents.
- Robert Raskin and Calvin S. Hall introduced the Narcissistic Personality Inventory.
- D. L. Paulhus and K. M. Williams identified the 'Dark Triad' of personality traits: narcissism, Machiavellianism, and psychopathy. This research highlighted the overlap between narcissism and other socially aversive traits, showing how individuals with prominent levels of narcissism often engage in manipulative and exploitative behaviours.

Additionally, the creation of the Pathological Narcissism Inventory (PNI) by Aaron L. Pincus and colleagues was designed to assess both grandiose and vulnerable aspects of narcissism, reflecting a more nuanced understanding of the disorder.

In the twenty-first century, advancements in neuroscience have equally provided new insights into the biological underpinnings of narcissism. Neuroimaging studies have identified abnormalities in brain regions associated with empathy, self-processing, and emotional regulation in individuals with NPD. For example, studies by Schulze et al. and Scalabrini et al. found differences in brain areas with those who demonstrated narcissistic personalities. These findings suggest that different forms of narcissism may have distinct neurobiological profiles.

More recent research has focused on explaining in more detail the subtypes of narcissism, particularly the distinction between grandiose and vulnerable narcissism. A study by Krizan and Herlache (2021) proposed a continuum model of narcissism, where grandiose and vulnerable traits are not seen as separate categories but as dimensions that can coexist within an individual. This model has implications for diagnosis and treatment, suggesting that therapeutic approaches should be tailored to the specific narcissistic profile of the patient.

The growing population of narcissism

If you want to heal from being parented by a narcissist, or help someone who has, you're probably keen to get to the more practical steps in this book. Have patience, because understanding the prevalence of narcissistic traits, Narcissistic Personality (NP), and Narcissistic Personality Disorder is important for grasping the scale of these conditions. Making an accurate estimate is a challenge, when we remember that narcissistic traits – which can be found on a spectrum from mild to severe – are quite common. Many people exhibit some level of narcissistic traits without meeting the criteria for NPD. The exact prevalence of these traits is difficult to pin down, but in an attempt to size this for you, here is a breakdown of estimates and diagnosed cases globally, and specifically for the UK and the USA.

Global surveys and studies estimate that around 10–15 per cent of the general population exhibits moderate to high levels of narcissistic traits. This is based on self-report questionnaires and personality assessments that measure traits such as grandiosity, entitlement, and a lack of empathy.

In the UK, it is estimated that about 12 per cent of the population may exhibit narcissistic traits based on similar survey methods and psychological studies.

In the USA, the figure is slightly higher, with approximately 15 per cent of people showing notable narcissistic traits, reflecting a culture that may promote individualism and self-focus.

On a global scale, NPD (the actual disorder) appears to be less commonly diagnosed than other personality disorders. The overall prevalence is about 1 per cent globally, which translates to about 1 in 200 individuals, though this number varies by region and income level. Research shows that high-income countries tend to have higher rates of personality disorders, very probably due to better diagnostic resources. For example, personality disorders in general are reported in 10 per cent of the population in high-income countries compared with 4.3 per cent in low- and middle-income countries.

In the USA, an estimated 0.5–6.2 per cent of the population may actually have NPD, depending on the diagnostic criteria used. A study found that about 6.2 per cent of people in the USA meet the diagnostic criteria for NPD, making it one of the more prevalent personality disorders in the country, following obsessive-compulsive and borderline personality disorders.

Men or women?

Interestingly, it is still reported that NPD may disproportionately affect men, with around 50–75 per cent of diagnosed individuals being male, although many academics, Prof. Sam Vaknin included, continue to dispute this. In undertaking the research for this book and from my own clinical experience, I am inclined to agree with him. As you will see, the impact of narcissistic mothers was noticeably prevalent in the research and case studies undertaken in preparing to write this book. We wonder as a therapeutic community whether women are more likely to be diagnosed with BPD and HPD than NPD given the partial crossover in presentation. Equally and importantly, the potential longtail of sexism given 'overly emotional' women (let's all collectively make an eye roll) seems a lazy and misogynistic diagnosis, no longer accepted by those of us aware of the complications in hand where women are seen as more 'emotionally dysregulated' (difficulty in managing and responding to emotional experiences) and so, are keener to look at BPD as a diagnosis when in fact it could be NPD. As already mentioned, we then need to explore the childhood history to understand whether there is trauma also present in the prognosis. With labels of both narcissism and borderline becoming more present in the everyday vernacular, this is a sensitive and delicate area which requires qualified and tender exploration, but one I wanted to highlight for you as you seek to understand further what you may be working with.

In the UK, estimates suggest that NPD affects between 1 per cent and 5 per cent of the population. This range highlights the variability in diagnostic approaches, as again not all individuals with narcissistic traits are formally diagnosed with the disorder. The symptoms in the UK population mirror those found elsewhere, including a lack of empathy, difficulties maintaining relationships, and an overt grandiose sense of self-importance or covert victimhood. While formal statistics on NPD are limited, anecdotal evidence suggests that the disorder remains underdiagnosed due to a combination of narcissists refusing to believe there is anything wrong with them, social stigma, and a lack of consistent mental health screening.

These figures offer you a general perspective and may vary based on diagnostic criteria, cultural context, and healthcare access.

What is important to understand is that if you are at a function, a party, or even on an office floor of over 100 people, there will be at least 12 people with narcissistic traits, and a handful who could have NPD. I suspect, given your interest in this topic, you have already identified a few of them and (if you are healthy of mind!) considered whether you might be in that set. Suffice to say, those who truly question themselves show a healthier sense of self-awareness and lack of defence than most narcissists, so I applaud your bravery in being willing to enquire within.

The challenge of diagnosis

In 2025, diagnosing NPD remains challenging, as many individuals with the disorder don't recognize their own problematic behaviours, making them less likely to seek treatment. The co-occurrence of NPD with other mental health conditions, such as depression, anxiety, and substance use disorders, complicates diagnosis further. Approximately 15 per cent of individuals with NPD also suffer from depression, and many exhibit symptoms of anxiety or substance misuse.

Treatment for NPD typically involves psychotherapy, but long-term success is difficult to achieve because patients often resist acknowledging the disorder. As a result, prognosis remains poor, with fewer than half of those affected receiving adequate mental health care.

Narcissistic Personality Disorder shares symptoms with several other psychological conditions, some within Cluster B, some outside, making it sometimes difficult to differentiate from other disorders. Differentiating NPD from these disorders requires careful assessment by mental health professionals, considering the individual's history, symptom duration, and context. Misdiagnosis can occur if clinicians focus solely on superficial similarities without a comprehensive understanding of the individual's personality structure and life history.

Here are some disorders that can be mistaken for NPD due to overlapping traits:

1 **Borderline Personality Disorder (BPD):** Marked by instability in relationships, self-image, and emotions, along with impulsivity.

   Overlap: Both NPD and BPD are Cluster B personality disorders, characterized by intense emotional experiences and unstable relationships. Individuals with BPD, like those with NPD, may display dramatic or erratic behaviour, a deep fear of abandonment, and a distorted sense of self.

   Differences: While those with NPD often have a grandiose self-image and seek admiration, individuals with BPD typically have an unstable self-image and may oscillate between extreme emotions, such as idealization and devaluation of others.

2 **Antisocial Personality Disorder (ASPD):** Defined by a disregard for the rights of others, deceitfulness, impulsivity, and a lack of remorse.

   Overlap: Both disorders involve a lack of empathy, manipulative behaviours, and a disregard for others. People with ASPD and NPD may engage in exploitative relationships for personal gain.

   Differences: The primary focus for individuals with ASPD is on deceitfulness, criminal behaviour, and a consistent pattern of violating the rights of others. Those with NPD are more focused on achieving admiration and may not engage in the same level of overtly antisocial behaviour.

3 **Histrionic Personality Disorder (HPD):** Involves excessive emotionality, attention-seeking behaviour, and a need for approval.

   Overlap: Both NPD and HPD are Cluster B disorders and can involve attention-seeking behaviour, superficial relationships, and a need for validation.

Differences: Individuals with HPD typically seek attention through dramatic, emotional, and seductive behaviour. While people with NPD also crave attention, their primary goal is admiration, often through perceived superiority rather than emotional or sexual allure.

4 **Bipolar Disorder (especially Bipolar I Disorder).**

Overlap: During manic episodes, individuals with Bipolar I Disorder may exhibit grandiosity, impulsivity, and an inflated sense of self, which can mimic the symptoms of NPD.

Differences: These symptoms in Bipolar Disorder are episodic and tied to mood swings, often alternating with periods of depression. In contrast, the traits of NPD are more stable and pervasive across time and situations.

5 **Obsessive-Compulsive Personality Disorder (OCPD).**

Overlap: Both NPD and OCPD may involve perfectionism, a need for control, and a preoccupation with orderliness and rules.

Differences: The motivation in OCPD is driven by a desire for order and perfectionism rather than the need for admiration or power. Individuals with NPD are less concerned with orderliness and more focused on status and external validation.

6 **Depressive Disorders (with Grandiosity).**

Overlap: Some individuals with depressive disorders may experience episodes of grandiosity or irritability, especially in atypical depression or when comorbid with other conditions.

Differences: In depressive disorders, the grandiosity is usually not a persistent trait and may be linked to specific episodes or triggers. In NPD, grandiosity is a chronic and pervasive feature.

7 **Substance Use Disorders.**

Overlap: Substance use, especially involving stimulants such as cocaine or methamphetamine, can cause behaviour that resembles NPD, such as inflated self-esteem, risk-taking, and lack of empathy.

Differences: These behaviours are typically substance-induced and may dissipate with sobriety, whereas NPD involves stable personality traits.

8 **Autism Spectrum Disorder (ASD).**

Overlap: Individuals with ASD might struggle with social interactions, and may appear self-focused or rigid, which can sometimes be mistaken for narcissistic traits.

Differences: The social difficulties in ASD stem from challenges in understanding and processing social cues, rather than a deliberate disregard for others' feelings.

9 **Attention-Deficit/Hyperactivity Disorder (ADHD).**

Overlap: ADHD can involve impulsivity, self-centred behaviour, and difficulty in maintaining relationships, which might be confused with narcissism.

Differences: The behaviours in ADHD are more related to inattention and impulsivity rather than a consistent pattern of grandiosity or lack of empathy.

10 **Schizophrenia (with Delusions of Grandeur).**

Overlap: In schizophrenia, particularly during psychotic episodes, individuals may experience delusions of grandeur, believing they possess exceptional abilities or importance.

Differences: These grandiose delusions are typically part of a broader pattern of psychotic symptoms, including hallucinations and disorganized thinking, which are not features of NPD.

The central question of nature or nurture

The enquiries that surface frequently with many clients I work with who are struggling with someone in their lives demonstrating NPD centre around the questions of how and why someone in their close circle is behaving in this way. Often curious to understand whether they are born with it, developed it, or something has happened to trigger it – often swiftly followed up with the concern that they too could be a narcissist. So be reassured if you are one of them.

Recent research into the development of NPD has delved deeper into the 'nature vs nurture' debate, with findings suggesting a complex interplay between neurobiological and environmental factors. Here are some of the questions and research that have been most recently undertaken:

Genetic predisposition: Studies have shown that NPD may have a heritable component. Recent studies have sought to understand the interplay between genetic and environmental factors in the development of narcissistic traits in children of narcissistic parents. A twin study by Rohrer et al. (2022) explored the heritability

13

of narcissistic traits and the role of parenting in their development. The study found that while there is a genetic component to narcissism, the parenting style of narcissistic parents plays a significant role in shaping the child's personality. The findings suggest that interventions targeting parenting practices could mitigate the transmission of narcissistic traits across generations. Twin studies, in particular, suggest that traits associated with narcissism, such as grandiosity and lack of empathy, have moderate genetic influence. Genes related to dopamine regulation and serotonin function are being studied for their role in NPD development, as they affect reward-seeking behaviour and mood regulation. This study showed that heritability estimates for narcissistic traits range from 40 per cent to 60 per cent.

Dopamine and serotonin genes: A study by Kastner-Bosek, Dajic, Mikus et al. (2019) exploring the role of dopamine receptor genes and serotonin transporter genes in narcissism suggested that variations in these genes may influence reward-seeking behaviours and emotional regulation, contributing to the development of narcissistic traits.

Neurobiological aspects: Recent neuroimaging studies by Griffith have revealed structural and functional abnormalities in the brains of individuals with NPD, particularly in regions involved in empathy, emotional regulation, and self-perception. The study found reduced grey matter volume in the anterior insula and prefrontal cortex, regions associated with empathy and self-regulation. This reduction may explain the emotional dysregulation and lack of empathy often seen in NPD.

Parental influence: A study by Dr Ananya Mandal, investigating how different parenting styles influence the development of narcissistic traits in children found that parents who overvalue their children or provide excessive praise can foster an inflated self-view in the child, while critical or neglectful parenting can also contribute to the development of narcissistic defences.

Additional research explored the role of inconsistent parenting – alternating between praise and harsh criticism – in fostering narcissistic traits. The study suggests that such inconsistencies can lead to a fragile self-esteem that may manifest as narcissism. In Chapter 4 we will look at this more closely.

Adverse childhood experiences: Studies have suggested exposure to childhood trauma, such as abuse or neglect, offer increased risk for developing NPD. Their findings suggest that narcissistic traits can emerge as a defence mechanism to cope with deep-seated feelings of vulnerability and worthlessness resulting from trauma.

Individuals with NPD often report higher levels of childhood trauma compared with non-NPD populations. This supports the hypothesis that trauma may lead to maladaptive coping mechanisms, such as the development of narcissistic defences.

Gene–environment interaction: Mandal's studies propose individuals with a genetic predisposition to narcissistic traits may be more sensitive to environmental factors, such as parenting styles or cultural influences. Their model suggests that these environmental factors can either amplify or mitigate the expression of narcissistic traits depending on the individual's genetic makeup.

Epigenetics and NPD: A 2023 study by Dr Ananya Mandal explored how childhood adversity can lead to epigenetic modifications that influence gene expression related to emotional regulation and self-perception. Epigenetics refers to how environmental factors can influence the way genes are expressed. For example, stressful or traumatic experiences can lead to changes in gene expression that might increase the likelihood of developing narcissistic traits, even in individuals who may not have a strong genetic predisposition.

Cultural and societal factors: Growing up in an environment that emphasizes individual success, competitiveness, and superficial values can also contribute to the development of narcissistic traits. Western cultures in particular have been noted for fostering narcissism through the glorification of self-promotion and material success. Western cultures, particularly in the United States, contribute to the rise of narcissistic traits, suggesting societal values that prioritize individualism, self-promotion, and material success may foster narcissistic traits in individuals.

Social media influence: The rise of social media has sparked interest in its potential role in exacerbating narcissistic traits. A study suggested that platforms such as Instagram, TikTok, and Facebook (Meta) may reinforce narcissistic behaviours by providing opportunities for self-promotion and validation through likes and followers, particularly in young adults.

The interaction between nature and nurture

So, as we look at many possibilities, the latest research suggests that NPD is not simply the result of genetic predisposition or environmental factors alone but is likely to be the outcome of their interaction. A child with a genetic vulnerability to narcissistic traits might be more likely to develop NPD if they are exposed to specific environmental triggers, such as poor parenting or traumatic experiences. Similarly, their personality traits can be amplified or mitigated by cultural and societal influences. It is a multifaceted interplay between genetic, neurobiological, and environmental factors. As the research speeds up and becomes more curious, we're seeing results which suggest there could be both a nature and a nurture element behind why such large numbers of the population now appear to be demonstrating a high number of narcissistic traits, or undiagnosed NPD.

Nature and nurture both contribute significantly, with environmental influences possibly playing a crucial role in the expression of genetic predispositions. Certainly, in my own clinical and lived experience of NPD, the nurture element, with the exposure to suboptimal emotional parenting, as well as close experience and observation of a child to a narcissistic parent, does seem to have an impact on the potential for narcissism to continue through families. As we will discuss in Chapter 4, the children of narcissists have different experiences which result in differing coping mechanisms and when a child is nominated and takes on the role of what we call the 'golden child', the one the narcissistic parent shows preference towards, there is sadly a greater chance of that child developing NPD themselves. The ongoing research is increasingly focused on understanding how these factors interact over time to shape the personality traits characteristic of NPD.

Limitations and challenges

Despite significant advances, research on narcissism and NPD faces several limitations and challenges. One of the biggest challenges is the huge amount of variety within the disorder. NPD encompasses a wide range of behaviours and personality traits, making it difficult to develop a one-size-fits-all approach to diagnosis and treatment. A prime example is the growing distinction between grandiose and vulnerable narcissism which, although useful, may not capture the full complexity of the disorder – leaving many still questioning whether a diagnosis is warranted or indeed accurate.

Another limitation is a reliance on self-assessment measures, such as the NPI and the PNI, which are subject to social desirability bias and may not accurately reflect the true extent of narcissistic traits. And while neuroimaging studies have provided valuable insights, they are often limited by small sample sizes and the difficulty of establishing causality.

The role of culture in shaping narcissistic traits is another area that needs further exploration. Most research on narcissism has been conducted in Western cultures, where individualism and self-promotion are more socially acceptable. Cross-cultural studies are needed to determine whether the findings from Western populations can be carried across to other cultural contexts.

It's hardly surprising that psychiatrists report only small numbers of individuals booking appointments for themselves, seeking diagnosis; people with NPD are reluctant to seek treatment, and those who do may struggle with the introspection and empathy required for therapy. As a psychotherapist, I remember in training being urged to swerve from treating those suspected of narcissism, so much had previous decades of therapists been burned by the experience of the idealization (love bombing) by the narcissistic clients in the early weeks, and then the demeaning and discarding phase as the months went on and the risk of the therapist's detection of their narcissism rose.

This can present as challenge to many therapists, given we are trained to 'hold hope' for every client we work with no matter their struggle. So, to either mentally or emotionally reject a client based on their presentation of Narcissism, somewhat goes against our heartfelt belief in being willing to help and treat everybody. For these reasons new therapies for NPD are always being trialed.

New therapies for NPD

Recent research has explored new therapeutic approaches. A study by Kealy et al. (2023) investigated the efficacy of schema therapy for NPD, a form of cognitive-behavioural therapy that focuses on identifying and modifying maladaptive schemas. The study found that schema therapy was effective in reducing narcissistic traits and improving emotional regulation, although long-term follow-up is needed to assess the durability of these effects.

Another promising approach is mentalization-based therapy (MBT), which aims to improve patients' ability to understand and interpret their own and others' mental states. A randomized controlled trial by Spinhoven et al. (2024) demonstrated that MBT significantly reduced narcissistic traits and improved interpersonal functioning in individuals with NPD.

The impact on the narcissist's family

As you probably know, Narcissistic Personality Disorder can have devastating effects on intimate relationships, especially on intimate partners, often leading to patterns of emotional abuse, manipulation, and control to the point of breakdown.

Living with a narcissist presents its own set of challenges and emotional pain, creating a parallel 'duplex of pain' for those in close relationships with them. The experiences of partners, family members, and friends who are involved with a narcissist are marked by emotional manipulation, inconsistency, and a lack of genuine connection.

One of the most striking aspects of living with a narcissist is the emotional roller coaster they create. Narcissists often engage in a cycle of idealization, devaluation, and discard in their relationships. Initially, they may shower you with admiration and affection, creating a sense of euphoria and validation. However, as the relationship progresses, the narcissist's need for control and dominance can lead to periods of devaluation and criticism. This inconsistency creates a destabilizing effect, leaving you feeling confused, hurt, and emotionally drained. Intermittent reinforcement can often be their favoured weapon of choice.

Living with a narcissist often involves the sacrifice of your own emotional needs in favour of catering to the narcissist's demands. You may find yourself constantly trying to appease the narcissist, seeking their approval, and avoiding conflict. This dynamic creates a huge emotional burden, as your needs and well-being are often disregarded in favour of maintaining the narcissist's self-image. The neglect of your own needs and the inability to establish healthy boundaries contribute to feelings of frustration, resentment, and emotional exhaustion.

Narcissists often create a sense of isolation for those around them, both intentionally and unintentionally. Their need for control and dominance can lead to the exclusion of friends and family members who do not align with their expectations or who challenge their authority. This isolation can result in a profound sense of loneliness in you, as you may feel cut off from meaningful social connections and support networks. The emotional isolation intensifies feelings of despair and helplessness, contributing and compounding the complex pain experienced by anyone living with a narcissist.

Individuals with NPD typically struggle with empathy, viewing relationships as a means to bolster their self-esteem, often at the expense of their partners and offspring. This dynamic can lead to a cycle of idealization and devaluation, where the partner or child is initially placed on a pedestal, only to be harshly criticized and discarded when they fail to meet the narcissist's unrealistic expectations. The narcissist sees other people as an opportunity to provide 'supply' to their ego – in the form of attention, validation, admiration, control, or emotional reactions that a narcissist seeks from others to maintain their inflated self-image and regulate their self-esteem. Once and if that individual/object does not comply, they risk being discarded – demonstrating how little true emotional connection the narcissist truly desires or creates. Partners and children are there merely to serve a purpose for the narcissist, until they no longer do so.

DARVO: Deny, Attack, Reverse Victim and Offender

One of the most harmful aspects of intimate relationships with individuals who have NPD is the phenomenon of DARVO and, related to it, gaslighting. DARVO stands for Deny, Attack, and Reverse Victim and Offender, describing the often swift pattern of behaviour when a partner or child seeks to resolve issues when a narcissistic partner or parent insults, offends, or upsets them. It is a manipulative tactic commonly used by the narcissist to deflect responsibility when confronted about their harmful behaviour. First, they Deny the wrongdoing, often dismissing or minimizing the issue. Then, they Attack the accuser, trying to discredit or shift the focus away from themselves. Finally, they Reverse the roles of Victim and Offender, positioning themselves as the victim of unjust accusations while painting the actual victim as the aggressor. This tactic is particularly damaging in relationships with narcissistic individuals, as it leaves the true victim feeling confused, guilty, and invalidated. This can lead to significant emotional and psychological distress for the partner or child, including anxiety, depression, and a diminished sense of self-worth.

Gaslighting and flying monkeys

Gaslighting, a term rooted in *Gaslight*, a 1944 film, describes a manipulative tactic where one person distorts another's reality to make them question their memory, perceptions, and sanity. In the film, a husband manipulates his wife by dimming the gas lights in their home and then denying any change when she notices, leading her to doubt her own observations and mental stability. Originally used to describe this extreme psychological abuse in intimate relationships, the term has since broadened to encompass various manipulative behaviours in different contexts. However, its recent overuse and casual application – often to describe minor disagreements or misunderstandings – risk diminishing the gravity of its meaning. This trivialization undermines the recognition of gaslighting as a deliberate, insidious form of emotional abuse that can devastate a victim's self-esteem and grip on reality, making it crucial to preserve the term's original significance.

Over time, this manipulation can erode any sane person's confidence and sense of reality, making them more reliant on the abuser for validation and control. This often becomes the cornerstone of what we will later discuss around 'trauma bonding' where the sense of reliance, guilt, and blame becomes a regular feeling alongside confusion and anger at the treatment from the narcissistic parent or partner.

Associated flying monkeys

In the realm of narcissism, the narcissist often needs and therefore recruits others to become their 'flying monkeys' – individuals who are manipulated by a narcissist to carry out their bidding, often without fully understanding the extent of the narcissist's manipulation or abusive behaviour. Borrowed from *The Wizard of Oz*, in which the Wicked Witch's flying monkeys enforce her will, these enablers can be friends, family, coworkers, or others drawn into the narcissist's web of influence, often through charm, lies, or guilt. They play a pivotal role in reinforcing gaslighting by validating the narcissist's distorted version of reality, spreading misinformation, and isolating the victim. This dynamic not only bolsters the narcissist's control but also deepens the victim's confusion and self-doubt, as the presence of seemingly impartial 'allies' lends false credibility to the narcissist's manipulative narrative.

Over time, with these behaviours in play, a child or partner may become isolated from friends and family, further exacerbating their dependence on the narcissist. What we call 'trauma bonding' is real, and some experts regard it as an addiction so powerful it is on a par with heroin. We are, sadly, now appreciating the effects of this in parental alienation cases, as well as in romantic relationships. Trauma bonding often infuriates friends and families who can see the destruction and encourage the child or partner to escape – but the bond may hold them in, continuing the abuse for years and even decades. Thankfully, as therapists we are educating ourselves around this phenomenon and there are a growing number of books and courses for those affected by this challenging psychological situation, which I hope in the future will bring help, hope, and support to those seeking to escape.

Despite the challenges, there are steps that anyone in a relationship with someone with NPD can take to protect themselves and their well-being. Establishing clear boundaries, seeking therapy, and building a dedicated support network are critical components of self-care – more of which we will discuss throughout this book. It is also important that you recognize you cannot change the narcissist's behaviour and that your priority should be your own mental and emotional health – regardless of how disheartening that may appear. Many go down with the ship, desperately trying to rescue the narcissists and the parental or romantic relationships they have with them, but in truth they often only further harm themselves in these valiant attempts.

Narcissist's impact on their children

Famous psychologist Carl Jung once said, 'The greatest burden a child must bear is the un-lived life of its parents.' Narcissistic parents have a profound effect on their children, no matter their age. Children of narcissistic parents experience a lack of emotional validation and support as the parent's focus is typically on their own needs rather than those of the child (although it may be disguised as such). This causes feelings ranging from worthlessness and a pervasive sense of inadequacy to co-dependency, enmeshment, and a fear of intimacy or abandonment – all of which may persist into adulthood. Parents with NPD often impose their own needs and desires on their children, viewing them as extensions of themselves rather than as independent individuals. This may lead to a range of developmental issues, including low self-esteem, difficulties with emotional regulation, and challenges in forming healthy relationships later in life. Some children of narcissistic parents may go on to develop narcissistic traits themselves, perpetuating the cycle of dysfunction, and this is a question or concern many self-aware clients ask me or raise in their earliest sessions.

The characteristics of narcissistic parents

Narcissistic parents often exhibit behaviours that are self-centred and manipulative, using their children as tools to fulfil their own needs rather than nurturing their children's individual growth and development. Common characteristics of narcissistic parents include:

- **Lack of empathy:** Narcissistic parents often struggle to empathize with their children's feelings and needs. This can lead to emotional neglect, where the child's emotional experiences are invalidated, ridiculed, or ignored.
- **Control and manipulation:** These parents may exert excessive control over their children's lives, dictating their choices and behaviours to maintain a sense of superiority and control – claiming it to be protection and guidance.

- **Conditional love:** Narcissistic parents often offer love and approval only when their children meet certain expectations, such as achieving success or behaving in ways that reflect well on the parent.
- **Projection and blame:** These parents may project their insecurities onto their children, blaming them for their own failures or shortcomings. This can create an environment of constant criticism, belittling, and fear.
- **Emotional exploitation:** Narcissistic parents may use their children to fulfil their own emotional needs, expecting them to provide admiration, validation, or even play the role of a caregiver. Enmeshment and emotional incest can occur, which is normalized by the parent, so the child is often unaware how unhealthy it is to them until later in life when their adult relationships become impacted.
- **Parental alienation:** Narcissistic parents may employ tactics such as gaslighting, triangulation (when the narcissist manipulates by drawing in a third person – real or implied – to create jealousy, rivalry, or confusion), and devaluation to turn the child against the other parent, projecting their own insecurities and need for control, distorting the child's perception of the alienated parent and fostering an unhealthy psychological environment. In such cases, the emotional and mental health of the child is at significant risk, as they are caught in a manipulative cycle that prioritizes the narcissistic parent's ego over the child's well-being.

Research on the impact of narcissistic parenting

The impact of narcissistic parenting on children has been a topic of research for several decades. Early studies such as those by Hewitt and colleagues focused on the psychological effects of growing up with a parent who exhibits narcissistic traits found that children of narcissistic parents often suffer from low self-esteem, anxiety, depression, and difficulties in forming healthy relationships.

Alice Miller is often credited with pioneering work in understanding the effects of narcissistic parenting. Her book *The Drama of the Gifted Child*, first published in 1979, explored how children of narcissistic parents often become overly attuned to their parents' needs, at the expense of their own emotional development. While Miller's work was not explicitly framed as 'narcissistic parenting', it laid the groundwork for understanding how narcissistic tendencies in parents could harm children's psychological development.

A later study, by W. Keith Campbell, found that children of narcissistic parents are more likely to develop narcissistic traits themselves, especially if they are what we term 'the golden child' – something we will come on to in Chapter 4 – perpetuating a cycle of dysfunction across generations. However, allow me to make it clear that this is by no means a given and with knowledge, awareness, psychoeducation, and compassion, we can begin to use all the research which has highlighted the role of parenting styles in the development of personality disorders and underscored the importance of early intervention.

Children of narcissistic parents often grow up in environments where their emotional needs are not met. As a result, they may develop a range of psychological issues. A study by McBride (2008) explored the emotional toll on children of narcissistic mothers. The study again found that these children often experience feelings of worthlessness, shame, and a pervasive sense of inadequacy. They may struggle with identity formation, as their self-worth is closely tied to their ability to meet their parent's unrealistic expectations.

Other, slightly more recent research such as that by Heather Hayes and Associates (2023) has found that children of narcissistic parents often exhibit poor self-esteem and have difficulty regulating their emotions. They are more likely to internalize negative self-concepts, leading to issues such as anxiety, depression, and perfectionism.

At the end of this book, I have listed the most up-to-date papers, studies, and books in this area in the hope that further reading and understanding will bolster your psychoeducation and offer you strength and proof that what you experience is real, has a name, a diagnosis, and an impact – all of which, I hope, will allow you to accept that there is a way forward for you.

With consciousness we have the tools for change, and that offers us all hope for better futures.

Long-term consequences: the lifelong impact

The effects of narcissistic parenting extend well into adulthood. Children of narcissistic parents often carry the scars of their upbringing throughout their lives. These long-term consequences can manifest in numerous ways, including difficulties in forming and maintaining relationships, persistent feelings of inadequacy, anger, fear, and broader mental health challenges. Indeed, within my clinical practice I have treated many glorious individuals who are the children of those displaying narcissism, with their ages ranging from 18 to 82. Some have only recently realized what happened to them, others have been seeking specific treatment to support them for many years. It has been a hidden and much misunderstood condition, and it is only in the last decade that psychotherapists have even been trained in how to treat the survivors.

Here are some of the most familiar challenges therapists see clients present with:

1 **Relationship difficulties:** One of the most significant long-term impacts of narcissistic parenting is the difficulty children face in forming healthy relationships. A study by Malkin (2015) found that adult children of narcissistic parents are more likely to struggle with trust and intimacy in their relationships. They may gravitate towards partners who exhibit narcissistic traits, repeating the patterns of their childhood. Alternatively, they may become overly self-reliant and avoid close relationships altogether to protect themselves from potential harm.

   Narcissistic parents can create rivalry and division between siblings by having favourites or pitting them against each other, a dynamic that can lead to long-lasting tension and resentment between siblings, further complicating their ability to form healthy relationships in adulthood.

   Cultural values, such as collectivism or individualism, can also influence the way narcissistic parenting affects children. In collectivist cultures, where family harmony is highly valued, the impact of narcissistic parenting may be less overt but still damaging. Children in these cultures may internalize their struggles to maintain the appearance of family unity, leading to suppressed emotions and a greater risk of mental health issues later in life.

2 **Identity and self-worth issues:** Children of narcissistic parents often struggle with their sense of identity and self-worth. These individuals are more likely to experience imposter syndrome, where

they doubt their achievements and fear being exposed as frauds. This is often a result of growing up in an environment where their worth was contingent on meeting their parent's expectations.

3 **Mental health challenges:** The mental health of individuals who grew up with narcissistic parents is often compromised. They are more likely to experience anxiety, depression, and other mood disorders. The constant criticism and lack of emotional support from their parents can lead to chronic feelings of shame, guilt, and low self-esteem, which can persist into adulthood.

4 **Perfectionism and fear of failure:** Narcissistic parents often impose unrealistic expectations on their children, leading to a pervasive fear of failure. Adult children of narcissistic parents are more likely to exhibit perfectionistic tendencies, which can lead to a cycle of overachievement and burnout, as these individuals strive to meet unattainable standards to gain approval and validation.

5 **Propensity for narcissism:** Again, one of the most troubling long-term impacts of narcissistic parenting is the increased risk of the child developing narcissistic traits themselves. It has been shown that children of narcissistic parents are more likely to exhibit grandiosity, entitlement, and a lack of empathy in adulthood. This perpetuates the cycle of narcissism across generations, as these individuals may go on to parent their children in similarly harmful ways.

Overcoming the impact of narcissistic parenting

Given the profound and long-lasting effects of narcissistic parenting, it is crucial to explore ways in which anyone experiencing them can overcome these challenges. While the scars of such an upbringing may never fully disappear, various therapeutic approaches and support mechanisms can help people heal and lead more fulfilling lives.

As you can imagine, whatever the flavour of narcissism or narcissistic behaviour displayed, observed or received by those living, working, or dealing closely with these individuals, one theme that is widely reported in many of the studies undertaken is that most individuals who display this behaviour are operating from a place of defence, defiance, insecurity, or false pride. It simply would not occur to them to choose to spend their good time and money visiting a psychiatrist to ask for an assessment or even a diagnosis. Many would find it almost comical. In fact, the very notion there is anything untoward about their behaviour is usually met with DARVO, and the very foundation of psychological safety, which can be underpinned with something in therapy we call 'rupture and repair', is simply unavailable to us. There is plenty of rupture if we dare to speak up, but no opportunity for repair, only retribution towards us. It is a desperate situation to endure no matter our age.

However, once diagnosed or even strongly suspected, the covert operational nature of the individual carrying these traits can often derail the therapeutic frame a psychiatrist or psychotherapist operates within. In fact, I would go as far as to say some psychotherapists will simply not collaborate with individuals demonstrating these behaviours for reasons which usually include a poor likely outcome to treatment, or a concentrated level of manipulation and aggression aimed at the professional.

So, we sometimes need to take on education for ourselves, and with depth of research, support groups, and professional therapeutic input, allow ourselves to trust what we experience and adopt whatever strategies we can to separate the incongruence of the narcissist's life and behaviours from our own. When we allow ourselves to separate from the noise and chaos they can bring, we can start to hear and heal ourselves.

In conclusion, Narcissistic Personality Disorder is a complex and multifaceted condition, of which we are gaining greater understanding. It has significant implications for anyone intimately involved with an individual who has the disorder. In my clinical experience it can often lead to long-lasting psychological and emotional consequences.

However, take heart – understanding the dynamics of NPD and seeking appropriate support can help mitigate the negative impact of the disorder and promote healthier, more fulfilling relationships. I promise you, it is possible.

2

Where does it all begin?
The formation of narcissism: theories, studies, and controversies

A whole stack of memories never equal one little hope.
Charles M. Schulz

When the people who are meant to love us the most choose consistently to hurt and abuse us (and consistently deny it), we start a quest that can become an exhausting, sometimes lifelong search for reasons to explain why. At times this becomes a desperate hunt to find an answer that allows us to stay in a relationship, in a family, or in a business and repeatedly to forgive when in fact the healthiest thing would be for us to leave or at least create a healthier boundary. Similar to a sunk cost fallacy, we have often worked so hard to find a way to cope with the narcissist in our lives that we can be unwilling to accept the truth of what they are, even when it is presented to us repeatedly. Finding the reason as to why and how this developed in them can offer us hope of change and deeper forgiveness, which is why I know this chapter is important for you.

One of the most treasured and celebrated traits of any empathic person is their desire and willingness to understand why another human being may be behaving the way they are. Before any judgement or condemnation, we first often seek to understand. Indeed, one of the most urgent questions I am asked by any client who comes to therapy with the story of a narcissistic parent or partner is, 'Why are they doing this? How did they develop this awful behaviour?'

Sadly, I must tell you now, in the many years I have existed on this planet and indeed practised as a therapist, I have found narcissism to be one of the most destructive, heartbreaking, and incurable personality types I have ever had to live around, work with, seek to understand, and even love. So, I stand with you in the pain and struggle we all endure in making sense of the living bewilderment that ensues when we have a narcissist entwined in our life.

As you will have seen by now, narcissism, and particularly Narcissistic Personality Disorder, has been the subject of intense psychological study and debate for decades and various theories have emerged to explain how and when narcissism develops. They focus on a combination of early childhood experiences, genetic predispositions, and environmental factors that may converge to form a narcissistic personality. Some explanations emphasize specific developmental stages, while others point to trauma or cultural influences. By examining the numerous factors involved – age, developmental stage, attachment styles, and societal trends – we aim to provide a comprehensive understanding of how narcissism takes shape and what might have happened to your parent that allowed the development of the behaviour you have endured for so long.

Early childhood and developmental theories

Many psychologists believe that narcissism has its roots in early childhood experiences, particularly in how the child's caregivers respond to their emotional and psychological needs. One of the most influential developmental theories comes from the psychoanalytic tradition, particularly the work of Sigmund Freud and later his follower, Otto Kernberg. Freud identified narcissism as a normal developmental stage, but one that, if not properly resolved, could lead to pathological forms of self-love. According to Freud, primary narcissism is an early stage in infancy where the child sees themselves as the centre of their world. In healthy development, this phase is outgrown as the child learns to form attachments to others. However, Freud suggested that when a child's needs are either excessively indulged or inadequately met by caregivers, their development can become arrested at this narcissistic stage.

Building on Freud's work, Otto Kernberg focused on the role of early object relations – specifically, how a child's interactions with primary caregivers shape their sense of self. Kernberg proposed that narcissism arises when the child's emotional needs are either excessively gratified or neglected, leading to an exaggerated sense of self-importance or a fragile self-concept. In his view, narcissism is a defence mechanism to protect the self from feelings of inadequacy or vulnerability.

'Maternal wounds', in the context of narcissism, refer to the deep emotional scars caused by an unhealthy or dysfunctional relationship between a mother and her child. These wounds can significantly shape the child's sense of self and lead to the development of narcissistic traits as a coping mechanism. For example, if a mother is emotionally unavailable – whether due to her own narcissism, depression, or preoccupation with external matters – the child may feel abandoned or unworthy of love. This lack of maternal attunement can lead to feelings of emptiness and a fragile self-esteem, as the child does not receive the necessary emotional mirroring and validation that are critical for developing a secure sense of self. In response, the child may adopt narcissistic defences, such as grandiosity or entitlement, to shield themselves from the pain of feeling unloved or unseen. Alternatively, the mother might impose unrealistic expectations or project her own unmet needs onto the child, forcing them to conform to a false self in order to gain approval. For example, a mother might praise her child excessively only when they excel in areas that align with her own desires or ambitions, teaching the child that love is conditional and tied to performance rather than inherent worth. This can lead to a cycle where the child, now an adult, seeks constant validation from others to compensate for the emotional void left by the maternal wound. The resulting narcissistic traits – such as an inflated sense of self, a desperate need for admiration or a lack of empathy – can be seen as protective mechanisms that the child developed to cope with the unresolved pain of not receiving unconditional love from their mother. Over time, these defences may harden into a narcissistic personality, rooted in the unresolved trauma of the maternal wound.

Heinz Kohut, another psychoanalytic theorist, argued that narcissism is not inherently pathological but rather part of normal development. He introduced the concept of 'healthy narcissism', which he believed every individual needs for self-esteem and self-cohesion. Kohut suggested that narcissistic personalities develop when a child's caregivers fail to provide what he called 'mirroring' responses – empathic validation of the child's needs and accomplishments. In such cases, the child develops an inflated sense of self to compensate for the lack of external validation. This theory is key in understanding how emotional neglect or inconsistency from caregivers can lead to the formation of narcissistic traits.

Early childhood narcissistic wounding

While it is always a challenge to expect someone with a narcissistic personality to report their past completely accurately, I have experienced several clients who assure me their parental upbringing was happy and secure but can point to a school or playground incident which they feel might have triggered a narcissistic injury and response in them as a child. Through a humiliation or pushback from another child or teacher they experience a deep wounding to their fragile sense of self, especially if the child already struggles with self-esteem or is overly dependent on external validation. Narcissists are extremely sensitive to anything that challenges their inflated self-image or threatens their sense of superiority, and these moments can trigger what is known as a narcissistic injury. Here are a few examples of what might be perceived as a narcissistic injury by someone with narcissistic traits:

Receiving constructive criticism: A narcissist might see even mild, well-meaning feedback as a personal attack. For instance, if a teacher or colleague suggests a small improvement to a project they are working on, instead of seeing it as helpful advice, the narcissist may interpret it as a direct challenge to their competence or intelligence. This perceived slight could trigger an intense emotional reaction, including anger, defensiveness, or attempts to discredit the person offering the feedback.

Being ignored or overlooked: Narcissists often crave attention and admiration, so being ignored or overlooked in social situations can trigger a narcissistic injury. For example, if they are at a party and the conversation shifts away from them, or they feel others are not giving them enough attention, they may feel slighted. This lack of attention can provoke feelings of unworthiness, which they often respond to with either sulking, withdrawing, or attempting to regain the spotlight with grandiose stories or behaviours.

With the rise in social media, the likelihood of a child being uninvited to a party, deleted from a WhatsApp group, or ostracized on a school trip can be high and for a child who has narcissistic tendencies, these can be escalated into major incidents – which if there is a narcissistic parent also involved can turn an everyday incident into a whole term of drama.

Losing to a peer: Competition often plays a significant role in a narcissist's self-concept, so losing to a peer in any context – whether it's a sports game, an exam result, or even a friendly debate – can deeply wound them. The idea that someone else could be superior in any way is intolerable to them. Instead of processing the loss in a healthy way, they may devalue the other person ('They only won because of favouritism') or exaggerate their own importance ('It's not a real competition without me anyway'). The covert narcissist might become even more focused and determined to double down their efforts next time, to the detriment of things they truly value and enjoy in life, wounded by the slight and driven by the need to return to pole position.

Alex's story

I was a child who prided themselves on being the fastest runner in their class. My self-worth was largely tied to this identity and I was proud of it. One day during lunch, a race was organized for years 8 and 9, and to my surprise, a boy in the year below me won by a large margin. In that moment, I experienced not just the loss of the race but a deep blow to my identity and self-image. This public defeat was so humiliating, especially as my mates and other children laughed and mocked me for losing. I claimed he had in fact cheated and remember muttering something about me being cleverer than any of the kids there anyway. I felt hatred towards that boy and fantasized about punching him.

For a child prone to narcissistic defences, this type of incident can feel like an intense injury to their ego, one that challenges their sense of superiority or specialness.

Rather than processing the event with resilience or understanding that losing is a normal part of life, the child might feel an overwhelming sense of shame or inadequacy. To cope with this, Alex showed a development of narcissistic defences, like devaluing the other children and inflating his sense of superiority in other areas by mentioning his own intellect. Over time, these defences had hardened into patterns of behaviour where Alex had become hypersensitive to any perceived slight or failure, unable to tolerate anything that threatened his sense of being the best.

This incident, while seemingly minor, could contribute to the development of narcissistic traits, particularly if the child begins to rely on these defences to protect themselves from feeling vulnerable or inferior. The narcissistic wound from such an event isn't just about the loss itself but about how the child interprets the experience as an existential threat to their self-worth.

Perceived lack of respect: Narcissists expect to be treated with deference and admiration, so when they perceive any disrespect – whether intentional or not – they are quick to feel injured. For instance, if someone interrupts them in conversation or doesn't acknowledge their opinion, they might take it as a severe insult. This can lead to disproportionate reactions such as silent treatment, outbursts of anger, or a need to dominate the next interaction to reassert their superiority.

Not being the centre of attention in a relationship: In close relationships, narcissists expect their parents or teachers to be fully focused on their needs and desires. If a partner or friend starts to focus on someone else's needs, or even their own, the narcissist might feel rejected or undervalued. For example, if their parent, teacher or even friend spends time with other siblings, pupils, or friends or pursues a personal interest, the narcissist might see this as a betrayal or sign of abandonment. They may react by becoming jealous, demanding more attention, or trying to undermine the partner's outside interests.

Being compared to others: Comparisons that show the narcissist as less than perfect are particularly triggering. For example, if a parent or friend casually mentions that someone else is more successful, more attractive, or better at something, the narcissist may feel deeply insulted. Rather than seeing the comment as benign, they might ruminate on it and become resentful or hostile towards both the person making the comparison and the person to whom they were compared.

Each of these examples highlights the fragility of the narcissistic ego. What might seem trivial or everyday events to others can feel like personal affronts to the narcissist, causing them to react with anger, withdrawal, or attempts to reassert their superiority.

Attachment theory and narcissism

Attachment theory, pioneered by John Bowlby, which you will see mentioned many times throughout the book, offers another framework for understanding the development of narcissism. Bowlby's attachment theory posits that early relationships with primary caregivers form the blueprint for how individuals relate to others throughout life. Secure attachment, characterized by consistent and responsive caregiving, allows the child to develop a stable sense of self and healthy relationships with others. However, when a child experiences insecure attachment – whether through emotional neglect, overindulgence, or inconsistency – their ability to form healthy relationships and a secure self-identity can be compromised.

Researchers have linked insecure attachment styles to narcissistic personality traits. Children with avoidant attachment styles, for example, may develop narcissistic tendencies as a way to avoid emotional intimacy and protect themselves from perceived vulnerability. Similarly, anxious attachment styles may lead to a fragile sense of self-worth, resulting in a need for constant validation from others, a hallmark of narcissistic behaviour.

Studies have shown that individuals with narcissistic traits often display avoidant or ambivalent attachment patterns. One study by Campbell et al. (2004) suggested that these attachment styles contribute to the development of grandiosity and entitlement, as narcissists use these traits to maintain a sense of superiority and emotional distance from others. We know, then, that the quality of early attachments may play a crucial role in the formation of narcissistic personality structures.

Genetic and biological factors

As I touched on in Chapter 1, while much of the focus on narcissism has been on environmental factors such as parenting and attachment, recent studies suggest that genetic factors may account for a huge portion of the variance in narcissistic traits. A landmark study in 2008 found that genetic influences accounted for approximately 50 per cent of the variance in narcissistic traits. These findings suggest that narcissism is not solely the result of environmental influences but that genetic predispositions play a substantial role.

In addition to genetic factors, some researchers have investigated the role of brain structure in narcissism. Across the various MRI imaging studies, they consistently found those with higher levels of narcissism had reduced grey matter volume in the prefrontal cortex, a region of the brain involved in empathy, decision-making, and self-regulation. This suggests that there may be biological differences in the brains of narcissists that contribute to their lack of empathy and grandiose self-image too.

Narcissism and cultural influences

Some people believe cultural factors such as social media, celebrity culture, and the emphasis on personal achievement have contributed to a rise in narcissistic traits among younger generations. With scores on narcissism inventories rising over recent years, the question is whether narcissism itself is on the rise or whether it is increasingly more broadly diagnosed.

However, the influence of cultural factors in shaping personality traits raises important questions about how societal values may impact the development of narcissism.

Controversial studies and diverging views

There are still many controversies around where narcissism comes from. Some researchers propose that children who are told that they are superior to others by their parents are more likely to develop grandiose views, but where does this leave the idea that narcissism stems from neglect and trauma?

Ultimately, as ever, it's complicated – parental overvaluation is only one factor and must be understood in the context of other emotional dynamics, such as inconsistency, conditional love, and neglect. While overvaluation may contribute to grandiose narcissism, it may not fully explain the more vulnerable forms of narcissism associated with emotional fragility and insecurity.

Another controversial area is the relationship between narcissism and self-esteem. While narcissism is often associated with high self-esteem, many studies suggest that narcissistic individuals may actually have fragile self-esteem that is dependent on external validation. This has led to the development of the 'mask model' of narcissism, which posits that the grandiose self-image of narcissists is a defence mechanism to hide deep-seated feelings of inadequacy. Again, my clinical lived experience supports this, and I find behind the mask (often at times it feels like a steel door) lies a ghost of an individual who feels empty and fragile, terrorized by the idea that they will be unmasked and revealed, which some clients have described as a near-psychological death.

So, what do we really understand about narcissists?

Despite the diversity of theories and ongoing debates, the most widely accepted view is that narcissism develops through a complex interaction of genetic predispositions, early childhood experiences, and environmental factors. The psychoanalytic theories of Freud, Kernberg, and Kohut have laid the foundation for understanding how early caregiver relationships shape narcissistic traits, while attachment theory has provided further insights into the role of insecure attachments in narcissistic development. Additionally, genetic and biological research has highlighted the importance of innate factors, while cultural theories emphasize the societal context in which narcissism may flourish.

While controversial studies, such as those focusing on parental overvaluation, offer valuable perspectives, they have not replaced the more comprehensive understanding that narcissism is multi-faceted, involving both internal and external influences. The most believed explanation remains that narcissism stems from a combination of childhood experiences – particularly inconsistent emotional validation – and innate personality traits that are shaped by genetic and biological factors. This integrated approach allows for a more nuanced understanding of narcissism, recognizing it as a spectrum of behaviours and traits influenced by various forces throughout development.

As research continues to evolve, our understanding of narcissism should grow more sophisticated, but for now, the intersection of early life experiences, genetic predispositions, and cultural influences offers the most complete explanation for how a narcissistic person is formed.

3

The challenge and spectrum of parental narcissism

Understanding different types and their formation

'Fifteen seconds, that's all it takes to change completely everything about a person.'

Colleen Hoover, It Ends With Us

Children raised by narcissistic parents often face the disorienting experience of living with a parent who exhibits starkly contrasting behaviours in public and private settings. This 'Jekyll and Hyde' dynamic – where the parent presents a charming, admirable façade in public while being harsh, dismissive, demanding, overwhelming, or abusive behind closed doors – creates a profound and confusing challenge for the child. The discrepancy between the public persona and private behaviour can significantly impact the child's emotional development and sense of reality, as they grapple with the complexities of their parent's dual nature.

In public, narcissistic parents engage in grandiose displays of charm, competence, and success, earning admiration and validation from others. This public persona is carefully crafted to reflect positively on the parent, highlighting their achievements, social status, or moral superiority. Back at home, of course, things are different, and the parent's public success and likability contrast sharply with the abusive or neglectful behaviour experienced by the child.

The parent's need for admiration and validation drives them to curate their public image meticulously, often resulting in a façade of warmth, generosity, or competence. The child sees their parent receiving praise and accolades from others, reinforcing their notion that their parent deserves admiration and respect.

Behind closed doors, the contrast with the public persona becomes increasingly more stark and painful. At home, narcissistic parents exhibit behaviours that are diametrically opposed to their public façade. They become abusive, controlling, inconsistent, or neglectful, displaying a lack of interest, empathy, or sensitivity towards their child's emotional needs. The private environment can be marked by disinterest, harsh criticism, emotional manipulation, neglect, or dismissal, creating a toxic atmosphere that is hidden from the outside world.

This duality means that the child is often left in a state of confusion and isolation. In private, their parent is emotionally volatile, inconsistent, and shows none of the support or affection expected in a nurturing parent–child relationship. The child learns to navigate a landscape where the parent's behaviour is unpredictable, swinging between extremes of outward charm and private cruelty. The child develops a profound sense of instability and insecurity as they struggle to understand why their parent behaves so differently in different contexts.

The hidden challenge: neglect in plain sight

One of the most challenging aspects of this dynamic is that the narcissistic parent's public persona shields them from scrutiny and criticism, making it difficult for others to see the underlying issues at home. This is especially the case in middle-class families, where the parent's ability to garner admiration and sympathy in public creates an illusion of normality or even perfection, masking the true nature of the family's internal struggles. Middle-class neglect and abuse often go hidden in plain sight, further leaving the child in a hopeless vacuum.

If you are the child, this hidden reality means you feel isolated and unsupported. The disparity between your parent's public image and private behaviour can lead to feelings of self-doubt and confusion. You may be reluctant to share your experiences with others, fearing disbelief or judgement, and struggle to articulate your difficulties in a way that makes sense to those who only see your parent's public face. This isolation can exacerbate feelings of helplessness and inadequacy as you are left to contend with your experiences without external validation or support – even from wider family members.

The experience of living with a Jekyll and Hyde parent can lead to significant emotional turmoil. The constant oscillation between the parent's charming public persona and their abusive private behaviour can create a profound sense of cognitive dissonance. You may question your own perceptions and feelings, wondering if you are imagining the differences or exaggerating the problems. This self-doubt can undermine your confidence in your own reality and judgement.

Additionally, you may internalize the conflict between the public and private selves of your parent, making it hard for you to establish your own sense of identity. Perhaps you are compelled to conform to the expectations set by your parent's public image, even while struggling with the negative experiences at home. This internal conflict can lead to emotional distress and a fractured sense of self as you navigate the demands of reconciling the disparate aspects of your parent's behaviour.

The Jekyll and Hyde paradox in narcissistic parenting presents a complex and challenging dynamic for children, who must navigate the stark contrast between their parent's public charm and private cruelty. The hidden nature of these difficulties, combined with the emotional impact of living with a dual-natured parent, can create a profound sense of confusion and isolation. Understanding this dynamic is essential for addressing the psychological impact on the child and for developing effective strategies for healing and recovery. By recognizing the complexities of the Jekyll and Hyde experience, we can better support individuals like you, who have been affected by narcissistic parenting, and help them reclaim their sense of self and well-being.

Understanding the distinct types of narcissism is crucial when dealing with narcissistic parents because it significantly impacts the dynamics of the parent–child relationship and the nature of the psychological harm inflicted. Each type of narcissism manifests in distinct behaviours and has unique ways of affecting others, so recognizing these variations can lead to more effective strategies for coping, healing, and intervention.

For example, **grandiose narcissistic parents**, who display overt arrogance and entitlement, may impose unrealistic expectations on their children and use them as tools to enhance their own self-image. This can result in a dynamic where the child is constantly pressured to achieve and validate the parent's sense of superiority, leading to chronic stress and feelings of inadequacy. Understanding this type of narcissism allows the child or therapist to recognize these patterns and address the impact of the parent's excessive demands and lack of empathy.

In contrast, **covert or vulnerable narcissistic parents** often present a more subtle form of narcissism, characterized by hypersensitivity and self-pity. These parents might seek excessive reassurance and sympathy from their children, placing an emotional burden on them and manipulating them into caregiving roles. Recognizing covert narcissism helps to identify passive-aggressive behaviours and emotional manipulation that might not be as immediately apparent as in the grandiose type. This understanding can help to set boundaries and manage the emotional demands placed on the child.

Malignant narcissistic parents, with their combination of grandiosity and antisocial tendencies, can be especially damaging due to their manipulative and aggressive behaviours. They use intimidation, deceit, or even emotional or physical abuse to assert control. Recognizing malignant narcissism is crucial for understanding the more severe and harmful aspects of the relationship and for implementing protective measures or seeking appropriate therapeutic interventions.

Overall, understanding the specific type of narcissism exhibited by a parent enables a more nuanced perspective on the dynamics at play, which is essential for effective treatment, healing, and fostering resilience in individuals affected by narcissistic parenting.

Grandiose narcissism: characteristics and behaviours

Grandiose narcissists are perhaps the most recognizable type of narcissist. They exhibit a pervasive sense of superiority, entitlement, and a need for excessive admiration. Their behaviour is characterized by overt arrogance, dominance, and a lack of empathy. Grandiose narcissists typically believe they are unique or special, and are preoccupied with fantasies of unlimited success, power, or brilliance. They seek to assert their superiority through achievements, status, and control over others.

The grandiose narcissist's need for validation and admiration can lead to difficulties in maintaining meaningful relationships. Their arrogance and lack of empathy can alienate others, leading to conflicts and strained interactions. Additionally, their constant need for external validation can create a fragile self-esteem that is highly susceptible to criticism or failure. When their grandiose self-image is threatened, they may react with intense anger, defensiveness, or even aggression.

Grandiose narcissism is often thought to develop from a combination of early childhood experiences and genetic predispositions. Overindulgent parenting, where children are excessively praised or shielded from failure, can contribute to the formation of grandiose traits. Additionally, environments that emphasize achievement and competition may reinforce the development of grandiosity. Genetic factors and temperament may also play a role, as some individuals are predisposed to develop narcissistic traits more readily.

In parenting, this type of narcissism manifests through unrealistic expectations and a demand for their children to meet their high standards. They often use their children as extensions of their own ego, pushing them to achieve and perform in ways that reflect positively on the parent's self-image. These parents may display arrogance and an inability to tolerate failure, leading to a controlling and perfectionistic approach to parenting.

Children of grandiose narcissistic parents may experience chronic pressure to succeed and perform, often at the expense of their own interests and well-being. The parent's lack of empathy and focus on their own needs can lead to feelings of inadequacy and a diminished sense of self-worth in the child. Over time, this dynamic can contribute to the development of anxiety, depression, and difficulties with self-esteem.

Meet Mark, 29

Mark came to me years ago, engulfed in a crisis of confidence and identity, feeling as if he were 'living someone else's life'. He had recently read about narcissism and wondered if his father, Simon, fitted the description. An executive investment banker, Simon had risen from a modest background but was prized (although without much love) as an only child by his parents. Attending a major public school on a scholarship, he became acutely aware of the class divide between his origins and his new elite peers. To mask the shame of his background, he crafted a false self, mocking those he deemed beneath him while feeling out of place in his new world. As Simon climbed the corporate ladder, his materialism blossomed – he amassed luxury cars, fine wines, and art, competing relentlessly with colleagues. His success fuelled a distorted image of himself as a golden boy, especially in his mother's eyes, but it came at the cost of emotional warmth and connection.

When Mark and his sister Joanne were born, Simon imposed his ambitions on them, insisting they would follow in his prestigious footsteps. He insisted his first wife both worked and ran the house, but given he was the major breadwinner, expected to rule the house given 'he was paying for everything'. After his first marriage predictably crumbled, Simon's embarrassment deepened, pushing him further into narcissism as he sought validation through wealth and status. Mark and Joanne became trophies for Simon's grandiose persona, their achievements in academics and sports celebrated while their emotional struggles went ignored. Mark developed a cough tic, raging psoriasis, and frequent bouts of nausea – physical manifestations of the anxiety simmering beneath the surface.

In Simon's second marriage, Mark felt the stark contrast between himself and his new stepbrother, Tim, who was encouraged by his parents to embrace his true self and was carefree and fun and accepted unconditionally. While Mark and Joanne mocked Tim's lack of intellect with their narcissistic father's encouragement, Mark envied his stepbrother's freedom and warmth, longing for the acceptance he never received. The tension escalated and ultimately Simon's second wife also left, unable to navigate the chaos of his domineering and narcissistic world.

Now in his late twenties, Mark mourns the childhood he never had, which he imagines could have been filled with joy and emotional expression. In therapy, he presents as brittle and defensive, struggling in romantic relationships where his 'learned' controlling nature is off-putting, regardless of his wealth. He has realized he has been merely fulfilling his father's unquenchable need for success, all while neglecting his own yearning for love and belonging. Mark epitomizes the son of a narcissistic father, trapped in a cycle where he was used to fill his father's void, forever living vicariously through his unfulfilled ambitions.

Covert narcissism: characteristics and behaviours

Covert narcissists, also known as vulnerable or introverted narcissists, present a different face of narcissism. Unlike their grandiose counterparts, covert narcissists are less overt in their arrogance and entitlement. They may exhibit a more subtle form of narcissism characterized by hypersensitivity, self-absorption, and a tendency to feel victimized. Covert narcissists often struggle with feelings of inadequacy and may present themselves as fragile or misunderstood. They may seek admiration in more passive or indirect ways, such as through self-pity or martyrdom.

The covert narcissist's struggles with self-esteem and hypersensitivity can lead to difficulties in interpersonal relationships. Their tendency to feel victimized or misunderstood may result in passive-aggressive behaviour or chronic dissatisfaction. Additionally, their lack of overt grandiosity can make their narcissistic traits less visible, leading to challenges in recognizing and addressing the underlying issues. The covert narcissist's emotional volatility and need for validation can create a cycle of dependency and resentment in relationships.

Covert narcissism often develops from early experiences of emotional neglect or inconsistency. Children who are not adequately validated or who experience inconsistent parenting may develop covert narcissistic traits as a way to cope with their underlying feelings of inadequacy. Experiences of chronic criticism or invalidation may contribute to the formation of covert narcissism. Genetic predisposition and temperament also play a role in shaping this form of narcissism.

Covert narcissistic parents exhibit a more subtle form of narcissism characterized by hypersensitivity, self-pity, and emotional volatility. In parenting, this type of narcissism manifests through passive-aggressive behaviours and a tendency to seek excessive emotional support from their children. Covert narcissistic parents may portray themselves as perpetual victims and rely on their children to provide reassurance and emotional validation.

Children of covert narcissistic parents may find themselves in caretaking roles from an early age, often being forced to manage the parent's emotional needs while their own needs go unmet. This can create an environment of emotional instability and confusion, leading to difficulties in establishing healthy boundaries and self-identity. The child may struggle with feelings of guilt, inadequacy, and difficulty asserting their own needs and desires.

Meet Olivia, 34

Growing up with my father, who I now understand was a covert narcissist, was a complex and painful experience, marked by emotional manipulation that left me confused and struggling to trust others and even myself. To the outside world, he presented as the perfect dad – charming and supportive – but at home, he wielded guilt and passive-aggressiveness like weapons. He was horrible to me and made me feel really useless academically, often changing my homework to 'make it better' and snorting or smirking at my struggle with maths. Whenever I pursued my own passions, such as art or ice skating, he would dismiss my passions, saying things like, 'That's nice, but you'll never make a living from that,' which planted seeds of doubt about my worth and abilities.

He often compared me to my very clever sister, making me feel inadequate and pressured to meet impossible standards. She supported his football team, so I was left at home while they went out together, and he would welcome her friends to visit while mine were never allowed. His emotional withdrawal was a constant threat.

If I didn't conform to his expectations, or agree with him, or even pay him attention when he came home, he would sulk and turn cold, leaving me feeling responsible for his unhappiness. I vividly remember the times I tried to express my feelings – only to be met with a condescending 'You're overreacting' or 'I don't like this version of you,' which invalidated my experiences and taught me to suppress my emotions. I remember begging him to just spend time with me at weekends and him telling me he worked hard all week for me and he deserved a nice weekend to himself, often reading in his room with the door shut, leaving me feeling rejected and somehow a disappointment. He once threatened to quit his job if 'that is what you really want' when I had just asked for us to go bowling together. It made me anxious and scared to ask him for anything after that.

I never knew what mood he would be in. Whenever I achieved something, rather than celebrating my success he would turn the conversation back to his own achievements or disappointments, putting the focus onto him and leaving me feeling guilty for even trying to shine. This emotional manipulation created a chaotic environment where I felt unworthy and constantly anxious about meeting his ever-shifting expectations, leaving me with a chronic sense of inadequacy that seeped into every aspect of my life. Now, at 34, I struggle to trust men, I worry I am not clever enough, or that I am seen as needy. Therapy is now helping me to see who I really am and what I have achieved in spite of my father, and to hear my inner voice once again. I find time with him brings anxiety and fear and I dread spending Christmas with him – I hope one day I will have a family of my own to feel safe in, but for now I am rediscovering who I am and what I am worth. None of my friends can see what the issue is and remember him as being friendly and normal, but none of them ever saw him behind closed doors and this makes me feel they still think I have made some of this up.

Malignant narcissism: characteristics and behaviours

Malignant narcissism is a more severe and dangerous form of narcissism that combines elements of grandiosity with antisocial and aggressive tendencies. Malignant narcissists exhibit a pronounced sense of entitlement, a lack of empathy, and a willingness to exploit or harm others to achieve their goals. They often display a sadistic streak, deriving pleasure from the suffering of others, and may engage in manipulative, deceitful, or destructive behaviour. Their actions are driven by a desire for power and control, and they may have a disregard for the well-being of others.

The malignant narcissist's harmful behaviour and lack of empathy can have devastating effects on those around them. Their manipulative and exploitative tendencies can lead to abusive relationships and a toxic environment. Additionally, their extreme aggression and lack of remorse can create significant challenges in managing interpersonal conflicts and addressing their behaviour. Malignant narcissists often resist treatment or intervention as their grandiosity and defensiveness prevent them from recognizing their need for help.

Malignant narcissism is thought to develop from a combination of destructive early childhood experiences and genetic factors. Childhood trauma, neglect, or abuse can contribute to the development of malignant traits as individuals may learn to cope with their pain through aggression and manipulation. Additionally, genetic predisposition and temperament may influence the development of malignant narcissism. The interplay between early experiences and genetic factors contributes to the formation of this more extreme and destructive form of narcissism.

Malignant narcissistic parents combine grandiosity with antisocial tendencies, exhibiting a dangerous blend of arrogance, aggression, and sadism. These parents often engage in manipulative, deceitful, and abusive behaviours to exert control and dominance over their children. They may use fear, intimidation, and emotional or physical abuse to maintain their authority and manipulate the family dynamics to their advantage.

Children of malignant narcissistic parents are likely to experience a highly toxic and abusive environment. The constant fear and manipulation can lead to severe emotional trauma and long-lasting psychological damage. These children may develop complex trauma, characterized by symptoms of post-traumatic stress disorder, chronic anxiety, depression, and difficulties with trust and self-worth. The abusive dynamics can severely impact their ability to form healthy relationships and maintain emotional stability.

Meet Jake, 41

Growing up under the watchful eye of his malignant narcissistic mother and aggressive father, Jake lived in a world where love was weaponized and affection was conditional, twisted into a tool of control and manipulation. From an early age, his mother would undermine his self-esteem with cutting remarks, such as telling him, 'You're just like your father – worthless' at the slightest hint of his independence. She would blame him when anything went wrong and play him off against his sister, with one of them being the scapegoat for just about anything. Both of them lived in fear and struggled at school. His father was aggressive and sullen. Mealtimes were especially terrorizing for both Jake and his sister, with his mother standing aside as their father physically abused them and their mother then 'coming to the rescue' later in the evening, making herself seem the hero.

Every achievement was met with a chilling indifference, overshadowed by his mother's need to assert dominance. When Jake won a school award, she'd merely say, 'Well, that's expected. You wouldn't want to disappoint me, would you?' Behind her polished exterior lay a deep cruelty, leaving Jake fearful of their interactions and burying his emotions. By the age of 12 he had started fighting at school for very little reason and could sense an inner rage that needed some level of expression. His mother crafted elaborate scenarios to pit him against his peers, often insisting he stay at home with her rather than playing in football matches or going out with his friends, ensuring he felt isolated, ridiculed, and dependent on her approval. Jake became adept at reading her moods, always walking on eggshells, knowing that any deviation from her expectations would result in emotional outbursts or icy silences that left him feeling unworthy and small. Her relentless need to control and belittle ensured that his sense of self was deeply fractured, a reflection of her malignancy that turned every moment of his childhood into a battle for survival rather than a journey of growth. It was only when he went to university (taking any course he could just to escape) that he began to see that all really was not well at home. When he met his first girl-friend's family, he finally realized the difference between a normal loving family and the abusive home he had endured for 18 years.

When he came to therapy, he spent many initial weeks having very little to say and when he did speak, I noticed him trying to please me as his therapist. It took brave work on his part finally to challenge me and realize he would be met with softness and curiosity rather than rage. Jake would find that after each session he felt sad, angry, and depressed and he actually stopped our sessions for several months as a result before his mother reappeared, reminding him of her insidious behaviours and manipulations, and he realized he had finally to address this wounding.

During our work together, he ventured to speak to his wider family, only to discover they were aware something didn't seem right but felt unable to intervene. This sense of secondary 'neglect by omission of protection' triggered Jake's inner anger and we spent time addressing what needed at long last to be expressed. He no longer has a relationship with his mother, choosing to set new personal boundaries for himself, and has managed to cultivate an alternative family with his partner and his friends' parents. In seeing there is a healthy and safe way to be in a family, and in separating what he had been told from what was the truth, he is now able, quite healthily, to observe the narcissism at play and take back control of who and when someone has access to him and his kind heart.

Social narcissism: characteristics and behaviours

Social narcissists are characterized by their need for admiration and validation in social settings. They are charming, outgoing, and focused on their public image. Social narcissists seek attention and recognition from others, and their self-worth is closely tied to their social status and popularity. They may engage in attention-seeking behaviours, such as boasting or exaggerating their accomplishments, to maintain their desired social image.

The social narcissist's reliance on external validation can lead to difficulties maintaining authentic relationships. Their focus on social status and image may result in superficial connections and a lack of genuine intimacy. Additionally, their constant need for admiration and attention can create challenges in managing relationships and navigating social dynamics. The social narcissist's preoccupation with their public image can lead to feelings of insecurity and dissatisfaction when they perceive a decline in their social standing.

Social narcissism develops in response to societal and cultural influences that emphasize the importance of social status and image. Environments that prioritize appearance and social success may reinforce the development of social narcissistic traits. Additionally, early experiences of validation or criticism related to social performance can contribute to the formation of social narcissism. Genetic predispositions and temperament may also play a role in shaping this type of narcissism.

Social narcissistic parents are characterized by their preoccupation with social status and public image. They seek admiration and validation through their social achievements and may push their children to reflect positively on their social standing. In parenting, this type of narcissism manifests itself through an emphasis on appearances, popularity, and social success, often at the expense of the child's individual needs and desires.

Children of social narcissistic parents may feel pressured to conform to social expectations and maintain a certain public image. The focus on social status can lead to a lack of genuine emotional support and validation for the child's personal interests and achievements. Over time, this pressure contributes to feelings of inadequacy, anxiety, and a diminished sense of self-worth, as the child's value is often tied to their ability to enhance the parent's social status.

Meet Stuart, 48

Growing up with a socially narcissistic mother, Stuart learned early on that his worth was a mere extension of her image, a pawn in her quest for social validation. She would often host lavish gatherings where her focus was less on nurturing her son and more on showcasing him as a trophy for her carefully curated life and wardrobe – he was paraded around like a prized possession, expected to charm her friends while she watched for any misstep that could tarnish her façade. Cruelty lurked beneath her polished surface; when he failed to impress, she would coldly dismiss him with comments such as, 'Buck up, no one wants to be around someone dull.' Each failure was magnified, fuelling her need to maintain her social status, while his emotional needs were systematically ignored. When he sought comfort or connection, she would deflect him with shallow praise, making it clear that his feelings were secondary to her ambitions. Her calculated behaviour ensured he never felt secure in her affection, teaching him that love was a performance – one that he was perpetually failing to master in her eyes. In this toxic dynamic, Stuart became acutely aware that his mother's desire for social superiority came at the cost of his own identity, leaving him trapped in a world where genuine connection was a distant dream, overshadowed by her relentless quest for admiration.

It was in his adult years that Stuart began to notice his own people-pleasing and partners accusing him of being false or shallow. In his heart, he felt the opposite, but he noticed that he was indeed adapting to others in an attempt to remain in their good books. In doing so he appreciated he had betrayed himself and his own wants and desires, which meant he harboured longing and also anger. With concentrated work in therapy, Stuart began to understand it could be safe to express his genuine feelings and preferences and in fact people moved more towards him the more they felt he was being truthful.

Communal narcissism: characteristics and behaviours

Communal narcissists present themselves as altruistic and concerned for the well-being of others, but they are often driven by a need for admiration and validation. They may engage in acts of kindness or charity as a way to gain recognition and approval. Communal narcissists often portray themselves as morally superior and self-sacrificing, using their perceived altruism to enhance their social status and self-image.

The communal narcissist's behaviour can create a façade of selflessness while masking underlying narcissistic motivations. Their need for recognition and admiration can lead to manipulative or self-serving behaviour, even in their altruistic actions. Relationships with communal narcissists may be marked by a lack of genuine empathy and an emphasis on self-promotion. The disparity between their public image and private motivations can create challenges in maintaining authentic connections and addressing underlying issues.

Communal narcissism often develops in response to early experiences of validation or reinforcement related to altruistic behaviour. Environments that emphasize the importance of moral superiority and social contribution may contribute to the formation of communal narcissistic traits. Additionally, childhood experiences of validation or criticism related to helping others can influence the development of communal narcissism. Genetic predispositions and temperament may also play a role in shaping this type of narcissism.

Communal narcissistic parents present themselves as altruistic and morally superior, often engaging in acts of charity or kindness to gain admiration and validation. In parenting, this type of narcissism manifests itself behind a façade of selflessness and concern for others, while the true motivation is self-promotion and social recognition. These parents may use their perceived altruism to control or manipulate their children, expecting them to uphold what they see as the family's moral image.

Children of communal narcissistic parents may struggle with the disparity between the parent's public persona and their private behaviour. The child might feel pressured to adhere to the family's moral standards and participate in activities designed to enhance the parent's social image. This creates confusion and emotional dissonance, leading to difficulties in understanding their own values and a diminished sense of self-worth. The child may also experience feelings of being used or exploited for the parent's social gain.

Meet Mia, 58

Growing up with a communally narcissistic mother, Mia was trapped in a suffocating cycle of performative altruism and emotional manipulation. Her mother presented herself as the ultimate caregiver, constantly volunteering and seeking praise from others for her 'selflessness', but behind closed doors she wielded guilt like a weapon. Whenever Mia expressed her own needs or desires, her mother would respond with a chilling sweetness, saying, 'Good girls like us will go to heaven,' twisting the narrative to ensure Mia felt responsible for her mother's future happiness. In public, she would boast about Mia's achievements while simultaneously undermining her self-esteem at home, belittling her accomplishments with dismissive remarks such as, 'You only succeeded because I pushed you.' This cruel duality left Mia feeling isolated and unworthy, trapped in a role that demanded constant sacrifice for her mother's approval.

While her mother thrived on being seen as a martyr, Mia's emotional needs were systematically silenced, forcing her to wear a mask of compliance and gratitude. As a result, Mia grew up feeling like an afterthought in her own life, her identity eclipsed by her mother's desperate need for admiration, and she often questioned whether she was worthy of love outside the confines of her mother's warped expectations. She also held deep resentment at all the giving she was forced to undertake, while never being the recipient.

During one session she recalled a summer during which they fostered a little girl for six weeks, and Mia watched her mother washing the little girl's hair and buying her clothes and cakes and reading her stories. Mia remembered feeling desperately sad and confused as to why her own mother never did any of these things for her and this left her feeling there was something not good about herself or that she was unlovable. It took some years in therapy to help her see this was no reflection on her whatsoever but in fact a pathway to narcissistic supply for her mother, who was admired and thanked for all she did for the fostered child.

Antagonistic narcissism: characteristics and behaviours

Antagonistic narcissists are characterized by their aggressive, confrontational, and antagonistic behaviour. They display a tendency to provoke conflict and assert their dominance through combative tactics. Unlike grandiose narcissists, who may use charm and manipulation to achieve their goals, antagonistic narcissists rely on intimidation, aggression, and hostility. They seek to undermine or dominate others, often using belittling or humiliating tactics to assert their superiority.

The antagonistic narcissist's aggressive and confrontational behaviour creates a hostile and toxic environment, leading to frequent conflicts and strained relationships. Their tendency to provoke and demean others can result in significant emotional distress for those around them. Additionally, their inability to manage conflict constructively and their lack of remorse makes it challenging to address their behaviour and maintain healthy relationships. The antagonistic narcissist's need for control and dominance exacerbates these challenges, creating a cycle of hostility and resentment.

Antagonistic narcissism may develop from early experiences of aggression or hostility in the family environment. Children who are exposed to chronic conflict, bullying, or punitive discipline may develop antagonistic traits as a way to assert control or protect themselves. Additionally, genetic factors and temperament may contribute to the development of antagonistic narcissism as some individuals may be more predisposed to aggressive or confrontational behaviour. The combination of early experiences and genetic predisposition contributes to the formation of this more aggressive form of narcissism.

Antagonistic narcissistic parents are characterized by their aggressive, confrontational, and antagonistic behaviour. They often use hostility and intimidation to assert control and dominance. In parenting, this type of narcissism manifests through a combative approach, marked by frequent conflicts, criticism, and attempts to belittle or undermine the child. These parents may create a highly contentious and volatile environment, where their need for dominance takes precedence over the child's emotional needs.

Children of antagonistic narcissistic parents are likely to experience a hostile and abusive environment, characterized by constant conflict and emotional distress. The aggressive behaviour and lack of empathy can lead to significant emotional trauma, including issues with self-esteem, anxiety, and depression. The child may also struggle with developing healthy conflict-resolution skills and maintaining positive relationships as their early experiences are marked by aggression and hostility, which leaves them hyper-vigilant.

Meet Liam, 39

Growing up under the thumb of his antagonistic narcissistic mother, Liam lived in a constant state of anxiety, acutely aware that her love was laced with hostility and manipulation. She thrived on conflict, frequently pitting him against others, relishing in the chaos she created; when he succeeded, she would undermine him with snide comments such as, 'You think you're special? Just wait until your friends find out how pathetic you really are.' Her need for control manifested in cruel games, where she would deliberately sabotage his friendships, feeding him lies about what others thought of him, leaving him isolated and uncertain. Each time he attempted to assert his independence, she would retaliate with a barrage of insults, claiming he was ungrateful and incapable of achieving anything without her guidance. Even moments meant for celebration were tainted. During his birthday, she would overshadow his joy by reminiscing about her sacrifices, saying, 'Giving birth to you ruined my body!'

This relentless cycle of emotional abuse chipped away at Liam's self-worth, forcing him into a role of perpetual subservience, where he was left to navigate the treacherous waters of her antagonism, always fearing the next eruption of her venomous wrath. In her eyes, he was merely a reflection of her own insecurities, a target for her cruelty, leaving Liam to grapple with a profound sense of unworthiness and a longing for the unconditional love he had never known.

Liam often considered suicide as a teenager: he felt there was no escape and was convinced it was all his fault. It was not until he was entangled in a physical fight at school and found he could not stop thumping his school friend that a wise teacher, knowing this was out of character, enquired as to what might be going on at home. The reactive rage that had built up inside him finally found a route out and his therapeutic journey began.

Conclusion

Understanding the different types of narcissism and their manifestations in parenting is crucial for recognizing the unique challenges and impact such parenting has on children. Each type of narcissistic parent brings distinct behaviours and dynamics into the parent–child relationship, shaping the child's emotional development and overall well-being. By identifying these patterns, we can tackle the effects of narcissistic parenting, seek appropriate support, and work towards healing and recovery. Recognizing these variations allows for a more tailored approach in both therapeutic settings and personal healing journeys, providing a deeper understanding of the complexities involved in navigating relationships with narcissistic parents.

The path to healing

Showing the different presentations of narcissism and the parenting styles that emerge alongside them will, I hope, offer you the opportunity to explore your own experiences and allow you to begin to feel some understanding and validation of what you have experienced. Once we begin to identify what we have been living through, we are better armed to enter therapy with a clear sense of what needs to be addressed and healed.

Additionally, becoming able to articulate the Jekyll and Hyde dynamic in narcissistic parenting is crucial for any child's healing and recovery, no matter their age. Acknowledging the discrepancy between the parent's public persona and private behaviour is a crucial step in validating a child's experiences and emotions. Therapy and support can help the child understand and process the impact of living with a narcissistic parent, offering strategies for managing the emotional fallout and rebuilding a sense of truth and self-worth.

In therapy, the child can work on recognizing the unhealthy dynamics and learning to set their own boundaries with the parent. It is also important to build a support system outside the family, where the child can find validation and understanding – potentially in siblings or family members or friends who had also privately observed or suffered as a result of the narcissist's behaviour. Developing a strong sense of self and self-compassion is crucial for overcoming the confusion and self-doubt that can arise from narcissistic parenting.

4

Narcissistic family constellations
The ties that bind

'It ran in the family, until it ran into me.'

Anon.

An understanding of our family constellation can visibly represent the intricate web of relationships that make up the core of human society. Whether nuclear, extended, blended, or chosen, families serve as the primary emotional hubs, shaping individuals' identities, values, and emotional well-being. These constellations provide both a sanctuary and a stage for personal growth, conflict, connection, and evolution. While families can be a source of unconditional love and support, they can also present significant challenges, given the complexities of human relationships and emotions.

There are as many types of families as there are individuals within them, each with its own dynamic and set of rules. The traditional nuclear family, consisting of two parents and their children, remains an ideal for many, but in reality, family structures are often much more fluid.

As of 2024, approximately 40–50 per cent of marriages in the United States ended in divorce. This figure has remained relatively stable over the last few decades, though divorce rates have slightly declined due to fewer people getting married in the first place. In the UK, around 41 per cent of marriages are expected to end in divorce before their 25th wedding anniversary.

Blended families, formed through remarriage, come with their unique dynamics, as stepsiblings and stepparents navigate their roles and relationships. Extended families, where multiple generations live together or remain closely knit, offer support and wisdom but also can foster a lack of autonomy or privacy. Chosen families, which often consist of close friends or other non-blood-related individuals, provide a powerful sense of belonging, especially for those whose biological families may be absent or dysfunctional.

Despite their differences, all family constellations share common elements: they are places where love, conflict, growth, and vulnerability intersect. In a healthy family dynamic, emotional support and love are paramount. Members of a healthy family system are given the space to develop their identities, practise self-regulation, and form secure attachments. However, even in the most harmonious families, conflicts arise. These conflicts, while challenging, are not inherently negative – they can offer opportunities for growth and deeper understanding. The way in which a family manages disagreements, stress, or trauma often defines the overall health of the emotional system within it.

On the other hand, families can present significant problems. Unhealthy dynamics, power struggles, or emotional imbalances create dysfunctional environments. When a family's emotional ecosystem becomes strained, individuals face feelings of isolation, resentment, or anxiety. At the core of many family conflicts lies the tension between individual needs and collective expectations. When a family fails to balance these dynamics, emotional turbulence follows, resulting in ruptures that are hard to heal – and never more so than when they are inhabited by an individual with a narcissistic personality.

The narcissistic family constellation

A parent with a narcissistic personality can corrode a once-healthy family structure, causing lasting effects which truly impact children as they grow and remain in the shadows or the forefront long into adulthood. There are many different constellations at play and I have been fortunate enough during the evolution of this book to sit with many adult children, who have generously allowed me to listen to their experiences and kindly offered for them to be shared with you, the reader, in the hope that you will feel less alone and increasingly validated by some of the stories, which might resonate with you. As you would expect, I have changed all the names to protect their identities, but I hope through their bravery and raw emotional storytelling you can begin to recognize the signs of narcissistic parenting. Later, in Chapter 10, we will return to them so they can offer their experience and insight into how gaining tools to heal has allowed them to rebuild healthier relational dynamics in their lives.

Families with a narcissistic parent often resemble a complex system in which each member assumes a specific role, consciously or unconsciously, to maintain a delicate and dysfunctional balance. The dynamics within such families are dictated by the narcissistic parent's need for control, admiration, and validation, often at the expense of the emotional and psychological well-being of the other family members. This introduction explores the common constellations or roles that emerge within these families, the psychological mechanisms driving these roles, and the broader impact on the family as a whole. Drawing on recent research, we will examine how these roles are formed, the challenges they present, and the long-term effects on individual family members and the family unit.

The narcissistic family system at work

The disruption: narcissistic parenting

In families with a narcissistic parent, the family system is typically organized around the narcissist's needs and demands. These families often exhibit characteristics such as enmeshment, lack of clear boundaries, and an overemphasis on external appearances. The narcissistic parent may use manipulation, guilt, and emotional abuse to control the family, creating an environment where members are forced to adopt specific roles to maintain harmony – or, more appropriately put, the appearance of it.

While emotionally balanced families thrive on self-regulation, clear boundaries, and mutual respect, these principles are often absent in families where one or both parents display narcissistic traits. Narcissistic parenting creates an environment of emotional imbalance, where the parent's needs take precedence over everyone's else's well-being.

The dominant parent may adopt many different methods to gain control, ranging from outright dictatorship, threats, coercive control, demands for admiration and respect, and outlandish expectations, to the opposite end of the spectrum, where they assume a victim mentality, seek sympathy, display an extraordinary need for attention and pity, and ensure all the efforts of the family are focused in their direction.

The children of these individuals will silently be given a role. It will have started early in life and you will most likely identify with one or several of these roles. Often the nominations can swing wildly depending on the frame of mind or individual circumstance, but often, over time, we will find we have been given and then assumed a regular role – one which will shape the way we experience the world, our later relationships, and the families we go on to create – and, indeed, the roles we assume in friendships and workplaces.

Recognizing narcissistic parents

The signs of a narcissistic parent can be subtle and difficult to identify, even for those who have grown up in such environments. Some common traits include:

- **Lack of empathy:** Narcissistic parents often lack the ability to empathize with their child's feelings. They may be indifferent or dismissive when their child expresses emotions, leading the child to feel invalidated or unworthy of care.
- **Grandiosity:** These parents often have an inflated sense of their own importance and may view their children as mere accessories to their own success. They often expect their children to reflect positively on them, not for the child's sake but to enhance their own self-image.
- **Manipulation and control:** Narcissistic parents often manipulate their children, using guilt, shame, or fear to control their behaviour. They might play one child against another or favour one child in a way that fosters sibling rivalry, all to maintain control over the family dynamics.
- **Conditional love:** Love and approval from a narcissistic parent are often conditional. Children learn early on that they must meet the parent's standards or perform in a way that pleases the parent to

receive affection or praise. This can lead to feelings of worthlessness if the child cannot live up to these often-unrealistic expectations.

- **Projection:** Narcissistic parents often project their own flaws and insecurities onto their children. For example, they may accuse their children of being selfish, lazy, or ungrateful, even when these traits are more reflective of the parent's own behaviour.

- **Emotional neglect and gaslighting:** These parents frequently gaslight their children, causing them to question their reality and emotions. The parent may deny past abuse or insist that their actions were justified, leaving the child confused and doubting their memories.

The roles within the narcissistic family

1 The golden child

The golden child is the one who receives the most attention and praise from the narcissistic parent. This child is idealized and viewed as an extension of the narcissist, embodying all the qualities that the parent values or wishes to see in themselves. Golden children are placed on a pedestal and are expected to excel in areas that reflect well on the narcissistic parent, such as academia, sports, or in their appearance.

While the golden child may appear to benefit from their favoured status, this role comes with significant pressure and unrealistic expectations. The child's self-worth becomes tied to their ability to please the narcissistic parent, leading to a fragile sense of identity. Golden children struggle with perfectionism, anxiety, and an inability to form authentic self-esteem, as their value is consistently measured by external achievements.

Their narcissistic parents' hobbies, favoured pastimes, belief sets, even music and fashion taste can become central to the connection, leaving the child no option but to mimic the parents' 'favoured' choices (given the lack of space for individualisation for the child). The result being the child finding common ground with the narcissistic parent's favoured things. At school, topics the parent enjoys become the child's priority, as with these the parent offers their attention for homework or projects – which the child of course appreciates.

Before they know it, the child is going to the university the parent always wanted to attend and pursuing a career in the area the parent always held unrealized ambition for. The child works harder and harder to please the parent, seeing and benefitting from every positive step they take to make the parent happy.

Being the golden child in a family with a narcissistic parent can feel like walking a tightrope between privilege and pressure. On the surface, you're showered with praise, attention, and approval – you're the 'chosen one' who can do no wrong. Yet beneath this veneer of favouritism lies a suffocating reality: your value is tied to your ability to reflect the parent's ego and fulfil their emotional needs. The love you receive feels conditional, based not on who you are but on how well you perform or uphold the family's image. The weight of perfection becomes overwhelming, as any mistake, no matter how small, threatens to strip you of the approval you've been trained to crave. You might feel trapped in an unspoken contract, where you must sacrifice your authenticity and desires to maintain the role of the golden child. The pressure to stay in the narcissist's good graces can lead to a deep sense of guilt, loneliness, neurosis, and anxiety as you're left wondering if you'll ever be truly loved for who you really are and not for the image you're forced to embody.

2 The scapegoated child

In contrast to the golden child, the scapegoat is the family member who is blamed for everything that goes wrong. The narcissistic parent projects their own faults and shortcomings onto this child, using them as an emotional punchbag. Scapegoated children internalize the negative messages they receive, leading to low self-esteem, depression, and feelings of worthlessness.

Scapegoats are the ones who resist or challenge the narcissistic parent's authority, which may make them targets for the parent's wrath. The scapegoat role can lead to chronic feelings of guilt and shame, as well as difficulties in forming healthy relationships outside the family. These children may either continue to attract narcissistic partners in adulthood or struggle to trust others altogether.

Being the scapegoated child in a family with a narcissistic parent is an experience filled with deep pain and confusion. It's as though you're living in a constant storm, where nothing you do is ever good enough and every flaw, real or imagined, is magnified and used against you. You grow up feeling isolated and unseen, as the narcissistic parent manipulates the family dynamic to cast you as the problem, the source of all tension, while others are often praised or shielded. This emotional burden leaves scars of self-doubt and insecurity as you internalize the blame for dysfunction you didn't cause. The love and validation you so desperately seek are withheld, leaving you to question your worth, while a quiet ache for acceptance and belonging grows within. Over time, the weight of being the scapegoat can erode your sense of self, making it hard to trust both yourself and others. Yet, amidst this darkness, there remains a small, resilient part of you that hopes for the day when you'll break free from the narrative imposed on you and discover your true worth.

3 The lost child

The lost child is often overlooked in the family dynamic. This child withdraws from the family drama, becoming invisible to avoid the wrath of the narcissistic parent. Lost children often develop a rich internal world, retreating into books, fantasies, or solitary activities to cope with their feelings of neglect and isolation.

The impact of being the lost child can be profound, leading to difficulties in expressing emotions, forming intimate relationships, and asserting oneself in adulthood. Lost children are more likely to experience social anxiety, low self-confidence, and a sense of purpose-lessness, as they were never given the opportunity to develop a strong sense of self within the family.

Being the lost child in a family with a narcissistic parent is an experience of profound invisibility and emotional neglect. While the golden child is praised and the scapegoat blamed, you feel like a shadow – unseen, unheard, and forgotten. In the chaos of the family dynamic, you've learned to stay quiet, to shrink yourself, hoping to avoid the manipulation or demands of the narcissistic parent. You become adept at fading into the background, not wanting to add to the turmoil, yet the silence is its own kind of pain. It's a lonely existence, where you might yearn for connection or recognition but instead are left to fend for yourself emotionally. No one notices your needs, your struggles, or your desires, and over time you may begin to doubt whether you even deserve attention or love. The isolation fosters a deep sense of abandonment and disconnection from others, making it difficult to form close relationships or trust in your worth. Yet despite the emptiness, there's a quiet strength in the lost child – a hope that one day, you'll find your voice and the world will finally see you for the unique and valuable person you are.

4 The enabler or co-narcissist

The enabler, often a spouse or another family member, plays a crucial role in maintaining the narcissistic parent's dominance. They may excuse or justify the narcissistic parent's behaviour, smoothing over conflicts and protecting the narcissist from the consequences of their actions. Enablers often have their own psychological issues, such as co-dependency, which drive them to support the narcissistic parent despite the harm it causes the rest of the family.

Enablers may also function as mediators between the narcissist and the other family members, reinforcing the narcissist's narrative and minimizing the impact of their abuse. This role can lead to a distorted sense of reality for the enabler, who becomes increasingly isolated from the rest of the family and dependent on the narcissist for validation. Enablers struggle with guilt, denial, and identity issues as they have sacrificed their own needs and values to maintain the family structure.

Being the enabler in a family with a narcissistic parent is a complex and exhausting role. On the surface, you may appear as the peace-maker, the one who holds everything together, smoothing over conflicts and justifying the narcissist's behaviour to others. But beneath that there's an inner turmoil as you constantly push your own needs aside in a desperate attempt to keep the family functioning. You might find yourself excusing the narcissist's cruelty, believing that keeping the peace is the only way to survive, or hoping that if you can just manage things well enough, the situation will improve. It's a role born out of fear and survival, where you're trapped between loyalty to the narcissist and a quiet guilt over enabling their behaviour. The pressure to maintain harmony takes a heavy emotional toll and over time you may feel resentful, drained, or lost in your own identity. Yet, breaking free feels terrifying because the narcissistic parent has very probably conditioned you to believe that without your enabling, the family would fall apart. Deep down, there's a yearning for release, a hope that one day you'll find the courage to stop carrying the weight of everyone's emotions and discover what it feels like to live for yourself.

5 The non-narcissistic partner or co-parent

Being the non-narcissistic co-parent in a family where your partner is a narcissist is a heartbreaking and often isolating experience. You find yourself constantly walking on eggshells, trying to protect your children from the emotional manipulation and control of the narcissistic parent while struggling to keep the family dynamic as stable as possible. You see the damage being done – the favouritism, the scapegoating, the emotional neglect – and it tears at your heart to watch your children suffer in ways that you feel powerless to stop.

You're caught in an agonizing bind, torn between shielding your children and not provoking your partner's narcissistic behaviour, all while dealing with the erosion of your sense of self-worth. The narcissist may undermine your parenting efforts, devalue your contributions, and manipulate your children against you, leaving you feeling as though you're constantly fighting an uphill battle, alone in the chaos. Despite this, you carry an immense amount of love and strength, trying to provide a safe space for your children, offering them the empathy and care that they so desperately need. The emotional toll is heavy, but the hope of breaking the cycle for your children keeps you going, even when it feels like you're barely holding on.

The impact on the family unit

The roles assigned or assumed by family members in a narcissistic family system create a rigid and dysfunctional dynamic that has long-lasting effects on the entire family. These roles are not static and shift over time, particularly as children grow and the family structure changes. However, the underlying dynamics of control, manipulation, and emotional abuse often persist, leaving deep psychological scars on all involved.

The rigid roles within a narcissistic family result in strained and superficial relationships. Family members may become estranged or maintain only superficial contact to avoid triggering conflicts. Adult children of narcissistic parents often struggle with trust and intimacy in their relationships as they have learned to associate closeness with manipulation and betrayal.

Communication in narcissistic families is often dysfunctional, characterized by passive-aggressive behaviour, indirect communication, and a lack of open, honest dialogue. Members of these families are often unable to express their true feelings or needs, leading to misunderstandings, resentment, and a lack of genuine connection. The need to maintain the narcissist's fragile ego often takes precedence over healthy communication.

The emotional toll on family members can be severe, leading to issues such as depression, anxiety, and complex trauma. Individuals raised in narcissistic families are at a higher risk for mental health disorders due to chronic exposure to emotional abuse and neglect. The constant tension and unpredictability in these families can create a pervasive sense of insecurity and fear.

The roles within a narcissistic family shape the identity and self-worth of family members in unhealthy ways. Individuals may struggle with self-esteem issues as their sense of worth has been tied to their ability to fulfil the roles assigned to them by the narcissistic parent. Whether it is the golden child's pressure to achieve, the scapegoat's internalized blame, or the lost child's invisibility, these roles have lasting effects on one's concept of self.

Sadly, dysfunctional patterns in narcissistic families are often passed down through generations as the roles and behaviours modelled by the narcissistic parent are replicated by their children in their own families. Children of narcissistic parents are more likely either to develop narcissistic traits themselves or enter into relationships with narcissists, perpetuating the cycle of dysfunction.

The constellation of roles in a family with a narcissistic parent creates a toxic environment that profoundly impacts the emotional, psychological, and relational well-being of all family members. These roles – whether as the golden child, scapegoat, lost child, or enabler – are strategies developed to survive in a system where the narcissist's needs dominate. However, these survival strategies come at a significant cost, shaping the identities and future relationships of family members in damaging ways.

Understanding these roles and their impact is crucial for both therapists and individuals seeking to break free from the cycle of dysfunction. Recent research underscores the importance of addressing these dynamics in therapy to help individuals reclaim their sense of self, establish healthy boundaries, and build more fulfilling relationships. By recognizing and challenging these roles, it is possible to heal from the trauma of a narcissistic family system and prevent the transmission of these patterns to future generations.

Narcissistic Personality Disorder can have profound and far-reaching effects on the family members of those afflicted, particularly on their children. When we are working with families where narcissism is suspected or known, this is an example checklist of what we would be noticing versus a healthier family.

Here are the top ten signs of a psychologically healthy family in operation:	Here are the top ten signs of a narcissistic family in operation:
Respect for hierarchy and equality: Healthy families maintain a balance of authority where parents guide but do not dominate. Family members are encouraged to express their views and decisions are made with collective input.	**Hierarchy and control:** The narcissistic parent maintains strict control, placing themselves at the top of the family hierarchy. Other members are expected to conform to their wishes, and any attempts to challenge their authority are met with anger or punishment.
Strong personal boundaries: Family members respect each other's privacy and autonomy. Individual boundaries, both emotional and physical, are acknowledged and upheld, fostering trust and independence.	**Lack of boundaries:** Personal boundaries are often disregarded as the narcissistic parent sees others in the family as extensions of themselves. Privacy is minimal and family members' emotional and physical spaces are frequently violated.
Equitable treatment: All children are treated fairly, with no clear favouritism. Siblings receive equal amounts of love and attention and no one is singled out for blame or over-praise.	**Favouritism and scapegoating:** One child may be treated as the golden child, showered with praise and attention, while another is scapegoated, blamed for family issues and subjected to criticism. This creates division and tension among siblings.
Unconditional love: Affection and love are given freely, without strings attached. Family members feel loved and accepted regardless of their successes or failures.	**Conditional love:** Affection is often conditional and based on whether family members meet the narcissistic parent's expectations. Love and approval are withdrawn when the parent feels slighted or criticized.

Emotional support: The emotional needs of each family member are prioritized. Parents empathize with their children and provide comfort, security, and validation during challenging times.	**Emotional neglect:** The emotional needs of children or partners are frequently neglected as the narcissistic parent prioritizes their own feelings and experiences. Empathy is minimal or entirely absent.
Reality affirmation: Family members are honest with each other, acknowledging each person's experiences and emotions. No one is made to feel confused or invalidated by manipulation.	**Gaslighting:** Narcissistic parents may engage in gaslighting, manipulating reality and making others question their perceptions, memories, or feelings. This often leads to confusion and self-doubt among family members.
Encouragement of independence: Family members support one another's autonomy and personal growth. Parents celebrate their children's milestones and encourage them to pursue their own paths.	**Enmeshment:** The narcissistic parent expects family members to be overly involved in their life and may discourage independence. They see others' autonomy as a threat to their control.
Self-reflection and accountability: Parents and family members acknowledge their flaws and work towards personal growth. Mistakes are owned up to and responsibility is not shifted onto others.	**Projection:** The narcissistic parent projects their flaws, insecurities, or feelings onto others, accusing them of the very behaviours they themselves exhibit. This deflects responsibility and blame.
Direct communication: Families manage conflicts with open, honest communication and do not involve others unnecessarily. Disagreements are resolved without manipulation or division.	**Triangulation:** The narcissistic parent may pit family members against one another to maintain control and create division. They manipulate relationships to keep power within the family, using tactics such as gossip and favouritism.
Consistency between public and private life: Healthy families present themselves authentically in both public and private settings. There is no need to maintain a façade as the emotional health of the family is sound both inside and outside the home.	**Public image vs private reality:** Narcissistic families often present a polished, idealized image to the outside world while concealing dysfunction within. This duality creates a confusing and isolating experience for family members who are aware of the hidden toxic dynamics.
This list reflects the positive behaviours of families that cultivate emotional health and well-being, in contrast to the dysfunctional traits found in narcissistic families.	These behaviours create a deeply unhealthy emotional environment, often leading to long-term psychological damage for the children and partners of narcissistic individuals.

Narcissistic mothers and their children

Narcissistic mothers on initial sight appear to be brought up in therapy more often than narcissistic fathers. While there is ongoing research to consider the pure data and statistics regarding this, my personal question is around whether the gender expectations on mothers versus fathers mean the mother is expected to provide more of the classic loving nurture to her children and therefore when her narcissistic traits come to the fore, a child will feel and suffer exponentially, due to not only the narcissistic abuse they experience but the delta between the expectations of a mother's love versus the reality of what they are experiencing.

Narcissistic mothers often exhibit a more covert form of narcissism, where their need for control and validation is manifested through emotional manipulation. Narcissistic mothers create a toxic and emotionally charged dynamic with their children, often treating them not as individuals with their own needs but as instruments to validate the mother's fragile self-worth – with each child assigned a role as we saw above. Such divisive treatment breeds resentment and confusion among siblings, driving a wedge between them and leaving them vying for a love that feels just out of reach.

The narcissistic mother controls through emotional manipulation, using guilt, shame, or conditional praise to keep her children compliant. Their achievements are either co-opted as reflections of her greatness or dismissed if they threaten her fragile sense of superiority. Over time, her children may struggle with self-esteem, constantly questioning their worth as they've been raised in a reality where love is earned, never freely given. This skewed version of love leaves deep scars, making it difficult for the children to trust, form healthy relationships, or even understand who they truly are outside the roles their mother imposed on them. The emotional damage ripples through their lives, and they may spend years untangling the complex web of loyalty, guilt, and hurt woven by the narcissistic mother's control.

Mothers and daughters

Narcissistic mothers often engage in subtle forms of emotional abuse, such as gaslighting, guilt-tripping, and conditional love. Daughters of narcissistic mothers often feel as though they can never be 'good enough'. This feeling of inadequacy can carry over into adulthood, leading to chronic self-doubt, anxiety, and a tendency to form unhealthy relationships where the dynamic of emotional manipulation is replicated.

The relationship between a narcissistic mother and her daughter is often fraught with tension, competition, and emotional manipulation. A narcissistic mother tends to see her daughter as both an extension of herself and a threat to her fragile ego. While the daughter might be groomed to reflect the mother's idealized image, she is also subjected to constant criticism and comparison. If the daughter shines too brightly, the mother may feel eclipsed and retaliate with jealousy, undermining the daughter's achievements or diminishing her sense of self-worth. If the daughter struggles or fails to meet her mother's impossible expectations, she may be dismissed or blamed, reinforcing a cycle of shame and inadequacy. The narcissistic mother projects her own unmet desires, paranoias and insecurities on to her daughter, shaping her identity in ways that strip her of autonomy. This constant tug-of-war creates confusion, as the daughter craves approval and love but finds that these are always conditional, contingent upon the mother's emotional needs. As a result, the daughter grows up internalizing feelings of never being 'good enough', questioning her worth, and struggling to find her own voice. The bond is a delicate, toxic dance – equal parts enmeshment and rejection – leaving the daughter to untangle a lifetime of complex emotions in search of her true self.

Mothers and sons

Sons of narcissistic mothers may experience enmeshment, where the mother relies on the son to fulfil her emotional needs. This can lead to a distorted sense of responsibility, where the son feels obligated to take care of his mother's emotional well-being at the expense of his own. A 2007 study by Levine and colleagues (*Journal of Counselling Psychology*) found that sons of narcissistic mothers often experience difficulties in establishing boundaries, leading to co-dependent relationships in adulthood.

Narcissistic mothers often forge a complicated, emotionally suffocating bond with their sons, shaping their identity in ways that can leave lasting scars. To the outside world, it might seem like the mother dotes on her son, showering him with attention and praise, but beneath that, her affection is often deeply conditional. She sees him not as an individual with his own needs and desires but as an extension of herself, expecting him to fulfil her emotional voids and mirror her greatness. This dynamic can create an impossible standard for the son, who grows up feeling the weight of unrealistic expectations while being denied the space to explore his own identity. If he complies, he may be praised as her 'golden boy', but at the cost of suppressing his true self. If he resists, he risks becoming the scapegoat, subject to criticism and emotional manipulation. The mother's need for control can foster a deep sense of confusion, as the son oscillates between craving her approval and feeling trapped by her demands. Over time, this relationship can profoundly impact his ability to form healthy connections with others, as he struggles with boundaries, self-worth, and understanding how love without strings truly feels.

Narcissistic fathers and their children

Narcissistic fathers create a complex and emotionally charged environment for their children. Driven by an insatiable need for admiration and control, these fathers impose rigid expectations, projecting their unfulfilled desires and ambitions onto their offspring. Children of narcissistic fathers feel they must constantly perform to earn approval, often at the expense of their own individuality and emotional needs. This dynamic leads to deep feelings of inadequacy, confusion, and self-doubt as the child navigates between seeking validation and fearing rejection. Over time, the father's lack of genuine empathy can foster emotional isolation, stunting the child's self-esteem and sense of worth. In such relationships, the father's image takes precedence over the child's authentic self, distorting their ability to form healthy attachments and understand their true identity.

Fathers and sons

The relationship between a narcissistic father and his son is often marked by competition and conditional approval. A father may view his son as a rival or as an extension of himself, expecting the son to achieve success in ways that glorify the father. Sons of narcissistic fathers often experience heightened levels of pressure and stress as they are constantly trying to live up to the unrealistic expectations set by their fathers.

The narcissistic father does not see his son as an individual with his own needs, dreams, and personality but rather as an extension of himself. This leads to a toxic blend of competition, control, and conditional affection, where the father may oscillate between criticizing and inflating the son's achievements based on how they reflect on his own ego. Sons of narcissistic fathers often struggle with identity, feeling pressured to meet unrealistic expectations or embody the father's image of success. This environment can foster resentment and a deep-seated fear of failure as the son is constantly measured against an impossible standard. Emotionally starved for genuine connection and validation, many sons of narcissistic fathers may either rebel against their father's dominance or internalize the pattern, repeating it in their own relationships while grappling with a sense of never being 'good enough'.

Fathers and daughters

Narcissistic fathers and their daughters often engage in a deeply unsettling interplay that profoundly shapes the daughter's self-worth and identity. In addition this critical relationship often serves as template for the daughter's future romantic relationships and how she expects to be treated. The narcissistic father may view his daughter as a reflection of his own desires or as a tool for bolstering his image, rather than as an individual with her own needs and aspirations. This can manifest in controlling behaviours, excessive praise when she meets his standards or harsh criticism when she fails to live up to his expectations. The daughter, caught in this emotional crossfire, may grapple with chronic self-doubt and an incessant need for validation. She might struggle with her self-image, oscillating between trying to fulfil her father's idealized vision and feeling inadequate when she falls short. This dynamic often leads to difficulties in forming healthy relationships as the daughter may either overcompensate by seeking external validation or subconsciously replicate the same controlling patterns in her own interactions. The narcissistic father's conditional love and approval create a volatile foundation for the daughter's self-esteem, shaping her emotional landscape long into adulthood.

Narcissistic grandparents: extending the cycle of abuse

The impact of a narcissistic parent can also extend to the next generation. Narcissistic grandparents may continue to manipulate their children through their relationships with their grandchildren.

Narcissistic grandparents often use their grandchildren as pawns in their ongoing manipulation of their adult children. For example, they may undermine the parent's authority by spoiling the grandchild or offering excessive praise, creating divisions between the parent and child. Dr Christine Hammond, in her 2016 article for *PsychCentral*, notes that narcissistic grandparents may try to turn their grandchildren against their parents by portraying themselves as the 'better' or more understanding figure, further destabilizing family relationships.

Narcissistic grandparents may engage in emotional triangulation, where they play the grandchild against their own children to maintain control over family dynamics. This leads to confusion and emotional distress for the grandchild, who is caught in the middle of conflicting loyalties. The grandchildren of narcissistic individuals often experience higher levels of emotional distress as they are subjected to the same manipulative behaviours their parents faced in childhood.

When we imagine a child experiencing narcissistic abuse at the hands of both their parent and a grand-parent, the enormity of the one-two-punch can leave that child trapped in a world of wall-to-wall gaslighting where their ability to develop trust and explore the truth becomes virtually impossible.

5

A narcissistic family case study

'In narcissistic families, abuse and neglect are permitted. Talking about it, however, is forbidden.'

Parental narcissistic dynamics in three generations of one family

This is the Halston family. The grandfather, Graham, had a double PhD and worked extensively abroad. He had been brought up by his father in the 1940s after his mother had unexpectedly walked out. While Graham was affectionately regarded, it had been noticed by members of the wider family that he displayed what they suspected to be high-functioning autistic traits, with fixations and patterns he liked to follow. Given he was frequently away or abroad with work, it often went unnoticed, but when home he often stayed in his private study for hours on end, opening the door only to receive food. After retirement he often played computer games until the early hours of the morning, spending little time with and paying little attention to Connie, his wife of 50 years.

Connie had grown up in London. Her mother had died when Connie was finishing school and she was therefore also left with just her father. She had a highly developed sense of style and though a little anxious, she left school to work in fashion. When she met Graham, they married within a year and she worked part-time, raising money for charity. Graham and Connie went on to have three children whom Connie brought up to a large degree on her own, given Graham's career. They managed to move from a semi-detached property to a large, detached house some years later and were well regarded in the community.

Their eldest child, Simon, was a welcomed baby. However, around the age of four, his parents started regarding him as a bit of a handful, initially not concentrating at school, then becoming angry and unmanageable at home. As a result, he was often hit and punished by both parents during adolescence. He developed an extraordinary talent for art, but by 16 he had left home and developed a drink and drug habit, telling others he thought he might have been sexually abused as a child by a man he could not identify. He was ridiculed and dismissed by the family for saying this, and his drinking was always used as a distraction. Simon's subsequent lack of responsibility was partially to blame for the failure of his first marriage, but in his forties he met and married a loving and emotionally strong and stable woman. With her support he was diagnosed with ASD and ADHD and started to control his drinking. Connie loved Simon but was always disappointed by him and did not trust him with any responsibilities, which he felt hurt by. She dismissed any neurodiversity diagnosis, claiming there was no history of ASD in the family and ridiculed any stories of child sexual abuse.

The middle child was Fiona, a well-behaved girl who witnessed the chaos around Simon's relationship with her parents and took the route of being good and quiet in order to pacify her mother and please her father. Aged just nine, Fiona was hospitalized for anxiety, something she now struggles to explain and which is never mentioned by the family. Fiona was of average ability at school and at 17 took on a caring role looking after other families. She met and married Peter in her late teens – he was in medicine and was away a huge amount of the time, mimicking her father's absence. They went on to have two daughters who followed their father into the medical world. The marriage was functional, but after 25 years they decided to divorce, to the huge shock of the immediate family – but it came as no surprise to the non-Halston faction who had observed dysfunctional patterns for some time.

The youngest child was Mike. Mike came along a lot later than Simon and Fiona and was regarded as the marriage-saving baby. Given the history of difficulty with Simon, Graham and Connie decided they would raise Mike differently. He was sent to private school and given a lot of attention and latitude. He displayed some interesting early traits, fixating on aeroplane seat configurations, for example, and memorizing hundreds of car numberplates – and insisting on naming all three of the sequential family cats 'Peter'. His mother regarded him as a genius, but his siblings called him Sir Mike given the favouritism displayed. When he was 17 (with Fiona and Simon now having left home) Mike's parents suddenly decided to move to Africa without him and arranged for him to live with a neighbour while he finished his A levels – something Mike still sees as completely normal, to the surprise of many of his friends. He was the first of the children to go to university, went on to build a successful career as an architect. He married Jenny in his late twenties, who he had dated on-and-off since childhood and was an outgoing charismatic and loving woman. Since Graham's death, Fiona had taken over the role of carer for Connie, but Mike had taken over the financial and legal work for his mother. He spent a lot of time with her and refused ever to spend Christmas anywhere but with her, even into his fifties, despite pleas from his children and partners.

Mike was married to Jenny for 10 years. However, Jenny eventually left him, after suffering multiple mental breakdowns and ill health, claiming psychological narcissistic abuse, concerns about his relationship with their eldest daughter, and that Mike was undermining her abilities as a mother. Mike hid this from his family, claiming instead that he was a victim of Jenny's unstable mental health and health anxiety, which he liked to describe as hypochondria, all of which they readily accepted. After the pair separated, Mike gained custody of the children, with Jenny seeing them at weekends while she tried to recover. Fiona, Connie and many of his female friends supported Mike and regarded him as both a victim and a hero.

Shortly after Jenny leaving, Mike commenced a secret 14-month relationship with Sarah, whom he had originally met during his university years, but told nobody, preferring to maintain his position as the victim in the divorce. However, Sarah too began to struggle, specifically citing his narcissistic behaviour. She had never been allowed into his house, nor met his children, and he made little time or space for her. She eventually decided to address this and Mike's response was simply to end the relationship via text and then ghost her.

A year later Mike met Ruth, a woman he had vaguely known and much admired professionally for 20 years. He proudly showed off about her accomplishments and appearance to his friends and family and swiftly introduced her to his children. He proposed after

18 months. Ruth immediately became aware of the children's struggles and Mike's bizarre behaviour at home and tried hard to help. They were together for six years until she also fled, claiming life-threatening psychological and narcissistic abuse as well as serious safeguarding concerns regarding Mike and his children.

Both Mike's children were identified by their schools as having emotional challenges, the blame for which he laid at their mother Jenny's door for having left. They were both on elevated levels of medication by the age of 11 and went to many therapists and psychiatrists over the years, but not once was Mike's role in their struggles ever discussed. He retained his position of the hero single father and all female partners, nannies or therapists who began to ask uncomfortable questions were bullied, diminished or sacked.

Let's take a look at what happened within this family, in and outside therapy, the effect that one covert narcissist had on three generations of the Halston family, and how the ongoing family dynamic allowed it to continue unnoticed, untreated, and unmanaged for three decades.

All names, vocations, geographies, and identifiable details have been changed to protect confidentiality, but this case study is based on a real family.

Mike Halston (father and covert narcissist)

Publicly, Mike described his childhood as idyllic, often recalling moments where he dictated exactly what he wanted – such as a specific, expensive bicycle – insisting his parents purchase it for him, and how he was supported, encouraged, and unconditionally loved by them. He spoke highly of them both, even if he did admit his mother was rather cold and negative.

Despite this external narrative, deeper examination revealed a less ideal upbringing. Mike frequently lied about sporting and academic accomplishments as a young child to impress others, most likely as a strategy to gain the emotional attention he felt was actually absent from his parents. His childhood was also marked by the discovery of his parents' extramarital affairs and their mutual threats of divorce. Conversations he overheard but topics that were never openly discussed then and remain under the psychological family carpet to this day.

By adolescence, Mike was displaying a pattern of taking criticism poorly and seeking revenge on those who slighted him. He recalled being hit at school by a teacher but not bothering to tell his parents, knowing they would not act. He got into some fights and always sought to 'pay back' those who had bullied him. He developed and exhibited obsessive behaviours and private rituals to control his anxiety, such as talking to 'devils' hidden in curtains and obsessing over the positions of items in his bedroom each night. When these behaviours were discovered and ridiculed by his peers, they caused Mike deep shame. He was painfully aware of his late development and coped by developing high ideals and an intense focus on his physical appearance, joining a muscle gym aged just 14 and demonstrating certain behavioural traits that he used to control his reputation. His relationships at this stage were marked by cycles of clumsy seduction followed by swift emotional detachment and sabotage, reflecting a growing avoidance of intimacy. Many commented that he had a blank stare and cold eyes, things he laughed off, often attacking that person's character in defence.

Mike's university years saw a significant shift in his persona. He adopted a false accent and sought to align himself with wealthier peers, further solidifying his focus on materialism and status. His condescension towards those he deemed 'unworthy' contrasted sharply with his performative charm towards those he viewed as useful to his ambitions. This was never more acute than in his intimate relationships with partners, where behind closed doors, his split personality would be revealed, and the kindly and respected Dr Jekyll would transform into the evil and violent Mr Hyde, something he would later occasionally admit in therapy. The man colleagues would describe as 'decent' and 'charming' appeared very different from the cruel, spiteful, and unsupportive shell of a partner Jenny and Ruth struggled with. Such a contrast left his loved ones confused, lonely, and feeling neglected and isolated, and his wider family rather bemused.

When Mike married Jenny in his mid-thirties, he had experienced no significant previous long-term relationships. On the surface, the marriage was functional, especially when they were both the centre of attention, but cracks soon emerged, particularly with the birth of their first daughter, Izzy.

The birth of Izzy seemed to exacerbate Mike's underlying anxiety. He became obsessively controlling over her routines, diet, and safety, yet relegated the bulk of parenting responsibilities to Jenny. This mirrored his father's traditional role of working long hours while being emotionally detached from family life. Jenny struggled with postnatal depression, but Mike showed no empathy or support, instead ridiculing and belittling her expressions of unhappiness.

When their second daughter, Suki, was born, some early but mild childhood illness placed further strain on the marriage. Jenny, now physically and emotionally depleted, experienced worsening mental health, leading to multiple hospitalizations. Despite this, Mike maintained his emotional distance, avoiding responsibility while framing himself as a sacrificial victim. He later admitted in therapy to 'checking out' of the marriage long before its dissolution, waiting for Jenny to leave him or engage in an affair to allow Mike to avoid any personal accountability.

Following Jenny's departure, Mike carefully curated a narrative of abandonment and self-sacrifice, portraying himself as a single father raising two daughters alone. However, within a week Mike had installed a full-time live-in nanny to undertake all parental responsibilities, from getting the children out of bed in the mornings while he went for a run, to cooking and eating supper with them because Mike wanted to relax alone – enabling Mike to maintain a detached and self-focused lifestyle where he neither ate with his children nor even put them to bed.

He used the claim of single parenthood to gain admiration and sympathy while employing manipulative tactics with his daughters. When the children themselves challenged him on his lack of involvement, Mike threatened dramatic consequences, such as quitting his job to be with them, telling them they would need to move house and school without his income, which frightened the children into compliance. This dynamic allowed him to maintain control while avoiding any meaningful engagement with them, something both the children spoke of with resentment in therapy. Mike used additional but subtle punishment tactics, including mood swings, silent treatment, neglect, sudden rage, emotional collapse, and absence. His control extended to shaping the family's public image, enforcing a façade of perfection that concealed the growing dysfunction underneath. Izzy would dutifully perform to please and align with her father as Suki was dragged along with threats to ensure she conformed.

By the age of just eight, as the divorce was being finalized, Izzy, the elder daughter, had become enmeshed with Mike, lured into adopting the role of his surrogate spouse. She had developed understandable anxiety through the disintegration of her parents' marriage and overhearing arguments and witnessing long-term silent treatment. With her mother in hospital or absent, she became hypervigilant as to the well-being of her father, her only remaining caregiver, and learned to monitor Mike's moods and provide emotional support, often at the expense of her own needs. Mike would go into her room when she was asleep and carry her into his bed, stating that he did not like sleeping alone, something that later alarmed Ruth when she discovered it.

Suki, the younger daughter, in turn became a pacifier and comic, attempting to soothe tensions within the household. Surprisingly, none of them had entered into therapy, despite the trauma of the last few years. By now, both girls were manipulated into defending their father publicly against any criticism, often through fabricated narratives about conflicts with their mother and, later, their stepmother too, despite their private experience of constant drama and arguments at home. Nothing could be Mike's fault as this would rock the only safety they had – their narcissistic father.

Mike kept his work and home lives segregated, ensuring neither ever merged in any meaningful way, with colleagues reflecting that while they knew him, they had never spent any time out of the office around him or been to his home. This allowed Mike fully to control the distortions he created and hide his abusive behaviour at home, while he wore the mask of a charming and single-parent victim at work. He was promoted at work and increasingly more absent at home. Professionally and socially he was presenting as happy and successful, but he was hiding a chaotic, angry, and incongruent home life, with his children mentally deteriorating.

Some years after Jenny left him, and around a year after he had abandoned Sarah, Mike pursued Ruth, a successful woman and mother whom he had admired for some time. He was initially surprised that she was open to a relationship with him and moved swiftly to secure things, introducing her to his family and children within weeks. However, within six months he was regularly abandoning Ruth at critical moments, not turning up to dates, not answering his phone for days, leaving her alone for weeks at a time unsure of whether the relationship was on or off. He even refused to support her at her mother's funeral or take her to the hospital for a major operation. Yet he lied to his friends and family about it all. Mike would end the relationship one minute and then write letters hoovering Ruth back in and even proposing – promising a life together, buying a home together, and having more children.

The intermittent affection and abuse Jenny had suffered was now being projected onto Ruth too and she found it bewildering, as did Suki and Izzy. They loved Ruth but were confused as to why she was often sad, quiet or upset with their father, not knowing how he had been psychologically and emotionally abusing her. Little did they also know how much Ruth was fighting for them to be loved and protected as vulnerable children by him. Mike would promise he would change and then do nothing at all to move towards it. He was the master of breadcrumbing – creating desire and plans and promises to be a better parent, none of which ever materialized or endured for more than a few days.

This would be the start of a painful six-year tussle for Ruth, who had sincerely committed to Mike and her stepdaughters, aware of the chaos and pain his divorce had created and determined to try to make things better. She would strive to figure out what was going on psychologically, including questioning whether Mike might actually be autistic or narcissistic. Running parallel with this she had begun to question both the inappropriate level of enmeshment she was observing between Mike and Izzy and his almost total lack of parenting – something his ex-wife was also calling out. Over time Ruth's mental and physical health, like Jenny's had, nosedived as she tried to cope and hold the family together. She admitted later that she had twice anonymously called social services with her concerns about the children and Mike, considered taking medication herself to cope, and spoken to Fiona, Mike's sister, asking her to come and observe the family over a weekend to see the truth for herself.

Throughout, Mike displayed little if no emotional response to either Jenny or Ruth's pleas for change, explanation or accountability and instead insisted all his punitive and at times bizarre actions and behaviours were 'in service to his children'. In fact his own children were also making increasingly distorted bids for his attention. He blamed his physical and emotional absence on work, becoming a credit-card father who batted away requests for time and attention by buying his children expensive items (which he then used against them when they complained about him) or taking them on five-star holidays, where he didn't need to take care of them himself.

The enmeshment with Izzy aside, he seemed to hold little genuine emotion or empathy towards his children, instead using his position as a parent to excuse and mask all his cruelty and abuse towards his partners – using them as a human shield further to mask his narcissism. Hidden in plain sight behind his parental peacocking façade.

Behavioural patterns and clinical observations

Emotional detachment: Mike exhibited a consistent pattern of emotional disengagement, both in his marriage and with his daughters. This aligns with an avoidant attachment style, potentially rooted in his early familial experiences.

Control and manipulation: His behaviours reflect covert narcissistic traits, including the need to control others while avoiding accountability, and the diminishing and discarding of his partners when they tried to expose him to protect his children and themselves.

Façade maintenance: The family's outward appearance of normalcy starkly contrasted with the reality of internal dysfunction. Mike's insistence on this image (utilizing his children to maintain it) served to shield his narcissistic behaviours from external scrutiny.

Interpersonal exploitation: Mike's relationships, including those with his daughters, were transactional, aimed at meeting his emotional needs rather than fostering mutual connection.

Partner abuse: The fact that all three intimate partners, across three separate decades, claimed he psychologically abused them raised major concerns with professionals.

Jenny Halston (Mike's wife, victim of narcissistic abuse and parental alienation)

Jenny Halston was an outgoing, vivacious, and highly capable individual known for her humour, determination, and warmth. She began a relationship with Mike in her late teens, which rekindled after his university years. The couple married a few years later and had two daughters, Izzy and Suki. However, the dynamics of their relationship, compounded by Mike's behaviours, eventually led to significant emotional and psychological distress for Jenny.

Following the birth of their first daughter, Jenny experienced postnatal depression, which marked the beginning of her struggles within the marriage. She sought medical advice for her condition but found little emotional support from Mike, who focused increasingly on work, sports, and his own interests. At home, his interactions with Izzy became obsessive and controlling, often undermining Jenny's parenting efforts. He triangulated their toddler daughter into conflicts, subtly encouraging Izzy to take his side, leaving Jenny isolated in her role as a mother.

Attempts to address these issues were met with emotional withdrawal on Mike's part. He responded to Jenny's bids for connection with silent treatment, sulking, or escalating minor disagreements into arguments. This behaviour further alienated Jenny and increased her sense of helplessness. Izzy later recalled these arguments as formative memories, perceiving a pattern of a constant bickering discord between her parents which caused her intense anxiety.

Jenny's health began further to deteriorate after the birth of their second daughter. Despite the joy Suki brought her, Jenny developed a range of physical and psychological symptoms, including difficulty swallowing, severe depression, anxiety, and gynaecological issues. Mike dismissed these concerns as attention-seeking behaviour, refusing to engage with her medical care or attend appointments. Jenny reported feeling entirely unsupported and emotionally discarded during this period.

Mike's controlling tendencies escalated. He forbade Jenny from attending social events with him, citing embarrassment, and removed her from their marital bed, placing Izzy in her place while Jenny was relegated to a spare room. His behaviour became increasingly hostile and dismissive, creating an environment of everyday aggression and invalidation for Jenny. At work he remained charming and generated a façade of deep care for his wife by garnering sympathy from those he told of her illnesses.

Over the years, Jenny's mental health declined significantly, culminating in multiple admissions to a private mental health facility. Attempts at family therapy during these admissions were unsuccessful; sessions were often ended mid-discussion such was the level of escalation between Mike, Jenny, and Izzy. Mike's primary concern was operational – ensuring childcare arrangements while Jenny was hospitalized – rather than addressing her emotional needs or the family's underlying dysfunction.

Following her fourth admission, Jenny decided she could no longer return to the family home, citing Mike's cruelty, coercive control, and emotional abuse as factors detrimental to her health. Mike's response was notably detached; he expressed outer coldness and no desire to reconcile and instead prioritized legal steps to protect his financial assets and secure full custody of their daughters.

After leaving the family home, Jenny attempted to maintain her relationship with Izzy and Suki. However, Mike's ongoing manipulation made this increasingly difficult. He actively alienated Izzy from her mother, portraying himself as the victim and Jenny as the cause of the family's problems. Over the first 18 months apart, Izzy, who had become enmeshed with Mike, adopted his narrative and distanced herself from Jenny.

When Jenny visited to collect the children, Mike refused to acknowledge her presence or even come to the door, further marginalizing her, and his family (her sister-in-law aside) stopped all contact. Over time, Jenny's ability to maintain contact with her daughters diminished, causing profound emotional pain for all involved. Her relationship with Suki, though initially stronger, was also strained by Mike's passive yet pervasive influence.

Jenny eventually found solace in a new relationship, building a stable and loving home environment with her partner. However, her health continued to decline and years later she was diagnosed with late-stage throat cancer. Notably, symptoms of this illness had emerged during her marriage to Mike but were dismissed by him as attention-seeking.

Jenny attempted to reach out to Ruth, Mike's new partner, to provide context for her experiences and help facilitate better relationships with Izzy and Suki. Ruth, while always being warm and welcoming to Jenny, initially remained loyal to Mike, believing his version of the story that Jenny was 'mad', and declined to discuss him specifically. But as a mother herself she did express willingness to focus on encouraging both the daughters to maintain relationships with their mother, with an awareness that parental alienation was setting in with Izzy.

It was only many years later, when Jenny learned Mike had also separated from Ruth, with Ruth citing psychological abuse and narcissistic behaviours, that Mike's partners reconnected. Ruth was shocked to learn of the extent of Jenny's experiences and, while aware of the alienation and the impact on her relationship with her daughters, now understood the horror of what had led up to their divorce. This shared understanding allowed Jenny, Ruth, and later even Sarah, all affected by Mike's identical behaviour, to recognize the pervasive and covert nature of his narcissistic and psychologically abusive tendencies and its impact on the children, which was horrific to them all.

Mike, however, cut contact with all three of his partners and stated to anyone who asked that he had ended all the relationships simply to support his children better, even suggesting he had had to sacrifice these love affairs for Izzy and Suki. And in the main, he was believed. He used, triangulated, and manipulated his own children to cover his abusive behaviour and even dispatched them as weapons against these women, leaving his daughters without any kind of safe mother or indeed an alternative parent that might uncover or quietly show the impact of the distortions their father continued to dictate. Any outsider in the home was a potential threat to him and his facade.

At the time Jenny sadly passed away (some years later) she had not been able to recover the relationship with her children or been given the opportunity to explain to them as adults why she really left and why she refused any contact with Mike. This story for Jenny is one great tragedy.

Clinical observations and implications

Coercive control: Mike's behaviour towards Jenny (and Ruth) included emotional manipulation, coercive control, triangulation, and efforts to isolate her from her own children and social supports.
Parental alienation: His tactics resulted in Jenny's estrangement from her daughters, particularly Izzy, who became enmeshed with Mike and developed identical hostility towards Jenny and later Ruth. She became a shield and a hiding place for his disfunction.
Medical neglect: Mike's dismissal of Jenny's physical and psychological symptoms reflected a broader pattern of invalidation and neglect. His lack of guilt a decade later when she died underlined his complete disregard for his part in her neglect.
Long-term impact: The covert nature of Mike's narcissistic abuse caused significant emotional and relational harm, extending beyond Jenny to subsequent partners and their shared children. With Jenny's death, Mike was quickly able to retell the story of himself as a widower, reaping even further attention, pity, and admiration – safe in the knowledge Jenny would never be able to tell the true story.

Izzy Halston (eldest daughter, golden child, and flying monkey)

Izzy Halston, by now a 16-year-old adolescent, had been deeply embedded in dysfunctional family dynamics since a young age. Highly intelligent, academically successful, and socially popular, Izzy's outward success had been overshadowed by the complex and enmeshed relationship she shared with her father. Following Jenny's departure from the family home, Izzy was swiftly placed in a surrogate role, replacing her mother in many emotional and relational capacities.

At the age of just eight, Izzy began taking on the role of emotional confidante and partner to Mike. She was given unrestricted access to his private communications, including emails and text messages, and was made privy to adult topics such as his finances and personal grievances. This dynamic blurred the lines between parental and peer relationships, with Mike treating Izzy as an equal rather than a child.

She began to call him 'Mike' instead of 'Dad' and exchanged romantic Valentine's cards with him, reinforcing the increasingly inappropriate emotional bond. Her younger sister, Suki, was often excluded from their relationship, deepening the rift between the siblings.

Izzy's relationship with her father developed into a co-dependent and enmeshed bond, which significantly impacted her psychological development. By the age of 13, she was diagnosed with severe anxiety and was prescribed high-dose sertraline to manage her symptoms. Her anxiety was accompanied by panic attacks, heightened emotional sensitivity, and hypervigilance. Izzy exhibited extreme difficulty coping with boundaries, showing marked aggression and distress when confronted with limits or disagreements, particularly from her peers or authority figures.

The dynamic between Izzy and Mike created a family environment characterized by tension, manipulation, and emotional dysregulation. Izzy was given special privileges, including the freedom to disregard conventional household rules such as mealtimes, bedtimes or chores. She displayed a lack of respect for other authority figures, including the nannies, whom she treated with disdain and disregard. Izzy's behaviour suggested early signs of narcissistic traits, especially in her interactions with others and her sense of entitlement. Mike would often tell sports or singing teachers Izzy must have a more prominent position or role in teams or shows, always using the absence of her mother as a need for special treatment.

The relationship between Izzy and Mike continued to evolve with increasing intensity, particularly after the introduction of Ruth, Mike's partner. Initially, Izzy and Ruth formed a bond, with Ruth providing the nurturing and maternal role that Izzy had missed given the absence of her mother. However, this dynamic shifted when Mike and Ruth became engaged. Izzy, feeling threatened by the growing seriousness of their relationship and therefore the potential loss of her unique position in Mike's life as his 'partner', began to project her unresolved feelings of abandonment and insecurity with her own mother on to Ruth. The enmeshment between Izzy and Mike was further reinforced as Mike failed to intervene or protect Ruth from Izzy's growing and open hostility, often even encouraging the fractures and subsequent attention.

Izzy's emotional manipulation of Mike was equally evident in her behaviours, which included openly mocking and disregarding Ruth and Suki in family therapy and attempting to intimidate Ruth physically. Mike, instead of setting boundaries or addressing Izzy's actions, reinforced the dysfunctional dynamic by siding with his daughter, blaming Ruth regardless of her input and thereby isolating Ruth (just as he had Jenny) further exacerbating the family's dysfunction. Izzy had begun to dress provocatively for her age, insisted on making adult decisions such as where to go on holiday and even which utility providers to use (aged 12), and constantly held hands with Mike in therapy sessions as if in a couple. The work was uncomfortable at times, even for the therapist.

Izzy admitted later in therapy that she was aware of her manipulative behaviour and, in her own words, expressed satisfaction in the control she exerted over her father. This control, she stated, helped reduce her anxiety and provided a sense of stability. Her actions demonstrated early signs of complex post-traumatic stress disorder (C-PTSD) but also emerging narcissistic tendencies, including the manipulation of others for personal gain and an inability to empathize with those who were negatively impacted by her behaviour.

As Izzy matured, her relationship with her father continued to deteriorate into a more pathological alliance. Mike allowed Izzy to share his bed and bathroom when Ruth was not present and made arrangements to exclude Ruth from family activities to appease Izzy's growing jealousy. Despite Ruth's efforts to address the unhealthy dynamic, Mike maintained the enmeshment, reinforcing his daughter's control over him. Mike would promise Ruth he would address the enmeshment and within days return to ostracizing Ruth and blaming her for any disruptions in the house, at times when she was not even there. This pattern persisted for years, with Izzy and Mike forming a 'secret club' of shared jokes, belittling others, and reinforcing their insular bond.

Izzy's social relationships began to suffer as a result of her dysfunctional home life. She was 'cancelled' by her peers in the year before she left for university after bullying and manipulating a male classmate. When her relationship with her boyfriend ended, she sought emotional support from Mike, further cementing their co-dependent bond, even persuading him to visit the boyfriend's parents and demand their son reunite with his daughter. When told 'no' by anyone (teachers, adults, even friends), Izzy would threaten suicide, which placed additional emotional strain on Mike. He was so enmeshed himself that he would suffer emotional collapse with Izzy. as if they were mirrors of each other, and this only perpetuated the cycle of manipulation.

When her mother died, Izzy began quietly to experience new feelings. A sadness, some guilt at her rejection of her mother, and spending less time with Mike, given her years at university, gave her an opportunity to appreciate that her life at home might not have been normal. It was at this point she ventured back to therapy.

Conclusion and clinical implications

Izzy's case highlights the profound psychological impact of enmeshment, narcissistic abuse, and parental manipulation. She was subjected to covert narcissistic behaviours by her father, which led to her becoming both a 'golden child' and a 'flying monkey', roles that enabled Mike to maintain control over the family dynamics. Her emotional dependency on Mike, coupled with her manipulation of others, reflected early signs of narcissistic traits and significant emotional dysregulation.

The family's dysfunction, particularly the lack of boundaries, emotional abuse, and triangulation, created an environment of ongoing chaos and instability for Izzy. Her relationship with her peers suffered as she was unable to navigate healthy age-appropriate interpersonal dynamics, and her mental health deteriorated as a result of the toxic family environment.

Therapeutic support: Izzy would benefit from individual therapy with a specialist therapist to address her anxiety, emotional regulation, and narcissistic traits. Equally, the death of her mother and lack of healthy parenting. Family therapy is also recommended to address the enmeshment and emotional abuse patterns, but only once she has recovered her independence from Mike.

Establishing boundaries: Interventions are needed to help Izzy and Mike understand the impact of their relationship on each other and on the wider family and to begin setting healthy boundaries.

Suki Halston (youngest daughter, lost child, and reluctant flying monkey)

Suki, the youngest daughter in the Halston family, was characterized by her creative, loving, and light-hearted personality. At 12 years old, she often found herself navigating the deep dysfunction of her family. Suki had a natural longing for connection and affection, especially from her father. However, she was largely neglected and emotionally overlooked, in stark contrast to her older sister, who enjoyed a more central and enmeshed role in Mike's life. This created a unique and painful dynamic for Suki, who longed for love, validation, and the attention that was consistently absent from her immediate family.

From a young age, Suki had struggled to sleep, concentrate or sit still for long periods of time, something Mike and Izzy ridiculed her for. Suki idolized Izzy, despite feeling hurt by her sister's behaviour and the preferential treatment she received from their father. Suki's emotional needs often remained unmet and she found herself yearning for recognition, particularly in her creative endeavours. Her artistic aspirations and need for nurturing support were ignored and instead Suki was subjected to a family dynamic that left her feeling isolated, neglected, and scapegoated.

Suki did attempt to maintain a relationship with her mother, Jenny, through secret emails, often being the only one in the family to defend her when she was scapegoated by Mike, Izzy, or their grandmother, Connie. Suki's emotional intelligence and empathy were in direct contrast to the cold, dismissive treatment she received from her father. She wanted harmony and connection within the family, but this was constantly thwarted by the chaos and emotional neglect around her.

Suki's mental health began to show signs of distress as early as the age of eight. Ruth noticed this within weeks of meeting her, and she brought it up with Mike, who instantly dismissed her, stating neither of his children had been to therapy and neither needed to. Suki admitted she was deeply affected by the loss of her mum and the emotional neglect and toxic environment in the home, resulting in severe anxiety and depression. By 12, Suki had begun to exhibit unhealthy coping mechanisms, including drinking, vaping, and spending hours alone in her room, disconnected from the family. She often engaged in inappropriate online behaviour, seeking attention and validation from people much older than her. She was aware of the risks, but secretly hoped her father would notice her struggles, which he did not. Ruth remained aware and often enquired or tried to intervene, but Suki admitted later in therapy she was torn between the unfamiliar but loving safety of Ruth and the disloyalty she experienced inside herself when she admitted her anger towards her father. A prime example of psychological splitting.

Suki's emotional dysregulation manifested physically as well. She developed a facial tic from the immense anxiety she was experiencing. She began to pull out large patches of her hair, a clear sign of the toll the familial dysfunction was taking on her mental and emotional state. When Ruth noticed the hair pulling, she privately suggested they should take her to see a psychiatrist. Mike, in keeping with his narcissistic tendencies, denied both the visible tic and the hair concerns – and the classic form of gaslighting deepened Suki's sense of isolation and confusion and left Ruth worried for Suki, angry with Mike, and ostracized within the family for speaking up.

As the youngest child, Suki found herself cast in the role of the lost child and at times scapegoat, frequently blamed for the family's problems. She was accused of being troublesome, argumentative, and rude, when in reality she was simply a child trying to navigate the neglect and emotional turmoil within her home. The responsibility for maintaining family harmony was placed on her shoulders alone, and when she failed to meet the impossible standards set by Mike, she was further alienated and dismissed.

The lack of care and attention Suki received from her father was stark. Mike ignored her basic needs and failed to show any real interest in her well-being. Most of the time, Suki was left to fend for herself, eating meals alone in her room and engaging in secretive behaviour in an attempt to gain the attention she so desperately needed. As Mike focused his energy on Izzy or himself, Suki's sense of worth continued to be eroded. The emotional neglect was compounded by a lack of supervision and boundaries, leading Suki to engage in unhealthy and unsafe behaviours.

Suki's struggles with concentration were becoming evident at school and at home. Ruth, recognizing the signs, suggested to Mike that Suki might have ADHD. However, Mike's narcissistic tendencies and obsession with perfection again prevented him from accepting this diagnosis. He became enraged by Ruth's suggestion and even ended their relationship for a brief period as punishment. Mike's inability to accept that his children might have challenges similar to his own led to a delay in addressing Suki's mental health needs.

It wasn't until three years later, when Suki again pleaded with Ruth to raise her concerns with her father once more, that Mike reluctantly agreed to seek a diagnosis. Suki was promptly diagnosed with severe ADHD and the medication she received resulted in an almost immediate and noticeable improvement in her quality of life. For the first time, Suki felt clear-headed, able to concentrate, and able to sleep properly. She expressed deep gratitude to Ruth for helping her navigate the system and gain the support she needed. Ruth as Suki's stepmother was left distraught that Suki had struggled unnecessarily for three years, something Mike forbade Ruth from ever discussing again.

The dysfunction in the Halston family continued to escalate. As Izzy prepared to leave for university, Suki feared being completely forgotten by her father. She struggled with feelings of loneliness and isolation, feeling as though she was invisible to everyone around her, except Ruth. But Suki felt torn. She loved both her father and Ruth but was often confused about what was really happening as her father (and by now Izzy), always blamed Ruth if there were any upsets at home.

Mike remained emotionally detached and neglectful. Suki's anxiety and depression worsened as she continued to be dragged into the family's problems. The girls were expected to provide validation for Mike: Suki through acting as his emotional support; and Izzy, by aligning herself with Mike and performing for his attention. Yet as Suki grew older, she realized that life in other families was vastly different from her own, something she would bring to therapy. The emotional neglect and manipulation she experienced at home were starkly contrasted with the more supportive and nurturing environments she observed in others. Suki's longing for stability, recognition, and love remained unmet as Mike continued to shift the blame for his failures onto others, particularly Jenny and Ruth.

Suki's experience in the Halston family highlights the devastating effects of narcissistic abuse, emotional neglect, and scapegoating on a child's psychological development. Suki was cast into the role of the scapegoat, blamed for the family's dysfunction, and largely ignored by her father. Her creative abilities, emotional needs, and mental health struggles were neglected, leading her to seek attention and validation in unhealthy ways.

The delayed ADHD diagnosis and lack of intervention exacerbated Suki's struggles, further impacting her self-esteem and ability to function in daily life. The absence of proper emotional and psychological support led to Suki internalizing the chaos around her and this manifested through physical symptoms such as anxiety and hair loss.

> **Therapeutic support:** Suki would benefit from individual therapy to address the emotional neglect, anxiety, and support through the ADHD diagnosis. Family therapy (with a narcissistic-aware practitioner) could also help address the dysfunction within the family and the dynamics of scapegoating and enmeshment.
>
> **Parental support and education:** Mike's narcissistic tendencies must be addressed through therapy and support, with a focus on learning to recognize and meet the emotional needs of his children.
>
> **School and social support:** Suki's school environment should be leveraged to provide ongoing support for her ADHD and mental health. Encouragement of positive peer relationships and hobbies would also help rebuild her self-esteem.
>
> **Awareness of narcissistic abuse:** Suki, along with Izzy, would benefit from understanding the long-term effects of narcissistic abuse and developing strategies for healing and moving forward.

Suki's case underscores the profound impact of narcissistic abuse on the emotional and psychological development of children. Suki's story is a tragic reminder of how emotional neglect, scapegoating, and a lack of appropriate support can lead to lasting mental health challenges.

Ruth (Mike's fiancée, Izzy and Suki's stepmother, scapegoat, and victim of narcissistic abuse)

At 44 years old, Ruth Halston had a successful career and had raised three of her own children, who were now at university. Ruth had known Mike for many years through their shared professional network and initially saw him as a charming, quiet, and reassuring individual. She was aware of his past marriage to Jenny, the mother of his daughters, and understood that Jenny had left the family, which contributed to Mike's image as a sympathetic single father admirably raising his daughters on his own.

Ruth's children were well adjusted and she had successfully co-parented with her ex-husband. When she began her relationship with Mike, Ruth took her responsibilities as a stepmother to Izzy and Suki seriously. She discussed the role with Mike regularly and expressed her commitment to co-parenting his daughters in a positive and supportive way. Mike initially seemed to be on board with this idea, reinforcing the relationship by telling Ruth that he had never introduced any woman to his daughters before, which gave Ruth the impression that Mike was serious about their future together. Early on, Ruth suggested the children showed signs of needing therapy given the loss of their mother, which Mike seemed unaware of. She equally appreciated she would see and experience less of Mike as her partner than in a normal relationship, given Mike's responsibilities. She had no idea, however, how little.

Within six months of their relationship, Ruth began to experience emotional abuse and psychological manipulation from Mike, which over time continued to escalate. He employed a strategy of alternating between hot and cold behaviour, creating confusion and instability in their relationship. Ruth was often left unsettled and uncertain of Mike's true intentions, feeling he changed personalities or mood states during evenings out, or became emotionally ice cold after a positive night out together. His lack of interest in spending any time alone with her, including spending weekends or holidays together as a family or special days such as Christmas or anniversaries with her, further deepened Ruth's sense of confusion and emotional neglect. Mike frequently used his children as an excuse to avoid spending time with Ruth, reinforcing his claim of being a devoted father while completely disregarding Ruth's emotional needs. In truth he was often at home alone and not even with his children, and Ruth would spend weekends by herself, feeling increasingly confused and lonely. To make matters worse, if she ventured to voice her hurt or anger, he would slam down the phone, or walk out, or ask her to leave, in front of his children, further punishing her for daring to challenge him and call out his behaviour. Most weeks he would 'allow' her just 3 hours alone with him. The coercive control was immense.

As Ruth observed the growing enmeshment between Mike and his eldest daughter, Izzy, she began to feel increasingly marginalized and isolated in the family dynamic. She adored both the girls and spent considerable time looking after them and getting to know them. Yet Mike seemed to encourage this enmeshment, promoting a surrogate spousal relationship between himself and Izzy, leaving Ruth feeling she was being invited to compete for Mike's affection and attention. Ruth's role as a stepmother became one of forced competition, not just with Izzy but also with Mike's emotionally manipulative behaviour.

Ruth did her best to raise both Izzy and Suki as if they were her own children, caring deeply for them despite the challenges within the family. However, after six years of trying to navigate the toxic family dynamics, Ruth became increasingly disillusioned. She saw firsthand the anxiety, panic disorders, and temper tantrums that both Izzy and Suki were experiencing as a result of Mike's narcissistic behaviour. The daughters were in constant competition for their father's attention and Mike used both of them as emotional shields to deflect any criticism or accountability for his actions.

Despite her efforts to intervene and help the family, Ruth found herself powerless in the face of Mike's manipulation and control and indeed his wider family's ability wilfully to ignore what was happening behind closed doors. She attempted to have difficult conversations with Mike about his narcissism and the detrimental effects it was having on his children, let alone herself. She tried many times to advocate for more appropriate parenting techniques, but Mike consistently dismissed her concerns, sabotaging any attempts to build a healthy family environment. At 14, Izzy was having unprotected sex and staying out all night, with Mike refusing to discuss contraception or allow Ruth to do so. By the time Suki was just 13 she was out until 2 a.m. with unknown friends while Mike would simply go to bed. Ruth would wait up in the dark alone, worried about the girls' safety, and she found her distress at the parental neglect unbearable. Having raised her own children, she knew this was simply not healthy and felt she was watching a car crash in slow motion.

Ruth's mental health began to deteriorate under the strain of the emotionally abusive situation. She developed depression and anxiety, feelings she had never experienced before. She found it unbearable to watch the emotional damage being done to the children, knowing she was powerless to stop it. The turning point came when Mike, during a moment of sexual intimacy, called Ruth 'Izzy'. This incident highlighted the now disturbing level of emotional enmeshment between Mike and his daughter. It left Ruth feeling physically sick and emotionally devastated. When confronted, Mike walked out on Ruth, claiming she was mentally unstable. He refused to acknowledge the true nature of the issue, instead gaslighting Ruth and accusing her of being unreasonable. The realization that Mike had crossed a boundary even if only mentally into an inappropriate erotic transference with Izzy led Ruth to make the painful decision to leave the family.

After years of trying to help the family and constantly salvage her relationship with Mike, Ruth could no longer withstand the emotional abuse and manipulation. She left Mike, retreating from the toxic environment in order to prioritize her mental health. Ruth also reached out to Mike's ex-partner Sarah, who independently corroborated patterns of narcissistic abuse. While supportive, Ruth found the trio of women who had suffered so deeply devastating to comprehend. It took her two years of intensive therapy with a specialist in narcissistic trauma to begin her emotional recovery. Through therapy, Ruth was able to process the years of emotional abuse she had suffered and start to heal from the psychological wounds inflicted by Mike. In addition, she lost two stone in weight and had to learn to manage a somatic trauma response if she ever bumped into him in the years that followed.

Although Ruth moved on with her life, she remained troubled by the issues she had witnessed in Mike's home. She often reflected on the emotional damage done to Izzy and Suki and hoped that one day they would find their own pathway to recovery and begin to understand her perspective and seek her out for support. Ruth was painfully aware of the anger and grief the girls very likely experienced as they processed their own trauma, especially when their biological mother,

Jenny, passed away. Ruth still carries the hope that she will be able to help Izzy and Suki heal, should they ever reach out.

Throughout her time in the relationship, Ruth felt silenced and isolated. She was scapegoated by Mike, who denied her any authority as a co-parent and undermined her at every turn. Ruth was trapped in a cycle of emotional manipulation and was made to feel responsible for the dysfunction in the family, despite her efforts to intervene and provide support. Mike's lies, gaslighting, and distortions of the truth further isolated Ruth from any potential allies, and the wider family failed to see the true nature of the abuse that was repeating behind closed doors.

It was not until years later, after Ruth had left Mike, that Mike's sister-in-law and brother-in-law reached out to her. They expressed concern over the incongruencies they had noticed over the years and were horrified when Ruth explained the truth of what had been happening within the family. Finally, Ruth received validation for her experiences and she was able to share the painful reality of the toxic and abusive environment she had endured.

Conclusion: Ruth's role in a narcissistic family system

Ruth's experience in the Halston family illustrates the devastating impact of narcissistic abuse on a co-parent and stepparent. Despite her best efforts to care for Izzy and Suki, Ruth was continually scapegoated and undermined by Mike's narcissistic behaviours. Her attempts at providing support for the children and advocating for healthier family dynamics were thwarted by Mike's manipulation and emotional control. He worked hard to diminish Ruth, knowing she was constantly on the brink of exposing him as a narcissist. Ruth's own mental health suffered as a result of the ongoing emotional abuse and she was ultimately forced to leave the relationship in order to protect herself – just as his wife Jenny had.

Ruth's case highlights the difficulty of co-parenting in a narcissistic family system and the emotional toll it takes on the individuals involved. Despite her eventual recovery, Ruth's experiences remain a painful reminder of how narcissistic abuse can distort family relationships and isolate those who try to intervene.

Counselling support: Ruth may benefit from counselling to process her own experiences of emotional abuse and isolation within the family dynamic. The unhealthy enmeshment between Mike and his eldest daughter, Izzy, placed Ruth in an untenable position. It not only created inappropriate dynamics but also left Ruth powerless to address boundary violations effectively.

Mike's alternating 'hot and cold' inconsistent behaviour very probably induced cognitive dissonance in Ruth, causing confusion and a prolonged attachment to the relationship (a trauma bond) despite clear red flags.

Ruth experienced gaslighting and psychological manipulation, leading to self-doubt, anxiety, and depression. This pattern is consistent with narcissistic abuse, which often destabilizes the victim's sense of reality.

Izzy's and Suki's roles in the family were distorted by Mike's emotional neglect and manipulation. Ruth's efforts to address these issues were consistently sabotaged, exacerbating her feelings of helplessness and distress.

Survivor guilt:

- After leaving, Ruth's lingering concern for Izzy and Suki reflects survivor guilt, as she feels responsible for their well-being despite having no control over their circumstances.

Therapeutic suggestions for Ruth:

- Engage in ongoing therapy with a specialist in narcissistic abuse and family systems. Techniques such as eye movement desensitization and reprocessing (EMDR) or trauma-focused cognitive behavioural therapy (TF-CBT) could help Ruth process her experiences and reframe her narrative.
- Grief counselling: Address the grief Ruth feels over the relationships she tried to build with Izzy and Suki, as well as the hopes she had for the family dynamic that didn't materialize.

Conclusion

Ruth's recovery underscores the profound emotional toll of narcissistic abuse within family systems. By prioritizing her mental health and seeking specialized therapy, Ruth can continue to heal and rebuild her life. Moreover, her resilience and efforts to intervene in the Halston family are a testament to her strength and commitment to creating healthy relationships, even in the face of adversity.

Connie Halston (enabler, flying monkey, and suspected social narcissist)

Connie Halston, Mike's mother, was in her eighties and remained active in her community despite the death of her husband years earlier from cancer. She had enjoyed a full life, maintaining strong social connections with her friends in Scotland. Connie's marriage had been marked by infidelity on both sides and constant arguing, rumoured to originate from her husband's lack of engagement and suspected ASD and Connie's frustration with boring family life. Yet these issues were never openly discussed or addressed within the family, even during the time we worked together. Their marriage appeared to be smooth on the surface but was deeply fractured beneath.

Mike, as the golden child, was the source of Connie's pride and admiration. She frequently boasted about his success to friends and family, seeing him as the embodiment of all that was good and accomplished. Simon, in contrast, was viewed as problematic, emotionally difficult, and an embarrassment to her, often being blamed for the family's dysfunction despite his emotional sensitivity and care. Fiona, the middle child, was largely neglected and left to fend for herself emotionally.

Connie's relationship with Mike was characterized by failed engulfment, with Mike being the favoured child in the family. She took extraordinary pride in Mike's success and status, holding him up as a model of what an ideal son should be. When Connie's husband died, she leant on Mike to undertake the physical and intellectual duties left needing attention and while Mike used to complain bitterly to Jenny and later Ruth, he always dutifully delivered for his mother. Jenny and Ruth both independently wondered if Mike's cruelty and neglect of his female partners was in fact a diverted suppression of his deeper rage at his mother for her emotional absence and later infidelity which he did not have the courage to express directly.

100

When Mike's first wife left him, claiming psychological and narcissistic abuse, Connie dismissed her allegations, instead blindly agreeing with his characterization of Jenny as mentally unwell and incapable of caring for their children. This set the tone for Connie's relationship with the women in Mike's life – she consistently sided with him and dismissed any concerns or accusations made by others despite undeniable nagging concerns.

Connie initially observed Ruth with a mixture of curiosity and wariness. Ruth was highly successful in her own right, and confident. Connie found herself somewhat intimidated but admiring of her. However, if Connie made a comment about the children not behaving well, Ruth would carefully but truthfully express concerns about the children's struggles with Mike and would confess how Mike neglected her too. Connie chose to ignore it, preferring to believe Mike was the victim of difficult women and dismissing their accounts of the issues within the family.

Connie's role within the family was that of an enabler. She refused to acknowledge or address any of the dysfunction within the Halston family, particularly the emotional abuse Mike inflicted on Izzy and Suki. When Ruth or the nanny raised concerns about the family's unhealthy dynamics, Connie ignored or dismissed those claims. This enabling behaviour contributed to the perpetuation of the dysfunctional family system.

Connie Halston's behaviour exemplifies the role of both an enabler and a flying monkey in a narcissistic family system. She consistently sided with her son, defending his actions and minimizing concerns raised by others. Her refusal to acknowledge the emotional abuse and dysfunction within the family allowed Mike to continue his manipulative behaviours unchecked. Connie's enabling actions reinforced Mike's narcissistic tendencies and contributed to the emotional harm experienced by his wife, his daughters, and Ruth.

Connie's own narcissistic tendencies, particularly her need to protect and idealize Mike, to dismiss Simon's diagnosis and abuse claims, and merely to utilize Fiona for care, prevented her from seeing the truth about the family's wider dysfunction. Connie's behaviour highlights the difficulty of breaking free from a narcissistic family dynamic, as she became deeply entrenched in the role of protector and defender of the narcissist.

Clinical implications

Therapeutic support for Connie: Connie's own narcissistic tendencies and enmeshment with her son may benefit from therapeutic intervention. A therapist could help her explore the dynamics of her relationships and the impact of her enabling behaviour on her family.

Family intervention: The family would benefit from intervention to address the toxic dynamics at play. Family therapy could help Mike, Connie, and the other family members recognize and address the patterns of narcissism, enabling, and emotional abuse.

Support for Izzy and Suki: Izzy and Suki would benefit from individual therapy to process the emotional damage caused by their father's narcissism and their grandmother's enabling behaviour. They need a safe space to understand their roles in the family and work through the trauma they have experienced.

Education on narcissistic family dynamics: Education and awareness of narcissistic family dynamics could help others, including Connie, recognize the harmful roles they may unknowingly play. This could open up opportunities for healing and breaking free from the cycle of abuse.

In summary, Connie's role as an enabler and flying monkey within the family served to perpetuate the narcissistic abuse inflicted by Mike. Her refusal to acknowledge the dysfunction allowed the family's toxic dynamics to continue, and her actions further isolated the victims of Mike's abuse, preventing them from seeking the help and support they needed.

Fiona Halston (Mike's sister, the lost adult child, and unconscious enabler)

Fiona Halston embodies the intricate roles of both an enabler and an adult lost child within her family's complex dynamic. As Mike's older sister, Fiona was seen as the dependable, sensible sibling who seamlessly absorbed the burdens of responsibility from a young age. The family's dysfunction often funnelled into her, as she navigated between silently supporting her parents, helping her scapegoated brother Simon out of trouble, and stepping in for Mike without hesitation when he needed support. However, this responsibility came at the expense of her own emotional needs, which were rarely acknowledged.

Fiona's childhood was marked by her role as the 'fixer' in the family – a child who never complained but quietly picked up the pieces. While others in the family received attention, albeit sometimes negative, Fiona's efforts went largely unnoticed. Her hospitalization for anxiety at age nine hinted at deeper cracks in the family structure, a signal that she bore a heavy emotional load even as a child. Despite her challenges, Fiona maintained her role, suppressing her own emotions in favour of fulfilling her family's expectations.

In adulthood, Fiona's marriage to an often-absent spouse mirrored the emotionally distant relationship dynamic she grew up observing between her mother and father. This suggests Fiona unconsciously sought out familiar patterns, aligning with her ingrained tendencies to support others at the cost of her own emotional fulfilment.

When Ruth turned to Fiona for help with the troubling situation involving Mike's daughters, Fiona's initial reaction was disbelief. She had long accepted Mike's carefully curated image of himself as a devoted, self-sacrificing father. Social media posts and rare family gatherings reinforced this narrative, leaving Fiona reluctant to consider an alternative reality.

Ruth's recounting of Izzy's risky behaviour and Suki's neglect painted a starkly different picture, yet Fiona hesitated to engage. Her loyalty to her brother conflicted with her emerging doubts and she promised Ruth she would talk to Mike. Fiona's conversation with Mike led to predictable results: Mike denied the issues outright, assuring her that everything was under control. Fiona chose to believe her brother, not only because it was easier but also because acknowledging Ruth's account would mean confronting deeper, more unsettling truths about her family.

Fiona's decision not to visit Mike's home despite Ruth's urgent plea to come and witness what was truly occurring behind closed doors reflects her role as an enabler. By avoiding direct involvement,

Fiona protected herself from confronting the dysfunction and preserved the family's fragile status quo. This pattern of avoidance, while seemingly passive, actively contributed to Ruth's isolation and perpetuated the harmful dynamics within Mike's household. Fiona's unwillingness to address the situation further entrenched the cycle of neglect and denial, leaving Ruth to bear the emotional burden alone.

Fiona's enabling behaviour stems not from malice but from years of conditioning to maintain family harmony at all costs. Her reluctance to challenge Mike or delve deeper into Ruth's concerns underscores her internal struggle: loyalty to her brother versus the discomfort of facing the truth. This conflict rendered Fiona incapable of offering Ruth (and therefore the daughters) the support she desperately needed.

Fiona's role as an enabler and lost child has taken a toll on her emotional well-being. Though outwardly composed, Fiona's lifelong habit of suppressing her own needs and emotions leaves her vulnerable to burnout and unresolved anxiety. Her role within the family, while externally functional, deprives her of genuine connections and personal fulfilment. Fiona's refusal to confront the truth may provide temporary emotional insulation, but it perpetuates a cycle of denial that prevents healing for herself and her family. Her marriage was equally one of avoidance and dysfunction, and a lifetime of people-pleasing and brushing problems under the carpet ultimately cost Fiona a huge amount of happiness.

For Fiona to break free from the enabling role and her lost child identity, she would need to confront the underlying dysfunction within her family system. This process would involve:

- **Acknowledging family dynamics:** Recognizing how her childhood roles shaped her current behaviour.
- **Seeking professional support:** Therapy could help Fiona explore her suppressed emotions, unresolved anxiety, and the impact of her enabling behaviour.
- **Setting boundaries:** Learning to prioritize her own emotional needs and establish limits with family members.
- **Developing assertiveness:** Gaining the confidence to challenge family narratives and confront uncomfortable truths.

By embarking on this journey, Fiona could not only address her emotional health but also potentially contribute to breaking the cycle of dysfunction within her family. Though the path forward is challenging, Fiona's willingness to confront her past could pave the way for a more authentic, fulfilling future.

Simon Halston (Mike's older brother, scapegoated adult child)

Simon Halston, Mike's older brother, occupies the role of the scapegoated child in the family system, a common position in dysfunctional families, particularly those with members who may display narcissistic tendencies. As the firstborn, Simon initially captured his parents' attention and fascination. However, over time, his behaviour became increasingly difficult for his parents to manage. This led to him being labelled as the problem child, with his actions interpreted as disruptive and unruly. As a result, Simon became the family's scapegoat, blamed for all the dysfunction and chaos, while his siblings, especially Mike, were afforded greater levels of validation and approval.

Despite being highly creative and successful in his early twenties, Simon struggled throughout his life with feelings of isolation and being misunderstood. These challenges were compounded by the family's inability to see him as anything other than a disruptive troublemaker. The narrative created around Simon – that he was the problem – contributed significantly to his emotional distress and feelings of alienation.

Simon's childhood was marked by an array of challenges. As an excitable and beautiful child, he was the initial focus of attention in the family. However, as he grew older, his behaviour, which showed signs consistent with autism, was viewed as problematic. Reports from school and home described Simon as difficult to manage, refusing to follow rules, and being disruptive. Rather than being understood as signs of underlying neurodevelopmental differences, these behaviours were framed by his family as rebellious and unruly.

As Simon navigated his adult life, he continued to struggle with alcohol abuse, a coping mechanism that may have been used to manage deep-seated anxiety and emotional pain. In his forties, he confided in his wife that he suspected he had been sexually abused as a child. He also wondered whether his siblings, especially Mike, had experienced similar trauma. This revelation came after years of internalizing the family's negative view of him.

Simon's wife, recognizing the depth of his struggles, encouraged him to seek therapy and consider also a parallel ADHD diagnosis. Simon eventually received a formal diagnosis of autism spectrum disorder, which helped explain many of his childhood behaviours. This diagnosis not only confirmed his suspicions but also provided a degree of validation that he had never received from his family. However, this new understanding of his neurodivergence came too late to alter the family's longstanding narrative about him.

By the time Simon reached his sixties, he had endured a lifetime of emotional hardship. The combination of his untreated ASD, childhood trauma, and the family's rejection had shaped his adult identity as the scapegoat. The role of scapegoat within a narcissistic family is typically one of profound emotional neglect, and Simon's experience exemplified this role's damaging effects.

As the scapegoated child, Simon was consistently blamed for the family's dysfunction, even as his siblings, especially Mike, were elevated to positions of approval and importance, particularly by their mother. The emotional neglect Simon endured in his childhood was compounded by the family's refusal to acknowledge his struggles. Instead of receiving support for his difficulties, he was branded as the problem and pushed further into the periphery of the family.

The emotional neglect and scapegoating Simon experienced had profound consequences for his mental health. His struggles with alcohol abuse were very probably an attempt to self-medicate the emotional pain caused by years of family rejection and misunderstanding. The undiagnosed autism further complicated Simon's ability to navigate social relationships and emotional expression, leading to increased feelings of isolation and alienation.

The family's lack of empathy and the long-term impact of the abuse and neglect Simon suffered contributed to his ongoing emotional struggles. His experiences highlight the devastating effects of being labelled as the scapegoat in a narcissistic family system, where one's pain is disregarded in favour of maintaining a false family narrative.

Simon's wife played a crucial role in helping him gain the diagnosis of autism, which provided him with a sense of validation and understanding. Her support was instrumental in Simon's ability to begin making sense of his life and his struggles. Without her encouragement, Simon may never have sought the help he needed and his sense of isolation would very probably have deepened.

Conclusion and clinical implications

Simon Halston's life story illustrates the profound emotional toll of being the scapegoated child in a narcissistic family system. His experiences of neglect, emotional abandonment, and substance abuse highlight the damaging effects of family dysfunction on an individual's mental health. The family's failure to address Simon's needs, coupled with the denial of his trauma and struggles, contributed to a lifetime of emotional pain and isolation.

Individual therapy: Simon would benefit from therapy to process the trauma he experienced throughout his childhood, including the emotional neglect, sexual abuse, and family scapegoating. Trauma-informed therapy could help him address the deep-seated emotional pain that has influenced his life choices, including his struggles with alcohol.

Autism spectrum disorder support: Simon's diagnosis of ASD would benefit from further therapeutic support tailored to neurodivergent individuals. This support could help him develop coping strategies for managing social interactions and emotional regulation.

Family therapy: Engaging in family therapy could help Simon confront the dysfunctional dynamics that shaped his family's treatment of him. It would also allow him to express his feelings of neglect and abandonment and provide a space for healing, although it would require the family to acknowledge their role in his emotional suffering.

Support networks: Strengthening Simon's support network beyond his family, including friends, support groups, or online communities, would provide him with the validation and connection he has long been denied.

By addressing the emotional wounds Simon carries, he can begin to heal from the toxic family dynamics that have shaped his life. However, healing from years of scapegoating, neglect, and trauma requires time, self-compassion, and a willingness to confront the painful realities of his past.

Recommendations for intervention

This case underscores the significant and long-lasting effects of covert narcissistic abuse and enmeshment on familial relationships and individual mental health. The dynamics within the Halston family exemplify the complexities of narcissistic abuse, which often go unnoticed until the damage becomes too profound to ignore.

Narcissistic abuse can happen in any family, no matter the class, religion, wealth, intellect or history. The well-meaning family circle can easily be manipulated by a skilful narcissist, especially a covert one, and the harder a brave voice may try to speak up, the tighter the distorted circle may become.

In Figure 5.1, you will see the broad constellation of a balanced and healthy family structure – and then the structure of the effects of Mike's narcissistic family. Here you can see the immediate distortions and over time you can start to comprehend the long-term effects this can have on the daughters who will one day come to understand what really happened and thus start their recovery journey.

If you or someone you know is living in one of these families and you are not being heard or you have struggled to believe what you are being told, I urge you to look and listen a little closer. Many victims of narcissistic abuse, in this case Suki, Izzy, Simon, Jenny, and Ruth, feel they are screaming behind soundproof glass. Narcissistic abuse has to be 'believed to be seen' and if only Fiona and Connie had taken a moment to believe and look a little harder, Mike could have been exposed – offering the children a chance at a healthier childhood.

Health Family – The nucleus of any healthy family should be the primary caregivers, who are supportive of each other and in sync around the way they raise and manage their family. The children are positioned as separate but close to their caregivers and additional family members such as grandparents and uncles etc provide orbiting support at appropriate distance.

Healthy Halston Family Constellation

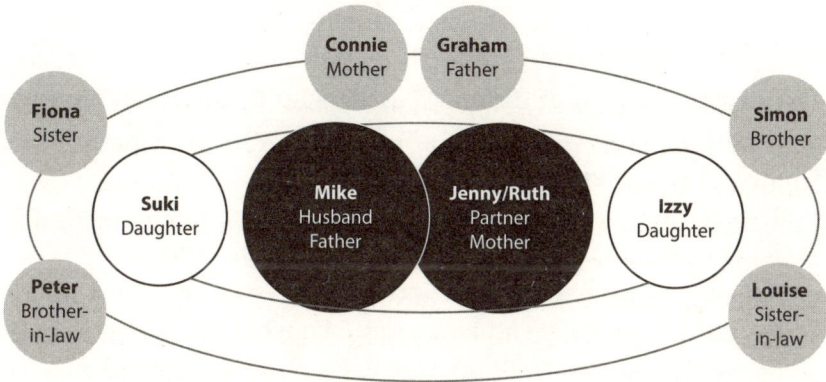

Narcissistic Family – In the Halston narcissistic family we clearly see the inflated presence and impact of the core narcissist with his golden child innapropriately enmeshed with him. His narcissistic mother and unconsious enabling sister surround and protect him, with his scapegoated child less visible. His two significant partners and mothers to his children are clearly ostricized and any uncomfortable or unconsious witnesses are held out from being able to assist.

Narcissistic Halston Family Constellation

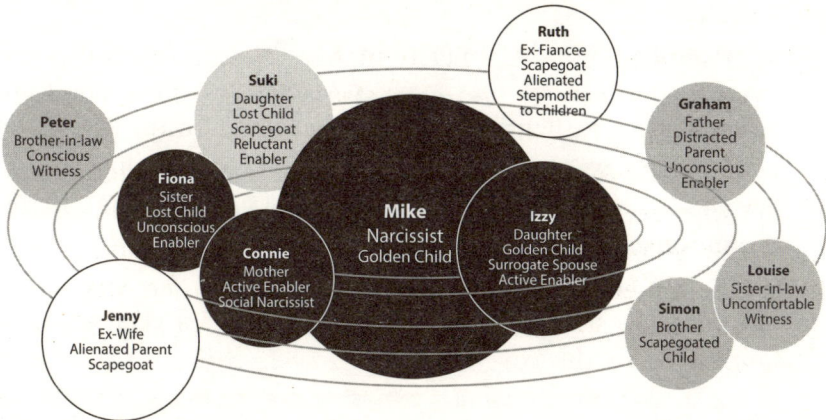

Figure 5.1 Contrasting constellations of a healthy family structure vs a narcissistic family structure
Source: Based on Bert Hellinger's family constellation framework

Key themes in the Halston family case study

1 The façade of normalcy
   o The description of the family as 'appearing to be happy and func-
     tioning' underscores a common hallmark of narcissistic dynamics –
     maintaining an external image of perfection or success to
     conceal internal dysfunction. Narcissists often prioritize this
     façade, manipulating others to support and sustain it and indeed
     threaten, dismiss or diminish those who threaten to demask the
     narcissist.

2 Collusion and silence
   o The family's collective collusion to avoid confronting pain-
     ful truths about issues such as addiction, affairs, and abuse
     reflects the psychological control a narcissist can exert. In such
     dynamics, family members may subconsciously adopt roles (e.g.
     enablers, scapegoats, flying monkeys, golden children) that rein-
     force the narcissist's control and deflect attention away from the
     real issues.

3 The role of the narcissist as a 'victim'
   o The central figure's ability to position himself as a victim is a clas-
     sic tactic of covert narcissism. By drawing sympathy and creating
     distractions, he redirected focus away from his own actions and
     onto others' perceived wrongdoings. This behaviour typically
     served to isolate and discredit anyone who might challenge his
     narrative.

4 Long-term impact on family members
   o The ripple effects of the narcissist's actions – whether through
     manipulation, gaslighting, or emotional abuse – often lead to deep
     psychological scars in family members. Over time, individuals may
     develop low self-esteem, anxiety, or trauma-related symptoms due
     to the constant upheaval and invalidation.

5 Breaking points and revelations
   o The marriage breakup seems to have acted as a catalyst for the
     unmasking of the covert narcissist. Such crises can disrupt the
     established family dynamics, exposing underlying issues that have
     long been hidden. However, they can also lead to greater chaos if
     the narcissist intensifies their manipulation to regain control.

Dynamics of Mike's covert narcissism

When a parent exhibits covert or malignant narcissistic traits, the impact on the family is particularly insidious:

1 **Parent–child relationships:** A narcissistic parent such as Mike often uses their children as extensions of themselves, demanding admiration, obedience, or validation. This can stifle the child's sense of individuality and lead to lifelong struggles with identity and anxiety.

2 **Triangulation:** Narcissistic parents may pit family members against one another to maintain control, fostering an environment of competition, distrust, and insecurity. In this case between his own two children, but also between his partners and children. Anyone close enough to Mike to know the truth about him presented a risk of exposure, so he sought to control or diminish them.

3 **Emotional neglect and abuse:** While overt narcissists may display obvious arrogance or cruelty, covert narcissists manipulate through passive-aggression, guilt, and victimhood, making it harder for others to identify the abuse. In Izzy and Suki oscillating between worrying about their father and feeling the inconsistency of his neglect and praise, their anxiety and confusion heightened, bringing drama and chaos to their home.

4 **Shielding the disorder:** Narcissistic parents often leverage their position to maintain their public image, making it difficult for outsiders to see the dysfunction. This can leave victims feeling isolated and unsupported. Jenny, Sarah, and Ruth were all victims of Mike's narcissistic abuse, being dismissed, bullied, and neglected as part of his defence against discovery.

5 **Perpetuating the problem:** The intergenerational trauma and learned behaviours played a perpetuating part in the family's collusion. Neither Jenny nor Ruth was understood or believed when they requested help within the wider Halston family, and this most certainly played into their mutual psychological demise.

This case study is a powerful reminder of the complexities of narcissistic family systems and the importance of addressing these dynamics with sensitivity and professional support.

Challenges in studying the mental health of children of narcissistic parents

While the mental health challenges faced by children of narcissistic parents are well documented in clinical settings, empirical research in this area faces several challenges. One major difficulty is the lack of clear diagnostic criteria for the impact of narcissistic parenting. Narcissistic Personality Disorder is often underdiagnosed, and many narcissistic behaviours exist on a spectrum, making it difficult to quantify and study the effects on children consistently.

Moreover, self-reporting biases can complicate research. Children of narcissistic parents may have difficulty recognizing or articulating the abuse they experienced, either because they have internalized the parent's distorted worldview or because they fear retribution or abandonment. This can lead to underreporting of symptoms or a lack of clarity in distinguishing between normal parental behaviour and narcissistic abuse.

Longitudinal studies, which follow this deep level of research, often in real time, over a long period are also limited in this area. Most research relies on retrospective reports from adults reflecting on their childhood experiences, which can introduce recall bias – where retrospective feelings and views can colour the initial factual evidence. Furthermore, the long-term impact of narcissistic parenting on mental health is challenging to isolate, as many factors – such as genetic predispositions, socioeconomic status, and other environmental influences – can also contribute to the development of mental health disorders.

Finally, the stigma associated with acknowledging parental narcissism can inhibit research participation. Admitting that a parent is narcissistic and that this has had a negative impact on one's mental health can be emotionally difficult, leading to denial or minimization of the problem.

And yet as our awareness grows it becomes even more urgent that we begin to understand the long-term impact on the mental and at times physical health of those abused by narcissistic parents.

Mental health challenges faced by children and grandchildren of narcissistic parents

1 **Low self-esteem and insecure attachment:** One of the most common issues among children of narcissistic parents is low self-esteem. These children often grow up feeling unworthy of love and approval as their parents may have provided positive attention only when the child served their needs. Children of narcissistic parents frequently struggle with self-worth because their value is often contingent upon how well they fulfil the narcissistic parent's expectations or enhance their image.

This conditional form of love and validation can lead to insecure attachment styles, particularly ambivalent attachment or avoidant attachment. Attachment issues may manifest in difficulties forming and maintaining healthy, trusting relationships. These children may constantly seek validation and fear abandonment, or conversely they may avoid close relationships altogether to protect themselves from anticipated rejection or emotional pain.

2 **Anxiety and depression:** Children of narcissistic parents are also at increased risk of developing anxiety and depression. The unpredictable and often emotionally abusive environment created by a narcissistic parent can lead to chronic stress, contributing to anxiety disorders. The constant need to navigate the parent's volatile emotions and avoid criticism or punishment creates a state of hypervigilance in children, which can persist into adulthood as generalized anxiety disorder or social anxiety disorder.

Depression is another common mental health challenge faced by these children. The lack of genuine emotional support and the internalization of negative parental messages often lead to feelings of hopelessness and worthlessness. Children of narcissistic parents report higher levels of depressive symptoms, particularly when they feel trapped in a cycle of trying to gain their parent's approval but never feeling good enough.

3 **Complex trauma:** The repeated emotional abuse, manipulation, and neglect that children of narcissistic parents often endure can lead to C-PTSD. Unlike traditional PTSD, which typically results from a single traumatic event, C-PTSD arises from prolonged

exposure to traumatic situations where the victim feels trapped, such as in the case of a child growing up in a narcissistic household.

The ongoing trauma experienced by these children can lead to symptoms such as emotional dysregulation, negative self-concept, and difficulty in maintaining interpersonal relationships. Children of narcissistic parents may struggle with feelings of chronic emptiness, dissociation, and difficulty controlling their emotions, often alternating between numbness and overwhelming emotional pain.

4 **Difficulties with boundaries and identity formation:** Another significant mental health challenge for children of narcissistic parents is the difficulty in establishing boundaries and forming a stable sense of identity. Narcissistic parents often violate their children's boundaries, seeing them as extensions of themselves rather than as individuals with their own needs and desires. Children raised by narcissistic parents often have poorly defined boundaries and may struggle to assert themselves in relationships, leading to patterns of co-dependency or submission in adulthood.

Additionally, the constant manipulation and invalidation by the narcissistic parent can hinder the child's identity formation. Kernberg (2018), in his work on personality development, explains that these children may grow up feeling confused about who they are, often adopting identities that are more acceptable to the narcissistic parent rather than developing their true selves. This can result in identity diffusion or a fragmented sense of self, making it challenging for these individuals to know what they genuinely want or need in life.

5 **Shame and guilt:** Children of narcissistic parents often carry a deep sense of shame and guilt into adulthood. The narcissistic parent may use these emotions as tools of control, making the child feel responsible for the parent's feelings or failures. Herman (2019), in her exploration of trauma and recovery, discusses how chronic exposure to shaming and guilt-inducing behaviours can lead to a pervasive sense of inadequacy and self-blame in the child. These individuals may become perfectionists, constantly striving to prove their worth, or they may develop self-sabotaging behaviours, believing they do not deserve success or happiness.

6 **Social and interpersonal difficulties:** Growing up in a narcissistic family environment can also lead to significant social and interpersonal difficulties. Children of narcissistic parents often struggle with trust and intimacy in relationships – they may either become overly dependent on others for validation or remain emotionally distant to avoid potential hurt. These individuals might also replicate the narcissistic patterns they learned from their parents in their own relationships, leading to cycles of dysfunction and emotional pain.

7 **Substance abuse and self-destructive behaviours:** In some cases, the emotional pain and unresolved trauma experienced by children of narcissistic parents may lead to substance abuse or other self-destructive behaviours as coping mechanisms. People with a history of parental narcissistic abuse are more likely to engage in substance abuse as a way to numb the emotional pain or fill the void left by unmet emotional needs.

Conclusion

Children and grandchildren of narcissistic parents may face a myriad of mental health challenges. The empirical research in this field highlights the profound and lasting impact of narcissistic parenting on a child's psychological development, though it is also clear that studying these effects presents significant challenges. Despite these difficulties, understanding the mental health consequences of growing up with a narcissistic parent is crucial for developing effective therapeutic interventions and helping these individuals heal from their early experiences.

How to deal with a narcissistic family dynamic

Learning how to deal with narcissistic family members in effective and healthy ways is different for each person, but it almost always involves developing strong boundaries, validating your truth, and decreasing opportunities for conflict. Someone who currently lives within the family will have to try harder to develop strong boundaries, as the close contact allows for more chance of manipulation.

Here are some tips for dealing with a narcissistic family structure:

- **Avoid conflict:** Narcissistic families thrive on conflict. Practise disengaging and releasing any feelings through keeping a diary or therapy.
- **Maintain emotional self-care:** This will help keep you emotionally strong to prepare for any triggers or manipulation and will help you release negative emotions.
- **Practise self-compassion:** Survivors of family trauma often have limited self-compassion due to a history of not being respected. Practise reversing that and take time to validate your feelings and learn how to love yourself.
- **Maintain strong boundaries:** Know what you are and are not comfortable with and practise sticking to them.
- **Recognize and acknowledge feelings of discomfort:** In the past, these feelings had to be dismissed or ignored. Acknowledge your truth and refuse to push your emotions away.
- **Use effective communication:** Keep it Necessary, Emotionless, and Brief – when able and appropriate, view communication in this frame. This will decrease chances for unintended emotional hijacking and manipulation of conversations and situations.

How therapy can improve narcissistic family structures

Many people ask if therapy can help improve narcissistic family structures, or if a narcissist can change. Due to the limited insight that is so pervasive in those with NPD, these people struggle to develop the self-awareness that would be necessary to improve in therapy. But if the individual is committed to change and growth, then healing is possible. If the person is not, family or marriage therapy can be dangerous and may not be recommended.

Most of the healing usually takes place in the survivors of narcissistic abuse, such as the children. In this case, the goals of treatment usually consist of developing insight into the unhealthy and abusive dynamics, working on improving boundaries and self-esteem and maintaining personal growth. Seek a therapist who has knowledge of intergenerational trauma and narcissistic families.

Therapy options to consider when dealing with a narcissistic family structure include:

- **Trauma-focused cognitive behavioural therapy:** TF-CBT is a therapeutic process that uses CBT to address difficulties that stem from traumatic life events.
- **Family therapy:** This form of therapy is beneficial when the whole family is willing to participate. It helps improve communication and understanding among the whole group.
- **Attachment-based therapy:** This method specifically focuses on exploring feelings, thoughts, and behaviours that clients have learned to suppress due to childhood trauma. The treatment addresses and explores early attachment experiences.
- **Eye movement desensitization and reprocessing:** EMDR is a form of therapy that was designed to alleviate the symptoms that come from memories of past traumas. This is great for clients who have post-traumatic stress disorder due to childhood trauma.
- **Psychodynamic therapy:** This method works best for people who have good insight and are in a safe space emotionally to revisit their trauma history and how it affects present behaviours and thoughts. It explores how unconscious motives and traumas contribute to behaviours and actions.
- **Group therapy:** In group therapy, people who have a shared experience come together for a group and peer session.

Ultimately, all families can be dysfunctional at times as no family system is perfect. However, the difference between a healthy and an abusive level of dysfunction is the amount of awareness and willingness to grow together. While no two dysfunctional families are the same, narcissistic family structures usually consist of specific family roles, as well as defined family rules and expectations.

Please do not hesitate to seek support or professional help if you are struggling to deal with a narcissist family structure or are working to address the resulting trauma. And, most importantly, be discerning in your selection of therapist – it is my humble opinion that your therapist needs deep experience of dealing with narcissistic behaviours and patterns truly be to of service to you.

6

Enmeshment, emotional incest, and alienation
When narcissism impacts the psyche

'A child that is being abused by its parents doesn't stop loving its parents. It stops loving itself.'

Shahida Arabi

In families where a parent is an especially potent narcissist, the toxic dynamics of enmeshment, emotional incest, and parental alienation can be disturbingly prevalent, weaving a complex web of emotional confusion and dependency.

Enmeshment occurs when boundaries between parent and child become dangerously blurred, leading to a lack of personal autonomy and identity for the child, who is often entangled in the parent's emotional needs and expectations. Children can grow to become co-dependent and lacking in a sense of self, no longer able to operate or make decisions without the approval or guidance of their parent – and over time the same in reverse for the parent. It's why therapists shudder when they hear a parent say their child is 'their best friend' – most often this is not a healthy dynamic.

Emotional incest involves the parent treating the child as a surrogate partner or confidant, thrusting them into inappropriate emotional roles that should be reserved for adult relationships. This exploitation of the child's emotional space can deeply undermine their sense of self and healthy relational development and also lead to levels of parentification, where the child assumes many roles and responsibilities of a parent, and in doing so, loses their opportunity to develop healthily and additionally loses their childhood. While they may believe they are enjoying the privilege and access to the adult's inner sanctum, they are in fact being robbed of their childhood and exposed to inappropriate emotional and sometimes even psychosexual harms.

Parental alienation can occur when the narcissistic parent manipulates a child's emotions, perceptions, or opinions post separation from the non-narcissistic parent. This manipulation can take many forms, such as badmouthing the other parent, limiting contact, or even fabricating reasons for the child to fear or resent the parent in the rejected position. Over time, the child may become estranged, which not only harms the relationship between the child and the other parent but can also have long-term effects on the child's emotional well-being, trust in relationships, and sense of self.

As delicate, controversial, and painful as each of these topics is to introduce and discuss, I felt it would be remiss of me to exclude them given the distortion and damage they can inflict on children, long into their adult life. My intention is both to validate those of you who have long suspected or known you have experienced these elements and, equally, to alert and bring to the attention the possibility of better understanding how to support and help families where narcissism is at play.

The phenomenon of enmeshment and emotional incest in narcissistic parent–child relationships

Emotional incest is a toxic dynamic where a parent uses a child to fulfil emotional needs typically met by a romantic partner. Unlike sexual incest, no physical boundaries are crossed (although inappropriate nudity, sleeping arrangements, and romantic gestures may be in play), but the psychological damage can be as profound. When the parent is narcissistic, the impact is even more destructive, as the narcissist is often oblivious or indifferent to the harm caused. In such cases, the child is treated as a surrogate spouse, expected to provide emotional support and validation, stunting their ability to form healthy boundaries and relationships.

This is especially common in relationships between narcissistic fathers and daughters or narcissistic mothers and sons, where the parent confides in the child about adult problems, relies on them for emotional validation, and holds them responsible for their emotional well-being. In a normal parent–child relationship, the parent provides protection, security, boundaries, and guidance. But in emotional incest, the child is forced into the role of emotional partner and caregiver, unprotected and overly exposed to adult matters for which they are simply not ready.

In narcissistic families, this dynamic is intensified by the concept of the 'golden child', a child assigned the role of meeting the parent's emotional needs. While this child may seem favoured, they are also subjected to immense pressure and manipulation, making it difficult to develop a true sense of self or establish healthy, independent relationships.

Why narcissistic parents enmesh with the golden child

Narcissistic parents enmesh with the golden child for several reasons, all of which are rooted in the parent's need for control, validation, and emotional fulfilment.

- **Validation and ego reinforcement:** Narcissistic parents often use their children as a means of validating their own self-worth. By elevating the golden child and tightly controlling their behaviour, the narcissistic parent can bask in the reflected glory of the child's achievements and attributes. This serves to reinforce the parent's sense of superiority and importance.
- **Control:** Narcissistic parents are often deeply insecure and feel a need to control those around them. Enmeshing with the golden child allows them to exert influence over the child's life, ensuring that the child remains dependent on the parent for approval and guidance. This control can be both overt and covert, with the parent manipulating the child through guilt, fear, or conditional love. It also strengthens the ability to control the wider family – with two members versus just one calling all the shots.
- **Fear of abandonment:** Narcissistic parents may also fear abandonment or rejection. By enmeshing with the golden child, they create a situation where the child feels obligated to meet their emotional needs, reducing the likelihood that the child will reject and distance themselves from the parent. This dynamic can create a toxic dependency that is difficult for the child to escape.
- **Lack of healthy adult relationships:** In single-parent situations, the narcissistic parent may lack healthy adult relationships and turn to the golden child to fulfil emotional needs that would

typically be met by an adult partner. This can lead to an inappropriate level of emotional intimacy between the parent and child, further deepening the enmeshment.

Narcissistic fathers and daughters: the surrogate wife

When the narcissist is a father, his daughters may experience unique challenges that can manifest in their future romantic relationships. The relationship between a narcissistic father and his daughters is often fraught with psychological complexity, including enmeshment and psychosexual implications.

As we've seen, narcissistic fathers often view their children as extensions of themselves rather than as independent individuals. This perspective can lead to unhealthy relationships where the father's needs, desires, and self-image take precedence over the child's emotional development. For daughters, this dynamic can be particularly damaging as it may distort their understanding of healthy boundaries, self-worth, and intimacy.

Narcissistic fathers may oscillate between idolizing their daughters and devaluing them, depending on how well the daughters reflect or support the father's grandiose self-image. In the examples of the siblings in Chapter 4, Izzy and Suki, Izzy aligns with her father's expectations. She may be excessively praised, leading to a fragile self-esteem built on external validation, which in turn can lead her to drive herself academically and physically to a point of extreme anxiety and near collapse.

Conversely, when Suki challenges her father or fails to meet his needs or expectations, she is criticized and emotionally abandoned, which fosters deep-seated insecurities and a lack of self-worth – only further developing her unhealthy trauma bond to him, especially given she has no mother to protect her or divert him. He has developed covert techniques in adopting the victim position, claiming he has 'sacrificed so much' for them and they should put him first. Izzy may bask in the sunlight of his attention and affection but has lost her sense of self and agency, trapped in the pleasing role to her narcissistic father as the golden child. Suki begins to shut down and retreat from the family dynamic, neglected and ostracized by both her father and Izzy – seeking unhealthy places away from the family circus where she can numb and subvert her sadness, anger, and loneliness.

In families where the father is the narcissistic parent, the daughter can become the target of emotional incest, particularly when she is the golden child. Narcissistic fathers may treat their daughters as surrogate wives, relying on them for emotional support, validation, and companionship, while neglecting or undermining the daughter's need for independence and appropriate boundaries. This can be especially problematic when the father is a single parent, as there is no other adult in the household to balance or counter the unhealthy dynamic.

In these emotionally incestuous relationships, the father may inappropriately confide in the daughter about personal issues, including financial problems, relationship difficulties, or even romantic interests. He may also expect her to provide emotional comfort and validation, much like a wife would in a traditional marriage. This puts the daughter in a position where she is responsible for her father's emotional well-being, a role that is far too burdensome and inappropriate for a child.

For example, a narcissistic father might lean on his daughter for advice on adult matters, such as his dating life, work stress, or personal insecurities. He may express jealousy or overprotectiveness regarding her relationships with boys or men, treating her as though she is his romantic partner rather than his daughter. This emotional enmeshment may give the daughter the impression of being special, 'grown up', and chosen, but he is fact stifling the daughter's development, making it difficult for her to form her own identity and establish boundaries in future relationships.

Long-term impact on daughters
Evidence of impact on future romantic relationships
Several studies and clinical observations suggest that daughters of narcissistic fathers often struggle in their romantic relationships later in life. These difficulties can be traced back to the distorted relationship with their father, which may affect their self-esteem, understanding of love, and ability to form healthy attachments.

Daughters of narcissistic fathers may develop insecure attachment styles, such as anxious or avoidant attachment. This can result in a fear of abandonment, an excessive need for validation, or an inability to trust partners. Daughters who grow up under the critical eye of a narcissistic father often internalize the belief that their worth is contingent on meeting the expectations of others. This can lead to low self-esteem and a constant need for external validation. In romantic relationships, these women may seek partners who mirror their father's behaviour – either by pursuing partners who are similarly narcissistic or by remaining in relationships where they are undervalued and mistreated.

Freud's concept of repetition compulsion suggests that individuals are unconsciously driven to repeat patterns from their past, particularly those that are unresolved or traumatic. Daughters of narcissistic fathers may find themselves drawn to partners who replicate the emotional unavailability, criticism, or manipulation they experienced with their father. This repetition serves as an unconscious attempt to resolve the past trauma, though it often results in perpetuating the cycle of dysfunction.

Enmeshment in the father–daughter relationship can lead to difficulties in establishing healthy boundaries in adult relationships. These women may either struggle to assert their needs or, conversely, may become overly rigid in an attempt to protect themselves from perceived threats. Psychosexual enmeshment with a narcissistic father can create a distorted view of intimacy, where love and affection are tied to control or manipulation. This may lead to a fear of true intimacy in adult relationships as the daughter associates closeness with losing her autonomy or being emotionally exploited.

Research suggests that daughters of narcissistic fathers may develop a conflicted sense of self-worth. A narcissistic father may alternately idolize and criticize his daughter, making her feel as though her value is entirely tied to how she reflects on him. Karyl McBride, a licensed marriage and family therapist and author of *Will I Ever Be Good Enough?* (2009), suggests that daughters of narcissistic fathers are more likely to struggle with low self-esteem and may seek validation from external sources, such as romantic partners, who mirror the unhealthy dynamics they experienced with their father.

The long-term psychological and emotional impact of being treated as a surrogate spouse can be profound for daughters of narcissistic fathers. Some of the most common effects include:

- **Identity and self-worth issues:** One of the most significant long-term impacts of emotional enmeshment is the daughter's difficulty in developing a strong, independent sense of self. Growing up in a relationship where her worth is tied to meeting her father's emotional needs, the daughter may struggle with low self-esteem and a lack of confidence in her abilities. She may also have difficulty making decisions or asserting her needs as she has been conditioned to prioritize her father's needs above her own.

- **Relationship difficulties:** Daughters of narcissistic fathers who have experienced emotional incest often have significant challenges in their romantic relationships. They may be drawn to partners who replicate the dynamics of their relationship with their father, seeking out men who are controlling, emotionally distant, or abusive. Alternatively, they may avoid relationships altogether, fearing the emotional intimacy that was so damaging in their relationship with their father. This can lead to a cycle of unhealthy relationships and emotional pain.

- **Difficulty establishing boundaries:** Because of the blurred boundaries in their relationship with their father, daughters may struggle to establish and maintain healthy boundaries in their adult relationships. They may have difficulty saying no or setting limits, leading to feelings of resentment, burnout, and emotional exhaustion. This lack of boundaries can also make them vulnerable to manipulation and exploitation by others.

- **Anxiety and depression:** The emotional burden placed on daughters in enmeshed relationships can lead to chronic anxiety and depression. The constant pressure to meet their father's needs and the fear of disappointing him can create a pervasive sense of unease and insecurity. Additionally, the lack of emotional support and validation in their childhood can contribute to feelings of worthlessness and despair in adulthood.

- **Emotional suppression:** The pressure to meet their father's emotional needs can lead daughters to suppress their own emotions, believing that their feelings are less important. This emotional suppression can contribute to issues such as depression, anxiety, and emotional numbness in adulthood. In my experience I have also seen this later display as outbursts of rage and anger in the company of safer adults, where the years of confusion and psychological splitting, (see p. 157) have left the inner child ready to explode.

- **Perpetuation of dysfunctional patterns:** Daughters of narcissistic fathers may also be at risk of perpetuating dysfunctional patterns in their own parenting. If they do not address the impact of their upbringing, they may unconsciously replicate the dynamics of their relationship with their father in their relationships with their children. This can perpetuate a cycle of emotional enmeshment and abuse across generations.

Narcissistic mothers and sons: the surrogate husband

In families where the mother is narcissistic, the son can become the target of emotional incest. Narcissistic mothers may treat their sons as surrogate husbands, relying on them for emotional support, validation, and companionship in a way that is more appropriate for a romantic partner than a child. This dynamic can be particularly pronounced when the mother is a single parent as there may be no other adult in the household to fulfil the emotional needs that the mother projects onto her son.

In emotionally incestuous relationships between narcissistic mothers and their sons, the mother may confide in the son about her personal issues, including romantic or financial problems, loneliness, or dissatisfaction with her life. She may also expect him to provide emotional validation and companionship, much like a husband would in a traditional marriage.

For instance, a narcissistic mother might express jealousy or possessiveness over her son's relationships with other women, acting as though she is competing for his attention and affection. She may also criticize or undermine his romantic partners, attempting to maintain control over his emotional world. This enmeshment can prevent the son from developing healthy boundaries and forming independent relationships outside the mother–son dynamic.

Long-term impact on sons

The long-term effects of being treated as a surrogate husband can be damaging for sons of narcissistic mothers. Some of the most common consequences include:

- **Difficulty establishing boundaries:** Sons of narcissistic mothers often struggle with setting emotional boundaries in their adult relationships. They may feel responsible for their partner's emotional well-being, just as they did for their mother, leading to co-dependent and unhealthy relationships.
- **Fear of intimacy:** The emotional burden placed on sons by their narcissistic mothers can lead to a fear of intimacy and closeness in adult relationships. These men may avoid emotional vulnerability, fearing that they will once again be trapped in an enmeshed and emotionally suffocating relationship.
- **Low self-worth:** Narcissistic mothers often project their insecurities onto their sons, leading them to feel inadequate or unworthy of love. This can result in low self-esteem and a tendency to seek validation through external achievements or approval from others.
- **Emotional burnout:** Being emotionally responsible for their mother's well-being can lead to emotional burnout in sons. They may feel exhausted by the constant need to care for their mother's emotional needs, leaving them with little energy or capacity for their own emotional growth and development.

Psychosexual implications

The concept of psychosexual enmeshment has its roots in psychoanalytic theory, particularly in the works of Sigmund Freud and Carl Jung. Freud's theory of the Oedipus complex suggests that children go through a stage where they develop subconscious sexual feelings towards the opposite-sex parent. In normal development, these feelings are resolved as the child identifies with the same-sex parent and matures. However, in a relationship with a narcissistic father, especially in Mike's case, where there is no mother to aid the balance back to centre, this natural progression can be disrupted.

Narcissistic fathers may unconsciously (or even consciously) foster a relationship with their daughters that blurs the lines between paternal affection and romantic attention. They may become overly involved in their daughters' personal lives, discouraging or even sabotaging the daughter's attempts to form healthy romantic relationships with age-appropriate partners. This can lead to a form of emotional incest, where the daughter is expected to fulfil emotional needs that should be met by an adult partner, not a child. While this relationship may not involve physical sexual abuse, it can have a profound impact on the daughter's psychosexual development and most certainly reverse into the father being unable to hold an adult intimate relationship of his own due to the jealous bind in which the golden child finds herself, should her position as his emotionally intimate mate be encroached upon.

This dynamic can cause the child, particularly during adolescence, to develop confusing feelings of attachment that may have a sexual or romantic undertone, even if no physical boundaries are crossed. The child, having been cast in a spousal role, may struggle to differentiate between familial love and romantic affection, leading to feelings of guilt, shame, or confusion. Therapists often note that these children may experience distorted views of relationships and intimacy later in life, making it difficult to establish clear boundaries or engage in healthy romantic partnerships. The risk of erotic transference underscores the profound psychological damage that emotional incest can inflict on a child's developing sense of self and relationships.

In my work as a psychotherapist to many stepparents, I have found this can also be a challenge if the parent has been single for some time. After separation, if a child is cast in the partner position they can later feel threatened by an incoming new partner for the parent. At this point, triangulation and jealousy in narcissistic families are rife and pervasive.

Additional risks in single-parent situations

The risk of emotional incest increases significantly when the narcissistic parent is a single parent. In such a situation, the narcissistic parent may have no other adult in the household to meet their emotional needs, making the child the sole target of their emotional enmeshment. This dynamic can be particularly damaging because the child has no escape from the emotional burden placed on them and may feel trapped in the role of the surrogate spouse.

In a two-parent household, the non-narcissistic parent may serve as a buffer, providing the child with a healthier emotional environment and preventing the narcissistic parent from fully enmeshing with the child. However, in a single-parent household, there is no such buffer and the narcissistic parent has free rein to project their emotional needs onto the child without interference.

Single narcissistic parents may also be more likely to confide in their child about adult problems, because there is no other adult to share these burdens with. This further blurs the line between parent and child, forcing the child to take on an inappropriate emotional role.

In single-parent households, the child may feel even more pressure to meet the emotional needs of the narcissistic parent. The parent may frame their emotional enmeshment as a necessity, telling the child that they are the only one who can provide support or comfort. This can lead the child to feel guilty or obligated to meet the parent's emotional needs, even at the expense of their own emotional well-being.

Emotional incest in narcissistic parent–child relationships is a deeply troubling phenomenon that can have long-lasting and damaging effects on the child's emotional, psychological, and relational development. When a narcissistic father treats his daughter as a surrogate wife or a narcissistic mother treats her son as a surrogate husband, the child is forced into an inappropriate and emotionally burdensome role that stifles their independence and disrupts their ability to form healthy relationships.

Recognizing the signs of emotional incest and understanding the long-term impact on the child is crucial for preventing this harmful dynamic and promoting healthier parent–child relationships.

When enmenshed children and new partners meet

When a new partner enters a relationship where the narcissistic father and daughter are enmeshed, they often find themselves in a difficult and challenging situation. The enmeshment between the father and daughter can create significant tension and conflict in the new relationship, as the partner may feel excluded, threatened, or manipulated by the dynamics at play.

- **Cognitive dissonance:** Emotional incest between a narcissistic parent and their golden child can create significant cognitive dissonance for an incoming partner. The dynamic can be deeply unsettling as the new partner is met with conflicting signals – the golden child may show love and commitment to the partner while simultaneously prioritizing the narcissistic parent's demands. The narcissistic parent may subtly or overtly undermine the new relationship, manipulating the golden child's loyalty and fostering guilt or obligation towards them. The partner, witnessing this emotional entanglement, may feel confused or threatened, recognizing the inappropriate level of closeness yet struggling to articulate the problem. This dissonance between the partner's expectations of a healthy relationship and the golden child's inability to detach fully from the parent can lead to frustration, conflict, and often a sense of competition with the narcissistic parent for emotional space in the golden child's life.

- **Safeguarding:** A non-narcissistic incoming partner may begin to sense a safeguarding issue between the narcissistic parent and the enmeshed child when boundaries in the relationship are consistently blurred or violated. The enmeshed child may exhibit behaviours that suggest an unhealthy level of dependence or inappropriate intimacy with the narcissistic parent.

  Most concerning is when the narcissistic parent's behaviour around the child mirrors that of a partner, such as spending excessive time together, intimate conversations or touch, or controlling behaviours that interfere with the child's ability to form their own independent identity and relationships. The partner may feel alarmed by the intensity of the narcissistic parent's involvement, particularly when it impacts the child's well-being, such as feelings of guilt for pursuing their own life or discomfort in setting boundaries around the adult relationship. This dynamic can raise red flags about emotional abuse or enmeshment that stifles the child's psychological growth, prompting the partner to see it as not just an unhealthy relationship but a potential safeguarding issue requiring intervention or outside support.

- **Feelings of exclusion:** New partners may feel excluded from the close and emotionally intense relationship between the narcissistic father and the daughter. They may struggle to find their place in the family dynamic and feel like an outsider in their own relationship. This can lead to feelings of isolation, frustration, and resentment, particularly if the father and daughter prioritize their relationship over the new partnership.

- **Competition for attention:** In some cases, the daughter may view the new partner as a rival for her father's attention and affection. This can lead to a sense of competition, where the daughter attempts to undermine or sabotage the new relationship to maintain her position as the primary emotional focus in her father's life. The narcissistic father may encourage this dynamic, either consciously or unconsciously, as a way of maintaining control over both the daughter and the new partner.

- **Manipulation and triangulation:** Narcissistic parents often engage in triangulation, a manipulative tactic where they create conflict or rivalry between two people to maintain control and power. In an enmeshed relationship, the father may use triangulation to pit the daughter against the new partner, creating a toxic and destabilizing dynamic. This can lead to significant strain on the new relationship as the partner may feel constantly undermined or manipulated by both the father and the daughter.

- **Impact on the new partner's mental health:** The stress of navigating an enmeshed relationship can take a toll on the new partner's mental health. They may experience anxiety, depression, or feelings of inadequacy as they struggle to cope with the challenges of the relationship. The constant emotional pressure and lack of support can lead to burnout, making it difficult for the new partner to maintain their well-being and stability.

- **Potential for relationship breakdown:** In some cases, the enmeshment between the narcissistic father and the daughter can lead to the breakdown of the new relationship. The new partner may find it impossible to compete with the intense emotional bond between the father and daughter, leading to feelings of hopelessness and despair. If the narcissistic father is unwilling to address the enmeshment or prioritize the new relationship, the partner may ultimately decide to leave the relationship to protect their own mental health and well-being.

The risk of emotional enmeshment between the golden child and the narcissistic parent, particularly in the context of narcissistic fathers and daughters, is a serious and complex issue. The dynamics of emotional incest, and the additional risks in single-parent situations can have profound and lasting effects on the child's development and well-being. Daughters who grow up in these enmeshed relationships often struggle with identity issues, relationship difficulties, boundary-setting, and mental health challenges.

Furthermore, the impact of enmeshment extends beyond the father–daughter relationship, affecting new partners who enter into the dynamic. These partners may experience feelings of exclusion, competition, manipulation, and mental health difficulties as they navigate the challenges of the enmeshed relationship. The potential for relationship breakdown is high if the enmeshment is not addressed and resolved.

Addressing the issue of emotional enmeshment requires a commitment to setting healthy boundaries, seeking therapeutic support, and fostering open communication in relationships. For daughters of narcissistic fathers, healing may involve breaking free from the enmeshed relationship, developing a keen sense of self, and learning to establish healthy, autonomous relationships in adulthood. For new partners, understanding the dynamics of enmeshment and advocating for their own needs and boundaries is crucial for maintaining a healthy and fulfilling relationship.

By recognizing the signs of enmeshment, seeking support, and working towards healthier relationship dynamics, it is possible to mitigate the impact of this toxic dynamic and promote emotional well-being for everyone involved.

Therapeutic interventions focused on helping these children recognize and break free from these patterns are crucial. By addressing the unresolved trauma and distorted beliefs formed in childhood, these children can begin to build healthier, more fulfilling relationships in adulthood. Recognizing the impact of a narcissistic parent's influence is the first step towards healing and reclaiming autonomy in their emotional lives.

The risks of parental alienation during/post separation with a narcissist

Divorce and separation are emotionally challenging experiences, but when one parent exhibits narcissistic traits, these already difficult processes can become even more damaging, particularly to the children involved. A narcissistic parent is likely to bring a toxic element to the post-separation family dynamic through the process of parental alienation – a situation in which one parent manipulates their child into rejecting or undermining the other parent. Parental alienation is particularly concerning when one parent suffers from NPD, as narcissists often use their children as tools to maintain control over their former partner and exact revenge.

When separation or divorce occurs, a narcissistic parent's manipulation can intensify as the narcissist seeks to maintain power over their former spouse and assert control through their children. Parental alienation occurs when one parent attempts to damage the relationship between their child and the other parent, often through emotional manipulation, negative comments, indifference, or exaggeration of the other parent's flaws. In cases involving narcissistic parents, the likelihood of parental alienation increases significantly because narcissists are motivated by a need to 'win' at all costs, often viewing relationships as competitions rather than partnerships. This need to win is transferred to post-divorce conflicts, where the narcissist might use the child as a weapon to punish or undermine the other parent and to seek attention for themselves.

The behaviours exhibited by a narcissistic parent attempting to alienate their child from the other parent often include subtle and overt manipulation, emotional extortion, and gaslighting. Some common signs include:

- **Negative comments:** The narcissistic parent will often make derogatory or negative comments about the other parent in front of the child, aiming to influence the child's perception. Over time, the child may adopt the same negative views, leading to resentment or estrangement from the other parent.
- **Triangulation:** Narcissistic parents are skilled at creating triangular relationships, where the child becomes the 'ally' and the other parent is portrayed as the 'enemy'. This dynamic fosters distrust and division, further alienating the child from the non-narcissistic parent and causing them to feel privately trapped in a false rejection of the other parent to support the narcissistic parents' wishes.
- **Distortion of reality:** Narcissists frequently engage in gaslighting, where they distort reality to serve their narrative. In cases of parental alienation, the narcissistic parent may rewrite history, telling

the child that the other parent has been neglectful or abusive, even if this is not true. This confuses the child, who may begin to question their experiences and memories.

- **Withholding access:** A narcissistic parent might restrict the child's access to the other parent, using excuses such as the child being 'too busy' or blaming the other parent for failing to uphold visitation agreements. Over time, this limited access can result in the child becoming increasingly distant from the alienated parent.

- **Emotional manipulation:** Narcissistic parents may guilt-trip or emotionally manipulate the child into choosing them over the other parent. For example, they might suggest that they will be hurt or disappointed if the child spends time with the other parent, forcing the child to choose sides.

- **False allegations:** Narcissistic parents may make false accusations of abuse or neglect against the other parent as a way to undermine that parent's credibility and limit their access to the child. These allegations, even when unfounded, can lead to legal battles and emotional stress for the alienated parent.

Psychological impact on the child

The link between narcissism and parental alienation has been the subject of growing interest in psychological and legal research. Although parental alienation can occur in any high-conflict divorce, narcissistic parents are particularly likely to engage in alienating behaviours due to their need for control, lack of empathy, and inability to tolerate dissent.

As new research and understanding emerges, I would encourage you to read the following:

Understanding Parental Alienation: Learning to Cope, Helping to Heal: Karen Woodall and Nick Woodall have become pioneers in the modern-day untangling of Parental Alienation Syndrome (PAS) and work within the parental alienation space, having previously focused on the separated parents' space. This book provides practical insights into parental alienation and how to navigate the emotional turmoil it causes, including steps to support healing for both children and alienated parents.

Parental Alienation Syndrome: Dr Richard A. Gardner introduced the concept of Parental Alienation Syndrome in the 1980s. According to Gardner, PAS is a disorder that arises when one parent attempts to alienate the child from the other parent, often through manipulation and psychological abuse. While PAS is not universally accepted as a formal diagnosis, the concept has been influential in understanding the dynamics of alienation, particularly in cases involving narcissistic parents.

Narcissism and Divorce: A 2017 study by Horan and Schmitt (*Personality and Individual Differences*) examined the relationship between narcissistic traits and conflict in divorce. The study found that individuals with higher levels of narcissism were more likely to engage in destructive post-divorce behaviours, including parental alienation. These individuals often view their former partner as an adversary and are more likely to use their children as a means of maintaining control or exacting revenge.

Impact of Parental Alienation on Children: A 2010 study by Baker and Verrocchio (*Journal of Child Custody*) explored the long-term effects of parental alienation on children's mental health. The study found that children who were alienated from one parent were more likely to experience depression, anxiety, and issues with substance abuse in adolescence and adulthood. The study also highlighted the role of narcissistic parents in perpetuating alienation, noting that these individuals are often unable to recognize the harm they are causing to their child's emotional well-being.

Legal recognition of parental alienation

While parental alienation is increasingly recognized as a form of emotional abuse, it remains a complex issue within the legal system. Courts are often reluctant to interfere in custody arrangements, and proving parental alienation can be difficult, particularly when narcissistic parents are adept at concealing their manipulative behaviour.

In recent years, however, there has been a growing awareness of the role that narcissistic parents play in parental alienation. Some family courts are beginning to recognize parental alienation as a form of emotional abuse and are taking steps to protect the child's relationship with both parents. In some cases, courts have awarded custody to the alienated parent or implemented interventions designed to restore the relationship between the child and the alienated parent.

The risks associated with narcissistic parents in single-parent or split-family situations are profound, particularly when parental alienation is involved. Narcissistic parents are more likely to engage in manipulative, controlling behaviours that undermine the child's relationship with the other parent, leading to long-term psychological damage for both the child and the alienated parent. Research supports the notion that narcissistic parents are more prone to engaging in parental alienation, driven by their need for control, lack of empathy, and desire for revenge.

While parental alienation remains a complex issue within the legal system, increasing awareness of the role that narcissism plays in this dynamic offers hope for more effective interventions. Recognizing the signs of parental alienation and understanding the psychological impact on both the child and the alienated parent is the first step towards mitigating the damage and fostering healthier post-divorce relationships for the entire family.

The psychological toll on children who are subjected to parental alienation by a narcissistic parent can be severe and long-lasting. Several studies such as those by Caitlin Bentley and Mandy Matthewson have highlighted the emotional and cognitive damage that occurs when children are manipulated into rejecting one of their parents.

Children who are caught in the middle of parental alienation often experience elevated levels of emotional distress. They may feel confused about their loyalties and develop feelings of guilt or anxiety when interacting with the alienated parent. This emotional strain can lead to long-term mental health issues, including depression, anxiety, and low self-esteem. They often internalize the conflict, blaming themselves for the dysfunction in the relationship between their parents.

Parental alienation can also lead to the child's becoming confused about their own identity, particularly when they are subjected to conflicting narratives from each parent. A narcissistic parent's constant undermining of the other parent can make it difficult for the child to form a coherent sense of self as they are torn between two competing realities splitting. Over time, this can lead to difficulty establishing a stable sense of identity, which may manifest in poor decision-making, difficulty forming healthy relationships, and chronic feelings of insecurity.

The most profound impact of parental alienation is the loss of a secure attachment with the alienated parent. Attachment theory, developed by John Bowlby in the mid-twentieth century, posits that children form emotional bonds with their primary caregivers that shape their ability to form relationships later in life. When parental alienation severs this bond, the child may grow up without a healthy model for relationships, leading to difficulties in forming secure attachments in adulthood.

A 2006 study by Harman, Kruk, and Hines (*Journal of Family Issues*) demonstrated that children who experience parental alienation are at a higher risk of developing attachment disorders, which can affect their ability to form meaningful relationships with peers, romantic partners, and even their own children later in life.

Psychological impact on the alienated parent

In addition to the harm caused to the child, parental alienation has a profound psychological impact on the alienated parent. Being cut off from their child, either emotionally or physically, can lead to intense feelings of grief, helplessness, and anger.

Alienated parents often describe their experience as akin to mourning the loss of a living child. The relationship they once had with their child is replaced by rejection, hostility, or indifference, leading to profound emotional pain. Alienated parents are at a higher risk of developing depression, anxiety, and even symptoms of PTSD as a result of the ongoing emotional abuse they experience during the alienation process.

Many alienated parents are forced to engage in prolonged legal battles to regain access to their children, which can be financially draining and emotionally exhausting. Narcissistic parents are often skilled at manipulating the legal system, using false allegations or exaggerations to restrict the alienated parent's rights. These legal battles can stretch on for years, further entrenching the alienation and causing significant financial strain for the targeted parent.

Finding help, guidance, and support

Navigating the complex and often distressing dynamics of narcissistic families can be overwhelming. With the evolving landscape of mental health and therapeutic practices, it is crucial to stay informed about the latest resources and specialists who can offer targeted support. Those seeking help for narcissistic family dynamics – particularly enmeshment, emotional incest, and parental alienation – have a variety of options.

Finding the right help for these issues requires an understanding of which professionals are equipped to address them. Below are some key avenues to explore.

Therapists and psychologists specializing in narcissistic abuse

Therapists with experience in narcissistic abuse are crucial for addressing the emotional and psychological impacts of growing up in such environments. When seeking therapy, look for professionals who specialize in the following areas:

- Narcissistic family dynamics:
  - Narcissistic Personality Disorder: Therapists familiar with NPD can help survivors understand the patterns and impacts of narcissistic behaviour.
  - Family systems therapy: This approach can help unravel the complex family dynamics and work towards healthier boundaries.
  - Trauma-informed therapy: Professionals who are trauma-informed understand the unique challenges faced by individuals recovering from abusive family environments.
- Specialists in enmeshment and emotional incest:
  - Family therapists: These therapists can work with the entire family to address and restructure unhealthy relational patterns. They often use techniques to help establish and maintain healthy boundaries.
  - Sexual abuse therapists: For emotional incest, therapists who specialize in sexual abuse or trauma can offer strategies to address and heal from these specific experiences – even when the abuse did not cross into physical or sexual.
- Experts in parental alienation:
  - Parental alienation therapists: These therapists focus on repairing damaged parent–child relationships and addressing the psychological impacts of alienation.

○ Family court consultants: In some cases, legal experts who consult on family court matters may offer additional support in addressing parental alienation.

○ Notable experts and their contributions: Karen and Nick Woodhall are prominent figures in the field of parental alienation. Their work is invaluable for understanding and addressing this complex issue. Karen Woodhall is a specialist in parental alienation and has contributed extensively to the field through her writing, workshops, and therapeutic practice as well as her representations in court cases. Her work focuses on the psychological effects of alienation and offers practical strategies for parents and children to rebuild relationships.

○ Nick Woodhall co-authors with Karen and brings additional expertise in family dynamics and therapeutic interventions. Together, they have developed resources and training programmes for professionals and families dealing with parental alienation. Their books and workshops through their Family Separation Clinic are highly recommended for those seeking to understand the nuances of parental alienation and explore strategies for intervention and recovery.

Additional resources

- **Support groups:** Joining support groups for individuals affected by narcissistic family dynamics can provide communal support and shared experiences. These groups often offer practical advice and emotional validation.
- **Online forums and communities:** Platforms such as Reddit and specialized forums can offer support and resources for individuals dealing with narcissistic abuse and related issues.
- **Books and literature:** In addition to the Woodhalls' work, several books provide valuable insights into narcissistic family dynamics. You will find them listed in the Further Reading section at the end of this book. Look for recent publications and updated editions for the latest perspectives.

Practical steps for finding help

When seeking help, consider these practical steps:

- **Research and referrals:** Start by researching into therapists and specialists in your area. Referrals from trusted professionals or organizations can be beneficial. Look on the British Association for Counselling and Psychotherapy and the United Kingdom Council for Psychotherapy websites where you can search by specialism and location.
- **Consultations:** Many therapists offer initial consultations to discuss your needs and determine whether their approach aligns with your goals.
- **Credentials and specializations:** Verify the credentials and specializations of potential therapists to ensure they are equipped to handle your specific issues.

In conclusion

Seeking help for narcissistic family dynamics requires a proactive approach to finding the right professionals and resources. By understanding the unique challenges of enmeshment, emotional incest, and parental alienation, and by turning to specialist individuals, you can access targeted support to navigate and heal from these complex issues. Staying informed and seeking specialized assistance can pave the way for recovery and personal growth in the aftermath of narcissistic abuse.

Being the individual who breaks a generational pattern, or recognizes narcissism in the family, or discovers the courage and bravery to start the work to find freedom and fortitude to live life the way you intend and need to, is what the next chapters are all about. In bringing what has happened in your family out into the open, you now have the opportunity to make the changes you desire to start the next, narcissistic-free chapter of your life.

7

Early life experiences of the true, false, and adapted selves
Discovering your true self: the path to authenticity and liberation

'To thine own self be true.'
Shakespeare

For those who have been raised in or around narcissism within a family constellation, it can be startling, shocking, and rather discombobulating to discover and then accept the truth about their family and upbringing. As we begin to untangle the truth behind the façade, it can be daunting to consider starting a journey to recovery and with it a potential reconstruction of the truth of where we have come from and, most importantly, who we truly are.

Many people go through life acting out roles, playing the part expected of them, whether it's in their family, their social circles, or their professional lives, and none more so than those with a peacock for a parent. But beneath all the masks and layers of expectations, there is something more profound and intrinsic – one's true self. Discovering and living in alignment with your true self is one of the most liberating experiences a person can have. It means living authentically, being fully present in your own life, and making decisions based on your values, needs, and desires, rather than the dictates of others. But this discovery is no small task, especially for those who have been subjected to environments that actively suppressed their true selves.

For many, the journey to authenticity is arduous and painful, particularly if they grew up in a family that imposed false roles and identities upon them and, of course, the most common environments in which this happens is in families with narcissistic parents. When a parent's needs eclipse those of the child, the child often learns to live a life that is not their own. They are conditioned to meet their parent's emotional, psychological, or even physical demands and often, as a scapegoated child, to hold the negative and difficult projections of accusations that have little if anything to do with them. Over time, they may lose sight of who they truly are.

The good news is that rediscovery of the true self is possible and the rewards are immense. Not only does it lead to greater personal fulfilment, it also fosters deeper, more meaningful connections with others.

The power of the true self

At its core, the true self is a reflection of your authentic desires, interests, and feelings – unfiltered by the opinions or expectations of others. It's the self you were born with before any external influence from life's pressures pushed you to conform to roles or expectations that weren't inherently yours. Your true self is not a static entity; it evolves with time, but it remains grounded in your core identity and values. Living as your true self means embracing your vulnerability, being honest with yourself and others, and having the courage to express your deepest needs, even when they may conflict with what others expect of you.

Living authentically allows you to make choices that align with your inner values, rather than ones that please others at the cost of your well-being. It fosters self-confidence, resilience, and a sense of inner peace. The false self, by contrast, is the façade we often construct to fit into societal, familial, or relational expectations. When you are disconnected from your true self, you may find yourself feeling lost, frustrated, or emotionally drained, even if you appear to be successful or 'normal' by external standards.

The strength of your true self is essential for living a liberated life. It allows you to create boundaries, say no to things that don't serve you, and say yes to opportunities that nourish your soul. It enables you to recognize when you are compromising your well-being for the sake of external validation and gives you the courage to prioritize your own needs and desires. This isn't selfish, it's self-preservation. Living as your true self leads to more authentic relationships, greater personal fulfilment, and a deep sense of purpose.

Donald Winnicott and the theory of the true, false, and adapted selves

Donald Winnicott was a prominent British psychoanalyst and paediatrician who made significant contributions to the understanding of early childhood development and the formation of the self. His work, particularly around the concepts of the 'true self', 'false self', and 'adapted self', has provided a profound framework for understanding how individuals develop their identities and cope with their environments. Winnicott's theories are especially relevant in understanding the dynamics within narcissistic families, where children often face intense emotional challenges and pressures that can lead to the development of a false self as a coping mechanism.

The true self

Winnicott's concept of the 'true self' refers to the authentic, spontaneous part of the individual that emerges naturally when a child feels secure and supported in their environment. The true self is associated with the child's core feelings, desires, and creativity – essentially, it is the person's genuine identity, free from external pressures or the need to conform to the expectations of others.

For Winnicott, the development of the true self is contingent upon a 'good enough' caregiving environment. A 'good enough mother' (a term Winnicott used to describe the primary caregiver, which can be any primary attachment figure) is one who is attuned to the child's needs and responds appropriately, fostering a sense of safety and allowing the child to express their true self without fear of rejection or punishment. This caregiver provides a secure base from which the child can explore the world and develop a strong sense of self.

Living as your true self, in the way Winnicott described, might look like someone who is deeply connected to their inner feelings and values, making choices that align with their authentic desires rather than external expectations. For example, consider someone who left a prestigious but unfulfilling career because they realized it wasn't aligned with their passion for creativity. Rather than being driven by societal pressures or the need for financial levelling or approval from peers or parents, they followed their true self's calling and pursued a career as an artist or writer, even if it meant taking risks or facing uncertainty. This person would demonstrate resilience and self-acceptance, embracing their imperfections and expressing their unique quirks without fear of judgement. They might marry someone they genuinely loved, regardless of religion, parental approval, or class. They would prioritize genuine relationships, surrounding themselves with people who support their growth and authenticity, and they wouldn't feel the need to hide their vulnerability. In daily life, this might manifest in how they communicate openly about their feelings, set healthy boundaries, and make decisions based on inner fulfilment, not external validation. Their life, though imperfect, would be deeply satisfying because it would be a true reflection of who they are at their core.

When the true self is allowed to flourish, the individual grows up with a strong sense of identity, capable of forming genuine relationships and navigating life's challenges with resilience and authenticity.

The false self

In contrast, the false self emerges when the caregiving environment is inadequate, overly controlling, or emotionally neglectful. This occurs when the child perceives that their true self is unacceptable or that they must suppress their authentic feelings and desires to gain approval, avoid punishment, or secure the love and attention of their caregivers. The false self is a defensive structure – a façade that the child constructs to navigate an environment where their true self is not welcomed or validated.

Living a false self life, as Winnicott described, might manifest in someone who appears highly successful or well-adjusted on the surface but feels disconnected from their inner emotions and true desires. For example, imagine a person who has pursued a career chosen by their parents, perhaps as a lawyer or doctor, not because it reflects their passion or interests but because it brings them external validation and meets family expectations. This individual might excel in their role and receive praise from others, yet inwardly they feel empty, anxious, or even resentful. They may be skilled at reading social cues and adapting their behaviour to fit what others want, often suppressing their own needs to maintain harmony or avoid conflict. In personal relationships, they might prioritize keeping others happy, neglecting their own emotional well-being and never expressing vulnerability for fear of being rejected or judged. Their life is outwardly smooth but marked by a pervasive sense of unease or dissatisfaction as their true self remains hidden behind the mask of a constructed, socially acceptable persona.

The false self is essentially a mask that the individual wears to meet the expectations of others. It is characterized by compliance, superficiality, and a lack of spontaneity. Over time, if the false self becomes dominant, the individual may lose touch with their true self, leading to feelings of emptiness, alienation, and a sense of not knowing who they truly are.

The adapted self

The concept of the adapted self can be seen as a middle ground between the true and false selves. It refers to the adjustments that an individual makes in response to their environment, which can be either healthy or unhealthy depending on the context. The adapted self is necessary for navigating social relationships and functioning within society, as complete authenticity (true self-expression) in every situation is neither possible nor desirable.

Living an adapted self life, as Winnicott understood it, involves someone who has made adjustments to their true self in order to function in their environment, often as a survival mechanism. This person may not be completely disconnected from their true self, but they have learned to compromise or modify it to fit social or familial expectations. For example, consider someone who loves art but works in a corporate setting because it provides financial stability and meets the practical needs of their family. They may still nurture their creative side in small ways, such as painting at weekends or decorating their home, but they don't fully express this aspect of themselves in their daily life. In relationships, this person may selectively share parts of their true self with trusted individuals but still avoid vulnerability in larger social settings or with family members who disapprove of their passions. They find a balance between living authentically and conforming to external demands, though this balance might leave them feeling constrained at times. Their life is not devoid of meaning or joy, but there is a constant tension between their inner desires and the adaptations they've made to fit into the world around them.

Winnicott's True Self & False Self Theory

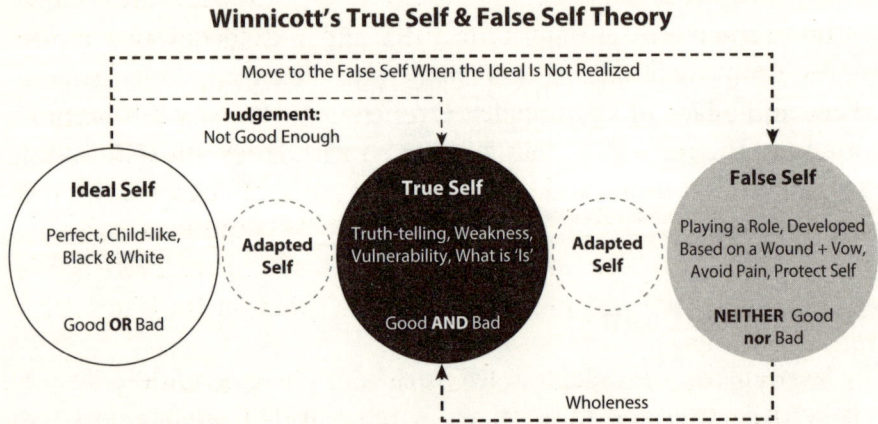

Figure 7.1 How the true self, idealised self, and false self interconnect
Source: Dr D.W. Winnicott

In environments where narcissism is prevalent, the adapted self may become overdeveloped as the individual learns to adapt excessively to the needs and demands of narcissistic figures, often at the expense of their true self. The adapted self in such contexts may involve adopting behaviours, beliefs, and attitudes that ensure survival and acceptance in a narcissistic family dynamic. See Figure 7.1.

Narcissistic families and the suppression of the true self

In narcissistic families, the dynamics are often centred on the needs, desires, and image of the narcissistic parent. The narcissistic parent may require their children to reflect their own grandiosity, success, or superiority, which places immense pressure on the children to conform to the parent's expectations. The child's role is not to be an independent individual with their own needs and desires but rather to serve as an extension of the narcissistic parent's ego.

The golden child and the false self

We know that the golden child is a common dynamic in narcissistic families. The golden child is often seen as an idealized version of what the narcissistic parent wants to see in themselves. This child may be showered with praise, attention, and privileges, but these are contingent upon the child's adherence to the parent's expectations and the suppression of their true self.

For the golden child, the development of a false self is almost inevitable. To maintain their favoured status, they must suppress their authentic feelings and desires and instead present a façade that aligns with the narcissistic parent's demands. This can lead to significant psychological distress as the child becomes increasingly alienated from their true self and trapped in the role that the parent has imposed on them.

In many cases, the golden child may not even realize the extent of their disconnection from their true self until later in life when they begin to experience feelings of emptiness, depression, or a crisis of identity. The false self, which was initially developed as a coping mechanism, becomes a prison that prevents the individual from living an authentic and fulfilling life.

The scapegoat struggles with true self suppression

As we have also seen, another common dynamic in narcissistic families is the scapegoating of one child. The scapegoat is often the child who, for whatever reason, fails to meet the narcissistic parent's expectations or who dares to express their true self in ways that challenge the parent's authority or image. The scapegoated child is typically subjected to criticism, blame, and emotional abuse, and is often held responsible for the family's problems.

For the scapegoated child, the true self is a source of pain and rejection, as it is constantly attacked by the narcissistic parent. This child may develop a false self as a means of self-protection, trying to conform to the parent's demands in a desperate attempt to gain acceptance or avoid punishment. Alternatively, the scapegoat may become rebellious, rejecting the false self and embracing a version of the true self that is defined in opposition to the parent's values and expectations. However, this rebellious stance is often more a reaction to the parent's narcissism than a true expression of the child's authentic self.

The scapegoated child may carry the wounds of this dynamic into adulthood, struggling with issues of self-worth, anger, and a distorted sense of identity. The suppression of the true self in childhood can lead to a lifelong battle to reclaim one's authenticity and overcome the internalized messages of worthlessness and inadequacy.

Coping with narcissism: the role of the false and adapted selves

In narcissistic environments, both the false and the adapted selves play crucial roles in helping individuals cope with the emotional and psychological challenges they face. These defensive structures, while often necessary for survival, can also create long-term difficulties in developing a healthy and authentic sense of self.

The false self as a coping mechanism

The false self is primarily a defence mechanism that allows the individual to navigate a hostile or emotionally unsafe environment. In the context of a narcissistic family, the false self is often developed in response to the overwhelming demands and expectations of the narcissistic parent. By adopting a false self, the child learns to suppress their true self and present a version of themselves that is more acceptable to the Peacock parent.

This coping mechanism can be effective in the short term, as it helps the child avoid conflict, rejection, or punishment. However, the long-term consequences of relying on a false self can be severe. As the individual grows older, they may struggle with feelings of emptiness, alienation, and a lack of purpose. The false self, while protective, prevents the individual from forming genuine connections with others and from living a life that is true to their own values and desires.

For individuals who have developed a strong false self, therapy and self-reflection can be essential tools in the process of reclaiming the true self. This often involves exploring the origins of the false self, understanding the dynamics that led to its development, and gradually dismantling the defences that have kept the true self hidden.

The adapted self and social functioning

The adapted self, while also a form of self-protection, is more focused on social functioning and maintaining relationships. In narcissistic families, the adapted self may be developed as a way to navigate the complex and often contradictory demands of the narcissistic parent. For example, a child may learn to be highly attuned to the parent's moods and needs, adjusting their behaviour to avoid conflict or to gain approval.

The adapted self is not inherently unhealthy as it allows the individual to function in social situations and to meet the expectations of others. However, in the context of a narcissistic family, the adapted self can become overdeveloped, leading to a pattern of people-pleasing, co-dependency, and a lack of boundaries. The individual may struggle to assert their needs and desires, instead prioritizing the needs of others to avoid conflict or rejection.

In adulthood, individuals with a strongly developed adapted self may find it difficult to establish healthy, autonomous relationships. They may be drawn to partners who are controlling or emotionally demanding, replicating the dynamics of their childhood. Over time, this can lead to burnout, resentment, and a sense of losing oneself in relationships.

Therapeutic work with the adapted self often involves learning to set boundaries, assert one's needs, and develop a stronger sense of self-worth. This process can help the individual balance the need for social adaptation with the need to stay true to their own identity.

The relevance of Winnicott's Theory in narcissistic families

Winnicott's theory of the true, false, and adapted selves is highly relevant in understanding the dynamics of narcissistic families and the long-term impact on the individuals who grow up in such environments. The pressure to conform to the narcissistic parent's expectations can lead to the suppression of the true self and the development of defensive structures that protect the individual in the short term but create significant psychological challenges in the long term.

One of the most significant long-term impacts of growing up in a narcissistic family is the struggle with identity and self-esteem. The false self, while protective, often comes at the cost of the individual's sense of authenticity and self-worth. The constant need to suppress the true self can lead to feelings of inadequacy, confusion, and a lack of purpose.

Children of narcissistic parents may grow up with a distorted sense of who they are, having internalized the parent's criticisms, expectations, and values. This can lead to a fragile sense of self-esteem that is highly dependent on external validation. In adulthood, these individuals may struggle with self-doubt, perfectionism, and a fear of failure, as they continue to seek approval and avoid the rejection they experienced in childhood.

The dynamics of the false and adapted selves also have significant implications for relationships. Individuals who grew up in narcissistic families may find it difficult to form healthy, authentic relationships as their ability to connect with others is often compromised by their defensive structures.

For those with a dominant false self, relationships may be characterized by superficiality as they struggle to reveal their true self to others. This can lead to feelings of loneliness and isolation as the individual may fear that others will reject them if they show their authentic self.

For those with an overdeveloped adapted self, relationships may be marked by co-dependency and a lack of boundaries. These individuals may prioritize the needs of their partner or friends at the expense of their own well-being, leading to patterns of unhealthy or abusive relationships.

The role of therapy in reclaiming the true self

Therapy can play a crucial role in helping those of us who grew up in narcissistic families reclaim our true self and heal from the psychological wounds of our childhood. This process often involves a combination of self-reflection, boundary-setting, and the development of self-compassion.

In therapy, we may explore the origins of our false and adapted selves, understanding how these defensive structures developed in response to our environment. This exploration can help us begin to dismantle these defences and reconnect with our true self.

Boundary-setting is also a critical aspect of healing, as it allows us to establish a sense of autonomy and protect ourselves from the demands of others. Learning to assert our needs and desires, and to say no, when necessary, can help us break free from the patterns of co-dependency and people-pleasing that often develop in narcissistic families.

Finally, developing self-compassion is essential for healing from the internalized shame and self-criticism that often accompany the suppression of the true self. By learning to treat ourselves with kindness and understanding, we can begin to rebuild our self-esteem and create a more positive and authentic sense of identity.

The idiosyncratic self

Winnicott also spoke of the 'idiosyncratic self', a term used to describe the parts of the self that are unique to the individual – quirks, preferences, and traits that don't necessarily fit into the socially prescribed mould but are integral to who the person truly is. The idiosyncratic self, when allowed to flourish, adds richness and colour to one's personality. However, in a family system dominated by a narcissistic parent, the idiosyncratic self may be stifled or ridiculed, forcing the child to hide or suppress aspects of their personality that don't conform to the family's expectations.

For individuals who grew up in a narcissistic family, the concept of the true self may feel foreign or elusive. They may have spent so long fulfilling roles imposed on them by their parent that they have lost touch with their own needs, desires, and even identity. They may have been the 'golden child', expected to live up to the parent's ambitious standards and reflect their success, or the 'scapegoat', blamed for the family's problems and subjected to emotional abuse. These roles, though powerful, are not reflections of the child's true self – they are constructs of the narcissistic family dynamic designed to maintain the parent's ego at the expense of the child's individuality.

The narcissistic family: roles and the suppression of the true self

In families with narcissistic parents, children often find themselves caught in a web of expectations that stifle their true selves. As we have discussed at length, narcissistic parents view their children not as individuals with their own needs and desires but as extensions of themselves. The child's worth is determined by how well they fulfil the parent's emotional needs, and any deviation from this is met with disapproval, manipulation, or outright hostility.

Children in narcissistic families may be assigned specific roles, as we have covered, and these roles are not based on the child's true personality or needs but rather on the parent's narcissistic desires. Over time, the child internalizes these roles and their true self becomes buried beneath layers of expectations and defences.

If you were the golden child, you may feel immense pressure to perform, achieve, and be perfect, constantly seeking the parent's approval at the expense of your own desires. If you were the scapegoat, meanwhile, you may become rebellious or withdrawn, believing that you are inherently flawed or unworthy of love. Both roles are equally damaging as they prevent the child from developing an authentic sense of self.

As these children grow into adulthood, they may struggle to identify their true selves. They may continue to seek external validation, believing that their worth is tied to their ability to meet others' expectations. They may feel disconnected from their own emotions, unsure of what they genuinely want or need. This disconnection can lead to feelings of emptiness, depression, and anxiety, as well as difficulties in forming healthy, authentic relationships.

Reclaiming the true self: the path to healing

The process of reclaiming your true self after growing up in a narcissistic family is a journey of self-discovery and healing. It involves peeling back the layers of false identities and roles that have been imposed upon you and reconnecting with your core self. This can be a challenging and painful process as it requires you to confront the ways in which you have suppressed or abandoned your true self in order to survive in a toxic environment.

One of the first steps in this process is recognizing that the roles you were assigned in your family are not reflections of who you truly are. You may have been conditioned to believe that your worth is tied to your ability to meet others' expectations, but this is not true. Your worth is inherent, and it is not dependent on external validation. Reconnecting with your true self involves rediscovering your authentic desires, interests, and feelings, and learning to trust your instincts and intuition.

Therapy can be an invaluable tool in this process as it provides a safe and supportive space for you to explore your true self and work through the emotional wounds of your past. Through therapy, you can begin to dismantle the false self that has been created in response to your family's expectations and start to build a more authentic sense of identity.

As you reclaim your true self, you may find that your relationships with others begin to shift. People who were comfortable with your false self may resist or even reject the changes they see in you. This is particularly true in narcissistic families, where your true self may no longer serve the family's dysfunctional dynamics. As you step into your authenticity, you may be met with anger, guilt, or manipulation from family members who are threatened by your newfound sense of self.

The challenges of living as your true self in a narcissistic family

One of the most difficult aspects of reclaiming your true self is dealing with the resistance and backlash that may come from your family. Narcissistic families thrive on control and when you begin to assert your needs and desires, you disrupt the family's established dynamics. Family members may accuse you of being selfish, ungrateful, or difficult, attempting to shame you into reverting to your old role. They may use manipulation, criticism, or emotional extortion to maintain control over you.

It is important to recognize that these reactions are not a reflection of your worth or your choices – they are a reflection of the family's dysfunction. As you continue to grow into your true self, you may need to set boundaries with family members, limiting contact or even cutting ties if necessary to protect your mental and emotional health. This can be an incredibly painful decision, but it is often necessary. By exploring and addressing the dynamics of the true self, false self, and idealized self, you can embark on a journey of healing and self-discovery, ultimately discovering and reclaiming your true self and fostering a more genuine and fulfilling sense of identity: the first step towards freedom.

8

Hearing your own voice; seeking the truth

'I am out with lanterns looking for myself.'

Emily Dickinson

One day you finally knew
what you had to do, and began,
though the voices around you
kept shouting
their bad advice –
though the whole house
began to tremble
and you felt the old tug
at your ankles.
'Mend my life!'
each voice cried.
But you didn't stop.
You knew what you had to do,
though the wind pried
with its stiff fingers
at the very foundations,
though their melancholy
was terrible.

It was already late
enough, and a wild night,
and the road full of fallen
branches and stones.
But little by little,
as you left their voices behind,
the stars began to burn
through the sheets of clouds,
and there was a new voice
which you slowly
recognized as your own,
that kept you company
as you strode deeper and deeper
into the world,
determined to do
the only thing you could do –
determined to save
the only life you could save.

Mary Oliver, The Journey

Narcissistic abuse, especially when inflicted by parents, is, in my view, a profound form of psychological identity theft. At its core, as these chapters have been describing, narcissistic abuse involves a systematic erosion of a child's sense of self, autonomy, and individuality in return for parental acceptance. This insidious form of abuse leaves deep scars, shaping how a child perceives themselves and navigates the world, which is why we need to go and retrieve that inner child and that true identity as we start our journey of recovery.

Seeking, finding, hearing, and beginning to trust your own voice and reconnecting with your true identity is central before we can begin the work of healing – something this chapter is going to address directly. Understanding Winnicott's 'true self'/'false self theory' is an essential – and sensible – starting point for us to begin to tune into the voice inside us, one we may have lost many years ago.

Psychological identity theft occurs when one's sense of self is co-opted, manipulated, or suppressed by another person. In the context of narcissistic abuse by parents, it involves a parent imposing their needs, expectations, and desires on to the child to such an extent that the child's individuality is overridden. The child is often denied the freedom to develop their own identity, leading to 'an adapted self' that exists to serve the parent's ego rather than the child's genuine personality and aspirations.

Narcissistic parents, as we now know, are either primarily driven by their need for validation and control, and an inflated sense of self-worth or a crippling fragile ego and narcissistic wound. Their children are seen not as individuals with their own thoughts, feelings, and potential but merely as objects or extensions of the parent. These parents often:

- **Project their desires:** They use their children to fulfil unfulfilled dreams or to bolster their image in society.
- **Demand perfection:** They expect their children to adhere to unrealistic standards, which reflect positively on them.
- **Control through manipulation:** Love, approval, and support are conditional, given only when the child behaves in ways that align with the parent's needs.

These behaviours stem from deep insecurity and a need to maintain dominance. By undermining their child's individuality, narcissistic parents ensure their authority remains unchallenged.

However, once we can understand and absorb the concept of true, false, adapted, and idealized selves, we can begin to search for the true self within, to listen out for our own voice, and begin to learn to trust that our body also knows the truth. With that as our aim and with the understanding of these earlier chapters now firmly in our pockets, we can start to reclaim our true identity.

For a child of a narcissistic parent or parents, this is not completely straightforward, but it is totally possible. No matter what position you may have played in the family to date, you will have been manipulated to behave in ways that please, calm, or avoid your abusive parent and you will have suppressed and given up or lost touch with some of your own true beliefs, and emotions in order to 'fit in' to the distortion of the controlling parent. After many years of this it can be hard initially to reach the core of ourselves because we begin to mistrust what we feel, think, and know any more. Our true identity is languishing and possibly hidden, yet waits longingly to be rediscovered.

Signs of psychological identity theft in the child

Recognizing that your identity has been co-opted by narcissistic abuse is the first step towards healing. Common signs include:

- **chronic self-doubt:** constantly second-guessing your thoughts, feelings, and decisions
- **difficulty setting boundaries:** struggling to assert your needs or to say no
- **overwhelming guilt:** a sense you are being unfair and maybe your memory is wrong
- **people-pleasing tendencies:** sacrificing personal desires to gain approval
- **disconnection from emotions:** difficulty identifying or expressing genuine feelings
- **lack of purpose or direction:** feeling lost or aimless, unsure of your true passions or goals.

In addition, we often detect 'splitting', which will further confuse your sense of truth and self. Psychological splitting is a defence mechanism often seen in children of narcissistic parents, especially those who have experienced abuse. It means that you may perceive people, situations – or even yourself – in extremes, such as entirely good or entirely bad, with little room for nuance. In the context of narcissistic abuse, children may 'split' as a way to manage the conflicting feelings of love for and fear towards their parent. The parent may oscillate between idealizing and devaluing the child, leaving the child with an unstable sense of self-worth and difficulty integrating these experiences. This coping strategy can persist into adulthood, influencing relationships, emotional regulation, and self-perception, as the individual struggles to reconcile the deeply ingrained dichotomy of admiration and rejection learned in childhood. For many of the adult children of narcissists I work with, their ability truly to trust and believe in themselves and what they have experienced can be one of the main and most important challenges.

Survivors of parental narcissistic abuse often adopt adaptations of the self – the false self, adapted self, and idealized self – to cope with their environment. These constructs serve as survival mechanisms in the face of a parent's manipulative and often invalidating behaviour. While these adaptations help the child navigate the abusive dynamics, they can distance the survivor from their true self, the authentic core of their identity. My role as a therapist is to hold the mirror steady as they start to recognize their true selves re-emerging after many years, often decades, of manipulation. I hope this can happen for you, too.

How and why we adapt for safety

To survive in a narcissistic family, you may well have developed an adaptive self – a persona tailored to meet the parent's demands and expectations. This adaptive self prioritizes survival over authenticity, often at great personal cost:

- **Suppressed authenticity:** Genuine interests, desires, and emotions are buried to avoid conflict or rejection.
- **Hypervigilance:** There is constant monitoring of the environment for signs of approval or disapproval.
- **Fragmented identity:** The adaptive self becomes so entrenched that the true self feels inaccessible.

While the adaptive self is a necessary survival tool in childhood, it becomes a hindrance in adulthood, preventing people from living authentically.

The false self emerges as a mask, tailored to meet the narcissistic parent's needs and avoid conflict or punishment. This self-suppresses authentic feelings, desires, and expressions to maintain the parent's approval or avoid their wrath. We can often see this in the lost child as a coping mechanism. Over time, the child may struggle to distinguish the false self from their genuine identity. Their thoughts and feelings are ignored, leaving them disconnected from their emotions. Their achievements and individuality are not acknowledged, leading to low self-esteem. As time goes on, they may struggle to articulate their needs or recognize their intrinsic worth, so finding their true self is paramount as they recover.

The adapted self develops as the child learns to conform to the parent's expectations, often at the expense of their autonomy. This self is rooted in hypervigilance and compliance, enabling the child to predict and placate the parent's erratic demands or indeed to rebel against them. We see this most often in the scapegoated child. They internalize shame and are made to feel inherently flawed or defective. They may choose rebellion or overcompensation, acting out or over-achieving to prove their worth. Reactive abuse, where the cumulative injustice or neglect at the hands of a narcissistic parent boils up in a child to the point that they act out, can occur, deepening the 'confirmation' of badness within the child, and their identity can become further fragmented where their sense of self is shaped by the constant invalidation and blame they receive. While adaptive in the short term, it can hinder the development of independence and self-trust, lowering the self-esteem to critical levels.

The idealized self is a version of the self that strives for perfection, reflects the narcissistic parent's unrealistic expectations. You will often notice the golden child adopts this version of self, which is driven by a need to earn love and validation through flawless performance or behaviour. Their worth is tied to their ability to meet the parent's expectations; they are burdened with maintaining the parent's image, leaving little room for personal exploration, and their individuality is subsumed by the parent's vision, creating a fragile, externally driven sense of self. It perpetuates a cycle of shame and inadequacy when perfection cannot be achieved.

Reconnecting all these abused children with their true selves is crucial for healing and involves peeling away the layers of adaptation. This process often requires therapeutic intervention, where survivors can explore their suppressed feelings, unmet needs, and authentic desires in a safe, validating environment. Techniques such as self-compassion, boundary-setting, and mindfulness can help survivors reconnect with their true selves, fostering a sense of self-worth and agency independent of their parents' influence. By embracing their true self, survivors can reclaim their identity and build healthier, more fulfilling relationships.

Narcissistic parents resist boundaries because they see them as a threat to their control and sense of superiority. When you assert your independence, they may perceive it as a personal attack or betrayal. Common responses include gaslighting, where they deny your experiences or emotions, making you question your perception of reality. They might ridicule your boundaries, dismissing them as overreactions or unnecessary. Emotional manipulation, such as guilt-tripping with phrases like 'After everything I've done for you,' or playing the victim to make you feel responsible for their emotional well-being, is also common.

Other forms of retaliation can include dismissing your feelings by labelling you 'too much'. Your parent may control your choices by micromanaging your decisions, leaving you unsure of your own preferences or abilities. Some might try to shape your beliefs about yourself further, imposing their views on who you are, creating a false narrative of inadequacy or dependency. Some may even exploit your vulnerabilities, using your weaknesses against you, leading to shame and self-doubt.

Over time, these behaviours can erode your sense of identity, leading you to ask, who am I, really? The answer feels elusive because your true self has been overshadowed by the narcissist's needs and expectations.

Many survivors of narcissistic abuse experience profound guilt when standing up to their parents. This guilt often stems from internalized conditioning, where you've been taught that prioritizing your needs is selfish or wrong. You may have grown up believing it was your role to appease or care for your parent, sacrificing your own well-being in the process. Cultural and societal expectations often compound this guilt, as filial loyalty and respect for parents are widely emphasized. Additionally, fear of rejection plays a significant role. Narcissistic parents often use love and approval as tools for control, which ultimately form a trauma bond, so standing up to them can trigger a fear of losing these entirely. Lastly, survivors tend to be highly empathetic, making it difficult to witness a parent's distress, even if it's only to manipulate, without feeling responsible.

Understanding trauma bonds in narcissistic abuse contexts

Trauma bonding is a psychological phenomenon that occurs when a person develops an unhealthy attachment to someone who is abusive or manipulative. In the context of narcissistic abuse, trauma bonding is particularly insidious because it intertwines love, fear, and dependency in a way that keeps the victim emotionally tethered to their abuser. To understand trauma bonding fully, it is essential to examine the dynamics that create it, recognize the signs that indicate one is trauma-bonded, and explore strategies for breaking free from these bonds.

An emotional attachment forms between the abuser and the abused, fuelled by a cycle of fear, neglect, and intermittent reinforcement and making it incredibly difficult to separate emotionally and mentally from a narcissistic parent. Studying of Prof Sam Vanknin's shared fantasy theory further illuminates the mutual (if unconsious) roles both parties play in maintaining this toxic bond. However, breaking this bond is essential for reclaiming your identity, which is why we must tackle it first.

How trauma bonds are created

Trauma bonds often emerge in relationships characterized by power imbalances and cycles of abuse. In narcissistic abuse, these dynamics are amplified by the abuser's deliberate use of inconsistent and manipulative behaviours to control their victim. The following factors contribute significantly to the creation of trauma bonds.

1 Inconsistent and hot/cold behaviours

Narcissists are notorious for alternating between extremes of affection and cruelty. This erratic behaviour creates a psychological rollercoaster that keeps their victim off balance. One moment, the narcissist may shower their victim with love, compliments, and attention (often referred to as 'love-bombing'), only to follow with criticism, neglect, or outright abuse.

This unpredictability triggers the brain's reward system, similar to the effects of gambling. The victim becomes addicted to the 'highs' of the abuser's positive attention and works harder to regain that fleeting affection during the 'lows'. Over time, this creates a craving for the abuser's approval, making it difficult for the victim to break free.

2 Intermittent reinforcement

Intermittent reinforcement occurs when positive reinforcement is given inconsistently, making it more powerful and addictive. In a narcissistic relationship, the abuser may occasionally provide acts of kindness or expressions of love, but only after periods of neglect or mistreatment. This unpredictability strengthens the emotional bond because the victim becomes focused on chasing those rare moments of affection, believing they can 'earn' the abuser's love if they try hard enough.

3 Gaslighting and manipulation

Gaslighting, a hallmark tactic of narcissists, involves distorting the victim's perception of reality to make them doubt their own experiences. The narcissist may deny their abusive behaviour, blame the victim, or rewrite events to suit their narrative. Over time, the victim becomes dependent on the abuser for validation and reality checks, deepening the trauma bond.

4 Isolation

Narcissists often isolate their victims from friends, family, and support systems. This isolation heightens the victim's reliance on the abuser for emotional fulfilment and creates a sense of entrapment. With fewer external perspectives, the victim may feel there is no way out of the relationship.

5 Fear and threats

Fear is a powerful tool in creating trauma bonds. Narcissists may use threats – overt or subtle – to instil fear of abandonment, retaliation, or social humiliation. This fear keeps the victim compliant and further entrenched in the toxic relationship.

Signs you are trauma-bonded to a parent

Trauma bonds are not limited to romantic relationships; they can also form between parents and children. When a parent exhibits narcissistic traits, the child may grow up feeling trapped in a cycle of seeking approval and enduring mistreatment. Here are some signs that indicate you might be trauma-bonded to a narcissistic parent.

- **Difficulty setting boundaries:** You find it challenging to say 'no' to your parent or establish healthy boundaries, even when their behaviour is harmful. You may fear their reaction or feel guilty for prioritizing your own needs.
- **Craving approval:** You constantly seek your parent's approval and validation, even if they rarely provide it. Their praise, no matter how infrequent, feels like a lifeline.
- **Feeling responsible for their emotions:** You feel obligated to manage your parent's emotions, often at the expense of your own well-being. You might blame yourself for their anger or sadness and work hard to 'fix' things.
- **Excusing or minimizing abuse:** You rationalize or downplay your parent's mistreatment, convincing yourself that 'They didn't mean it' or 'It's not that bad.' You may also idealize them, focusing on their positive traits while ignoring the harm they cause.
- **Fear of abandonment:** You are afraid of losing your parent's love or approval, even if maintaining the relationship causes significant emotional pain. This fear can prevent you from confronting their behaviour or stepping away.
- **Feeling trapped:** You feel as though you cannot escape the relationship, due to emotional, financial, or social constraints. The thought of severing ties may fill you with guilt or anxiety.

Steps to break the trauma bond

Healing from a trauma bond is a complex process that requires time, self-awareness, and deliberate effort. Here are five techniques to help you break free from a trauma bond with a narcissistic parent.

1 Educate yourself about narcissistic abuse

Understanding the dynamics of narcissistic abuse and trauma bonding is a crucial first step. Educate yourself about the tactics narcissists use and how trauma bonds develop. Knowledge can empower you to recognize the patterns in your relationship and validate your feelings. At the end of this book you will find a selection of resources from online support groups to further reading and workshops to validate your experiences further through education on the possibilities of healing.

2 Practise no contact or low contact

If possible, consider a no-contact boundary with your narcissistic parent. This involves cutting off all communication to create space for healing. If no contact is not feasible, implement low contact by limiting interactions and maintaining strict boundaries. Low contact can help reduce the emotional hold your parent has over you and allow you to focus on your own well-being. This might take the form of limiting occasions, time length, and topics of contact. For example, only communicate about essential matters and avoid engaging in emotional conversations. This can take 'training' not only of yourself but of members of the wider family. Teaching them you will not be drawn in, by consistently refusing to engage unless you wish to, will slowly educate them to stop trying to involve you when you have no desire to be involved. Siblings may be quietly jealous of your ability to hold your line and others may resent you for 'leaving them to deal with' the narcissistic parent, but you must follow your own path – and they theirs. Remembering that no one is your responsibility is key here.

3 Seek professional support

Working with a therapist who specializes in trauma and narcissistic abuse can be immensely helpful. Therapy provides a safe space to process your experiences, rebuild your self-esteem, and develop coping strategies. Therapists can also guide you through inner-child work, which involves addressing the unmet emotional needs from your childhood and nurturing yourself in ways your parent did not. There is a beautiful example of this in Chapter 10.

4 Build a support system

Breaking a trauma bond is challenging, but having a strong support system can make it easier. Surround yourself with people who validate your experiences and encourage your healing. This might include friends, family members, or support groups for survivors of narcissistic abuse. Sharing your story with others who understand can provide comfort and perspective.

5 Practise self-care and self-compassion

Reclaiming your sense of self is a vital part of healing. Prioritize self-care activities that nurture your physical, emotional, and mental well-being. These might include exercise, meditation, writing a diary, or creative hobbies. Additionally, practise self-compassion by challenging negative self-talk and affirming your worth. Remind yourself that you deserve love and respect, regardless of your parent's behaviour.

Breaking free from a trauma bond with a narcissistic parent is a journey that requires courage, patience, and persistence. While the process can be painful and overwhelming, it is also an opportunity to reclaim your autonomy and create a life rooted in self-love and healthy relationships. By educating yourself, seeking support, and implementing healing strategies, you can break the cycle of abuse and move towards a brighter, more fulfilling future.

Understanding that guilt is a natural response to breaking free from a lifetime of conditioning is essential. It doesn't mean you are doing something wrong; rather, it signals that you are doing something necessary for your growth and well-being.

To set and maintain boundaries effectively, clarity, consistency, and resilience are key. Start by defining your boundaries clearly. Write down what you will and won't tolerate in specific terms to reduce ambiguity and reinforce your resolve. Communicate assertively using 'I' statements to express your needs without blame. For instance, you could say, 'I feel disrespected when my experiences are dismissed.

I need you to listen without interrupting.' Staying calm and focused, even in the face of an emotional reaction, is crucial.

Expect pushback when setting boundaries. Narcissistic parents are likely to test your resolve with gaslighting or guilt-tripping. Preparing your responses in advance can help. For example, if they gaslight you, you might respond with, 'I know what I experienced and I won't debate it.' If they guilt-trip you, a calm response such as 'I'm sorry you feel that way, but my decision stands' can help you remain firm.

Here are some other examples that may support you in your responses.

Manipulative comment by narcissistic parent	Healthy, boundaried response
'If you loved me, you'd help me like your brother/sister does.'	'I love you, but I have to make decisions based on what works for me, not comparisons with others.'
'You'll regret not spending more time with me when I'm gone.'	'I value our time together, but I need to make space for my life too. Let's enjoy the moments we do share.'
'You never do anything for me. Your sibling would have done it by now.'	'I'm sorry you feel that way. I help when I can, but I also need to take care of my priorities.'
'You know my health isn't great, but you still make everything harder for me.'	'I'm sorry to hear about your health. I'm doing my best to balance everything in my life right now.'
'Your siblings always make time for me. Why can't you?'	'I'm happy they can help in the ways they can. I'm doing what works for me and my circumstances.'
'All the other kids call me every day. Why don't you?'	'I'm glad you're staying in touch with them, but I can't commit to daily calls. Let's set a routine that works for both of us.'
'I feel so lonely when you're not here. Don't you care about me?'	'I care about you, but I also have responsibilities and need to balance my time. I'll visit when I can.'

Limiting exposure is another essential strategy. If your parent refuses to respect your boundaries, as we saw above, reducing contact may be necessary to protect your mental health. In these moments, seek validation from trusted friends, therapists, or support groups who can affirm your experiences and decisions. External validation can help counteract the self-doubt instilled by your parent's gaslighting.

Grounding techniques are invaluable when faced with gaslighting or emotional manipulation. Practices such as deep breathing, progressive muscle relaxation, or repeating affirmations such as 'I trust my perception of reality' can help you stay centred. You will find an example of a grounding technique in the Further Reading section to get you started. Recording your feelings and experiences is another effective way to process events objectively and affirm your reality.

Consistency is critical when dealing with a narcissistic parent. They may repeatedly test your boundaries, hoping you will back down. Remaining steadfast reinforces your resolve and sends a clear message that you won't waver. Avoid justifying or over-explaining your decisions as this opens the door to further manipulation.

Overcoming guilt is an ongoing process, but it is possible with the right tools. Reframing your perspective is a powerful technique. Remind yourself that boundaries are an act of self-respect, not selfishness, and view guilt as a sign of growth. Breaking free from unhealthy patterns often feels uncomfortable at first. Practising self-compassion is equally important. Acknowledge the courage it takes to set boundaries and treat yourself with the kindness and understanding you may not have received as a child.

Visualizing your goals can also help you stay motivated. Imagine a life defined by autonomy, self-respect, and emotional safety, and use this vision to guide you when guilt arises. Challenge any false beliefs that fuel your guilt, such as 'It's my job to keep my parent happy,' and replace them with empowering truths such as 'I am responsible for my happiness, not theirs.'

Creating a supportive inner dialogue can strengthen your resolve. Counter negative self-talk with affirmations and self-reassurance, such as 'It's okay to prioritize my needs' or 'I deserve relationships based on respect and mutual care.' Reflecting on why you are setting boundaries – to protect your mental health, reclaim your identity, and break the cycle of abuse – can anchor you in moments of doubt.

Gaslighting, one of the most insidious tactics used by narcissistic parents, requires a strategic response. Recognizing its signs is the first step. Statements such as 'You're imagining things' or 'You're being dramatic' are classic gaslighting techniques. Trust your instincts when something feels off. Keeping a record of interactions that feel manipulative or dismissive can provide clarity and reinforce your perception of events. Avoid engaging in debates about your reality as this only fuels the gaslighting. Instead, respond with phrases such as 'That's not how I remember it' and disengage. Affirming your reality through grounding techniques or keeping a record can help you stay connected to your truth.

Setting boundaries around gaslighting is essential. Let your parent know that dismissing your feelings or experiences is unacceptable. If they persist, end the conversation or remove yourself from the situation. This reinforces your boundaries and protects your mental health.

Emotional manipulation is another common tactic used by narcissistic parents. Recognizing patterns such as guilt-tripping (e.g. 'I guess I'll just be alone') or emotional extortion (e.g. 'If you loved me, you would …') is key to resisting their influence. Detaching emotionally from their behaviour is crucial. Understand that their manipulation reflects their issues, not yours. Focus on your values and goals rather than their reactions.

When dealing with manipulation, respond rather than react. Take a moment to pause and reflect before replying to their tactics. Practising these strategies consistently will empower you to establish and maintain healthy boundaries, protect your well-being, and reclaim your autonomy from a narcissistic parent.

Rediscovering and listening to your own voice

Reclaiming your identity involves rediscovering your own voice – the thoughts, feelings, and values that are uniquely yours. This process takes time, but it is deeply rewarding as you learn to trust yourself again.

In some cases, as you start this work, the parent may react with anger, using tactics such as the silent treatment or threats to withdraw love and support. These strategies are designed to make you doubt your decisions and revert to compliance, reinforcing their control. Don't give in.

Recovery from narcissistic abuse involves dismantling the adaptive self and rediscovering the true self. This process is challenging but transformative, requiring self-awareness, self-compassion, and often professional support.

1 Acknowledging the abuse

The first step is recognizing and validating the impact of narcissistic abuse. This involves:

Educating oneself: Learn about narcissistic dynamics and their effects. The earlier chapters of this book have been written especially to further your psychoeducation on this condition and its origins and impact; additionally, I have provided more links and signposting to further studies in the Further Reading section so if you feel you'd like to delve even deeper, you can. While we can be glad the awareness of NPD has grown, the popularization and misinformation have somewhat diluted and undermined the facts, so I urge you to stay abreast of developments and be sure your sources are backed up with research – it will help you stay grounded and determined when others seeks to minimize, especially the narcissist themselves, and indeed their enablers.

Breaking denial: This involves accepting that the abuse occurred and acknowledging its consequences. Sometimes in life it can be easier to dismiss, ignore, or suppress memories, experiences, and wounds that we feel. After all, if we had a peacock for a parent we will be used to having our thoughts and feelings undermined, so it can become second nature to deny how deep we might have felt their neglect or abuse. Learning slowly and gently to accept what you experienced and what happened to you is critical for your own peace. Like any toxin that we suppress, it will find its way out in other, sometimes destructive ways. Acknowledge the discomfort at accepting the truth but honour and respect yourself enough to know you deserved better. The discomfort can at times be so strong that we reject the notion of the work and shut it down, only to discover some weeks later that the initial need to resolve this pain reoccurs. Be brave and start. Something in our body is being called upon. Go gently, go slowly, and do a little of the work every day – in time you will be able to tolerate a little more. The technique 'widening the window of tolerance' is mentioned in Chapter 10 and is also linked in the Further Reading section.

Naming the experience: Giving language to one's pain helps make sense of it. Finding and meeting other people who have experienced narcissistic parents has been, in my professional experience, one of the most healing aspects of all. Not only are you immediately believed and understood, but you can share and hear stories that you relate to and make you realize you are not alone. Language is a shorthand which can help you find and accept intervention and support as you discover and seek to recover, and I hope the explanations in these chapters can form part of your vernacular when telling your own story now.

2 Reconnecting with emotions

Reclaiming the true self requires re-establishing a connection with one's emotions. Techniques include:

- **Mindfulness practices:** Meditation and keeping a journal can help identify suppressed feelings. At the end of this chapter you will find a starter meditation which will allow you to invite your inner self to access your deeper feelings and beliefs. Tuning into ourselves provides an opportunity to identify what we are really feeling and where in our bodies we are holding it. In time it becomes a fruitful habit to allow you to feel and speak your truth and to connect to yourself in a way you may not have done before. Keeping a journal also offers the opportunity to get down on paper (and out of our minds and bodies) all the thoughts and feelings we are having. It allows a process to occur and equally an awareness of what is really happening and in time opens up a pathway to seeing our progress.
- **Therapeutic support:** This involves working with a therapist to process and release pent-up emotions. This work can be truly transformational with a narcissistic- and trauma-informed therapist to run alongside you, like an athlete's coach or pacesetter. Intervention and thoughtful provocation can help you access not only the sadness and pain but also the anger and frustration you may have felt. You may be so conditioned to worry about the reaction of others, given your upbringing with a narcissistic parent, that finally to be allowed to speak your truth freely may feel foreign and overwhelming. A good therapist will invite you to express your feelings in the safety of their presence and guide and encourage you as you do the work.
- **Body awareness:** Practices such as yoga or somatic therapy can reconnect the mind and body. The mind and body are completely

connected, so ensuring we are not hiding in the confines of our glorious brain is important. Feeling and breathing into the work will ensure the whole self is getting relief and healing along the way. Sitting and tuning into aches and pains, gut reactions, reoccurring ailments, and the physical impact of just the thought, never mind the presence, of your narcissistic parent tells you the body already knows what needs attention and healing.

3 Challenging internalized beliefs

Narcissistic abuse often instils deep-seated beliefs about unworthiness or inadequacy. To heal, one must start by:

- **Identifying false narratives:** Recognize and challenge the messages implanted by the narcissistic parent. In the beginning, to search and connect to your true self will mean an awakening within of what really has been happening and the truth of many situations. Beginning to disseminate truth from fiction (and recognize gaslighting) is critical in starting to see the disparity between the false mask and narrative of the narcissistic parent versus your lived experience. Facts, timings, witnesses, and record keeping can feel primitive yet are informative as you begin to reveal the genuine truth of your life being brought up by this individual.
- **Replacing negative self-talk:** Develop affirmations and positive self-statements. Re-parenting ourselves is an important part of healing and yet can present a challenge. When you have been raised by a narcissistic parent you may have ingested so many untruths about yourself or constantly been told you were never good enough that you may have been led to believe many things about yourself that are simply untrue. Starting to talk to yourself in a way you would as a loving and encouraging parent is a critical early step in changing the tone and narrative by which you (and your central nervous system) hear your own voice and start to observe yourself.
- **Setting realistic expectations:** Allow yourself to grow and make mistakes without fear of rejection. You may have suffered decades of abuse under a narcissistic parent, so this work is tender and gentle and gradual. It takes intent, practice, encouragement, and experimentation to find your voice and begin to express yourself for the first time. You may falter now and then, or retreat to old patterns when

things get tough, but gradually, as you stay focused on recovery, you will make ground. Set small but meaningful steps (from setting one boundary, to practising one meditation, to talking to one other survivor) and before you know it, change will be afoot within you.

4 Setting boundaries

Learning to establish and maintain boundaries is essential for reclaiming your autonomy. This involves:

- **Recognizing boundary violations:** It is critical to identify when others overstep or manipulate, whether it be through a text exchange, a phone call, a visit, or simply an action that oversteps your wishes. When you know this is happening, you can decide what you might prefer to do about it. Start by thinking what the bravest part of you would say or do. Practise speaking that truth, even if simply to yourself, and in time allow that voice to begin to take action. Imagine a physical shield around you, protecting you from any retort – and voice your boundary. Each and every time you consistently enforce that boundary, you send a clear and new message – one that in time will be accepted, even if not liked. Start – you will surprise yourself how, over time, it gets easier and clearer. But start.
- **Practising assertiveness:** This means communicating needs and limits clearly. Start easy if needs be – setting or voicing boundaries with friendly people. Ask to meet a friend at a time that better suits you. Say 'no' to requests to attend a party or work meeting or to help a friend when in truth you either don't want or need to. Begin to ask for what it is you truly want – a seat on a train, that cake in the shop, the running machine you like at the gym. Start to speak your truth.
- **Minimizing contact:** In some cases, reducing or severing ties with abusive family members may be necessary. As discussed already, no contact or low contact may be the best way forward for you – only you can decide. Either way, the question to ask yourself is, 'Would I accept this behaviour from anyone else?' Just because someone is your parent or part of your family does not give them 'access all areas' to you. Quietly move away or loudly declare you're moving out, but be sure to know you have the choice.

5 Exploring authentic interests

Rediscovering the true self involves exploring activities and passions that align with your genuine interests. This can include:

- **Trying new experiences:** Experiment with hobbies, careers, or creative outlets. As we begin to seek and acquaint ourselves with our true self, we may find exploring new areas in life can be important. As you venture out from under the cloak of narcissistic deflection, you become free to experiment and to hear your inner curiosity and desires as they bubble up to the surface – offering you the opportunity to discover unlived parts of your life that have been waiting for you.

- **Reflecting on childhood joys:** Revisit interests or activities that brought happiness before the abuse took hold. Many of my clients will tell me about hobbies, interests, and passions they once had that were forbidden, discouraged, or marred by their narcissistic parent or family. Often, reconnecting with an interest can be important as you further identify your true self. Spending time enveloped in a world or project you love will soothe you and allow you to spread your wings as you find life after this upbringing with the peacock.

- **Seeking community:** It's always important in life that we 'find our people' and never more so than when recovering from this type of abuse. Surround yourself with supportive and like-minded individuals, who can identify with your story, share their own in service to you, and love and support you as you find your new voice in recovery. In my experience it remains one of the most healing elements from this level of psychological abuse. To be seen and truly believed is like reaching a safe shore having swum through rough seas.

6 Embracing self-compassion

Healing requires treating yourself with kindness and understanding. Practices include truly listening to what you need. An example of the 'prescription of kindness' I wrote myself when I was recovering from narcissistic abuse was:

- allowing myself to know it would take 1–2 years for recovery and I needed to go slow

- accepting my recovery was my own private mission to pursue
  - actioning
  - a long hot bath after tough episodes so I could talk to my inner child and soothe her
- buying and preparing my favourite food, from a nutritious supper to confectionery treats (my frightened inner child had a very sweet tooth!)
- a long call with a friend who truly understood even though he had heard my pain many times already – validation to undo the gaslighting was central
- making space to cry when I needed to release the sadness – the grief for what has happened to you, and what will no longer be, can feel immense at first
- long hugs with loved ones who quietly knew I was in deep pain
- clean sheets to snuggle into and envelop my tired and exhausted body when sleep came
- watching or listening to joyful films or music and avoiding aggressive or depressing material
- only doing exercise I actually enjoyed, such as boxing or dancing
- cuddling and talking to the dog

Reminding myself that I knew the truth and that was good enough

- saying good morning and good night to myself as if I was my own child – with a kind smile in the bathroom mirror and a summary of what had happened that day
- acknowledging what had been tough and what had been better that day – every single small step and every single element helped.

Other practices include:

- **Self-care routines:** It is important to prioritize physical and emotional well-being. Some days we can feel as if we have been run over, especially just before or just after interaction with the abusive parent. Agree with yourself, especially around those days, to look after yourself carefully, with routine and boundaries: early nights, always showered, a good body stretch, a breathing moment before leaving the house and a good check-in with your hand on your heart. I would ask myself most days, 'How are you doing today?'

Please stop to listen to the answer and respond as if you were your own child.

- **Forgiving oneself:** Let go of guilt or shame tied to the abuse. Guilt is a perverse and persistently reported side-effect of having suffered a narcissistic parent. Un-enmeshing yourself from an overwhelming peacock may bring a sense of guilt as they manipulate you with their performative sadness or claims of abandonment. Equally, standing up to a critical parent or vulnerable victim parent can bring about a guilt or shame response. It shows what a wonderful human being you are to be so empathetic to their perceived pain, but in order to break the cycle you need to stand firm in your boundary and 'sit in the fire' of discomfort. It will subside.

- **Celebrating progress:** Acknowledge and honour your growth, no matter how small. Every step, large or small, is a triumph – something to be acknowledged and accepted. A high five in the mirror before bed or a note in your journal – just keep moving in the right direction and before too long the awkward crank of the wheel of change will start to feel like a smooth habit. You need to become your greatest cheerleader – the parent you deserved all along.

Conclusion

Narcissistic abuse by parents is a devastating form of psychological identity theft, stripping children of their autonomy and individuality. Whether cast as the lost, golden, or scapegoated child, survivors face unique challenges as they navigate the aftermath of this abuse. However, by recognizing the impact, stepping away from the distorted bond, reconnecting with their true selves, and embracing the journey of healing, they can break free from the constraints of their adaptive or even projected idealized selves and reclaim their authenticity.

As a child of a narcissistic parent, you may have perfected the art of hiding your true self as a coping mechanism to dodge their rage, engulfing, or manipulations, but I urge you now to reconsider. As you commence your journey of recovery you will rediscover the magical parts of who you were always meant to be in the world. Recovery is a courageous and transformative process, one that leads to a life of greater freedom, fulfilment, and self-acceptance. So as Donald Winnicott famously said:

'It's a joy to be hidden, and a disaster not to be found.'

Embracing the journey of healing

Healing from narcissistic abuse is a journey – one that requires courage, patience, and self-compassion. By breaking the trauma bond, rediscovering your voice, and forming an authentic and compassionate identity, you reclaim the parts of yourself that were lost. This process is not only a return to who you are but a chance to become the person you were always meant to be.

You are not defined by the narcissist's narrative. You are worthy, whole, and capable of creating a life that reflects your true self. As you walk this path, remember: every step you take towards healing is an act of profound self-love.

Guided visualization: finding your true self

When we have endured a lifetime of being gaslit or manipulated, the idea of finding our true self can sound very encouraging but may initially be quite challenging to engage with. To that end, I wanted to offer you an example of an inviting guided visualization. One that once you've learned it, you can read to yourself and have played back to you while you have your eyes shut. I offer it to you here as a start and I promise, when you engage with it on a regular basis, your true self and your true voice will be easier to find, easier to hear, and more likely to engage with you once it learns it is safe.

Take a moment to settle in. Find a comfortable position, whether you're sitting or lying down. Let your hands rest gently on your lap or by your sides. When you're ready, softly close your eyes.

Take a deep breath in through your nose ... and let it flow gently out through your mouth.

Feel your chest rise as you inhale ... and fall as you exhale.

Let your breath find its natural rhythm, slow and steady, like the gentle ebb and flow of a calm ocean.

Now, bring your attention inward. Begin to notice the sensations in your body. Start at the top of your head and slowly move downwards, scanning each part of yourself.

Notice the weight of your body resting against the chair or the floor beneath you. Feel the support it offers, holding you safely in place.

Bring your focus to your chest, just over your heart. Place your hand there if it feels right for you. Take a moment to notice the gentle rhythm of your heartbeat – steady, constant, always present.

Breathe deeply and with each breath, feel yourself connecting more deeply to this rhythm. Imagine that your heartbeat is like a quiet, reassuring beat within you, anchoring you to the here and now.

As you listen to this rhythm, picture a warm, golden light glowing softly at the centre of your chest. This light represents your true self – the part of you that is pure, authentic, and unshaken by the world around you.

With each breath, this golden light glows a little brighter. Feel its warmth spreading outwards, filling your chest, flowing down your arms, and radiating into your entire body.

Now, ask yourself: What does my true voice sound like?

Perhaps it feels like a whisper, a soft murmur deep inside. Or maybe it is clearer, a shout, more distinct. Whatever you hear, trust that it is yours.

Let this voice speak. It doesn't need to be loud or certain – it only needs to be heard. What does it want to say to you right now? What do you need to know? To be reminded of? To admit for the first time?

Take a few moments simply to listen. You don't need to force anything or search for answers. Just hold space for this quiet voice, letting it emerge naturally.

If emotions arise – from rage to sadness – welcome them with compassion. If silence is what you hear, let that be okay too. Sometimes silence speaks volumes – it may be the space your true self needs to grow stronger.

As you continue to breathe deeply, feel your feet firmly connected to the ground beneath you. Picture roots extending from the soles of your feet, sinking deep into the earth. These roots anchor you, grounding you in safety and stability.

Know that this connection is always here for you. Your heartbeat, your breath, your true voice – they are all parts of you, waiting for you to return whenever you need them. They may have been waiting a long time for you to come and find them.

When you feel ready, gently begin to bring your awareness back to the room. Wiggle your fingers and toes. Notice the sensation of your body and the space around you.

Take one final deep breath in and as you exhale, carry with you the warmth of your inner light and the strength of your true voice.

When you're ready, softly open your eyes. Welcome back.

Some other ideas for your journey

- **Keeping a journal:** Write about your thoughts and feelings without judgement. Explore questions such as, What do I want? What brings me joy? What do I value?
- **Mindfulness practices:** Learn the meditation at the start of this chapter. Engage in meditation or deep-breathing exercises to quiet external noise and tune into your inner self. Use body scans to reconnect with physical sensations and emotions.
- **Inner child work:** Imagine nurturing and comforting your younger self. Acknowledge the unmet needs from childhood and seek to fulfil them as an adult.
- **Creative expression:** Explore art, music, writing, or other forms of creativity to give voice to emotions and experiences that may be difficult to articulate.
- **Define your values:** Reflect on what matters most to you – independent of the narcissist's influence. Write a personal mission statement to guide your decisions.
- **Practise self-compassion:** Treat yourself with kindness, especially when feelings of shame or self-criticism arise. Use affirmations such as 'I am enough' or 'My worth is not determined by others.'
- **Build your adult and compassionate identity:** Once you've started to hear and trust your own voice, the next step is to build an identity that reflects your authentic self. This involves developing self-awareness, self-acceptance, and self-compassion.
- **Form your adult identity:** Explore your interests. Try new hobbies, activities, or experiences to discover what excites and fulfils you. Revisit passions that were dismissed or discouraged by the narcissist.
- **Set personal goals:** Define short- and long-term goals based on your aspirations. Break them into actionable steps to build confidence and momentum.

- **Develop autonomy:** Make decisions – even small ones – without seeking external approval. Celebrate your ability to choose for yourself.
- **Practise assertiveness:** Communicate your needs, boundaries, and desires clearly and respectfully. Learn to tolerate discomfort when others react negatively.
- **Cultivate emotional intelligence:** Identify and express your emotions in healthy ways. Empathize with yourself and others without losing your sense of self.
- **Reframe your story:** See yourself not as a victim but as a survivor and thriver. Use your experiences as a foundation for resilience and growth.
- **Consider evidence-based approaches to healing:** Research supports several therapeutic and self-help strategies for survivors of narcissistic abuse:

  o **Trauma-informed therapy:** Therapists trained in trauma can help survivors process their experiences and develop coping strategies.
  o **EMDR therapy:** This is effective for reducing distress associated with traumatic memories.
  o **Somatic experiencing:** This focuses on releasing trauma stored in the body.
  o **Cognitive behavioural therapy:** CBT helps reframe negative thought patterns and develop healthier behaviours.
  o **Dialectical behaviour therapy:** DBT teaches skills for emotional regulation, interpersonal effectiveness, and mindfulness.
  o **Peer support groups:** These provides connection, validation, and shared wisdom from others who understand. Foster relationships with people who respect and affirm your autonomy.

9

Healing mind, body, and spirit through validation

'Good things come in threes.'
Aristotle

Recovering from narcissistic abuse at the hands of a parent is not only possible but can lead to profound healing and growth. As your true self begins to re-emerge, recovery can begin, with the understanding that your experiences are real and deserve validation – a cornerstone of the process. Being truly seen and believed by those who acutely understand is, in my professional view and lived experience, the most transformative element in helping to rebuild the trust in yourself that the abuse may have eroded.

Choosing the right paths to healing is essential and I strongly suggest there are three fundamental elements. The cognitive and emotional combination of seeking support from compassionate, trauma-informed therapists in combination with connecting with other discerning, empathetic survivors can provide the safe space needed for your voice to emerge. When you then add the third element of somatic connection and healing, you have a fighting chance of regaining your mind, body, and spirit. This journey, though challenging, is an opportunity to reclaim your worth, rediscover your inner strength, and create a life filled with the love and peace you deserve.

Before you begin: accepting what happened

Recovery from narcissistic parental abuse begins with a critical and often challenging first step: accepting the reality of what has happened. This process involves confronting painful truths about your childhood, acknowledging the abusive behaviours of your parent, and understanding the impact these experiences have had on your emotional and psychological well-being. For many survivors, this step is complicated by years of gaslighting, manipulation, and societal expectations that idealize the parent–child relationship.

Collaborating with a therapist or professional who can help you begin to separate your truth from your parents, gaslighting, your true self from the adapted self, and your inner child from your lost/scapegoated or golden position in the family, allows you to start to observe what really happened. In helping you to build a solid foundation of truth to stand on, you gain clarity and cognitive appreciation for the truth, and sadly with it a sense of the delta between what you have been told happened versus what really transpired. It is at this point that the gaslighting, manipulation, and enmeshments begin to come into full view.

Why acceptance is crucial

Denial is a common coping mechanism for survivors of narcissistic parental abuse. As children, survivors often rationalize their parents' behaviour to preserve a sense of safety and attachment. This rationalization can carry into adulthood, manifesting as minimization of the abuse or persistent feelings of self-blame. Acceptance dissolves this protective denial, creating the foundation for genuine healing. Without acknowledging the abuse, it is impossible to validate your experiences fully, set boundaries, or rebuild your sense of self.

Denial may look or sound like an ambivalence to addressing what happened, but may actually be masking understandable fear. In early sessions with a client looking to address their narcissistic parent but facing their first encounter of change I often hear:

'I'm not that bothered, I can put up with it.'
'Maybe I was a handful as a child.'
'He says I have a warped memory – maybe I do?'
'They are so nice to everyone else, maybe it is something about me?'
'What's the point in dealing with it now, she/he is old?'
'I don't think I've got the energy, to be honest.'
'I have mates who got beaten black and blue, so maybe this wasn't that bad.'
'It was a generational thing.'
'My sister/brother seem to get on with them just fine.'
'I was fed and clothed and they took me on holiday – maybe it wasn't that bad.'
'They had a difficult childhood themselves, maybe they couldn't help it.'

Research in trauma recovery underscores the importance of acceptance in healing from abuse. A study published in *Psychological Trauma: Theory, Research, Practice, and Policy* found that acknowledgement and validation of trauma are associated with decreased symptoms of depression and anxiety in survivors of childhood abuse. The study highlights that survivors who recognize and name their experiences are better equipped to rebuild their self-esteem and develop healthier coping mechanisms and I would encourage you to do the same.

The psychological challenges of acceptance

Accepting the reality of a narcissistic parent's abuse often means grappling with conflicting emotions. Survivors may feel grief, anger, guilt, and even a sense of betrayal. Grieving the loss of the nurturing parent they hoped for is a common part of this process. Dr Karyl McBride (author of *Will I Ever Be Good Enough?*), emphasizes that acknowledging the parental limitations and abusive behaviours is a critical step in breaking free from their control and beginning the healing journey.

In the context of narcissistic abuse, Dr Christine Courtois, an expert in trauma and attachment, writes that acceptance is necessary for survivors to reframe their experiences. She notes that reframing helps survivors shift the narrative from 'What did I do to deserve this?' to 'What happened to me was not my fault.' This reframing is a powerful tool for breaking the cycle of self-blame and opening the door to validation.

Survivors also face the challenge of dismantling the narrative the narcissistic parent created. Narcissistic parents often project their flaws onto their children or the co-parent, leading survivors to internalize feelings of inadequacy, shame, and guilt. Acceptance requires separating the truth from the distortions instilled by the parent, a process that can be emotionally intense but liberating.

A powerful way to address this challenge and something to return to each time you recommence any conversation with yourself, with others, or even with the parent themselves, is the phrase 'They had a duty of care.' This is the most wholesome truth that allows for the denial and the defence and excuses to subside, allowing the truth to be seen and accepted in you. Your parents did have a duty of care to you – and if they failed in that, you have a solid and valid place from which to start.

Steps to facilitate acceptance

There are various steps to help you on the road to acceptance:

- **Education:** Learning about narcissistic abuse, even reading this book, for example, can be an eye-opening step towards acceptance. Understanding the traits of narcissistic parents and their tactics (e.g. gaslighting, scapegoating) can help survivors see their experiences more clearly.
- **Naming the abuse:** Giving a name to the abuse, whether it be emotional manipulation, neglect, or control, can validate feelings and experiences that may have been dismissed or minimized.
- **Seeking validation:** Sharing your story with trusted individuals or support groups who understand narcissistic abuse can affirm your reality and reduce feelings of isolation.
- **Therapeutic support:** Working with a trauma-informed therapist can provide a safe space to explore and process difficult emotions associated with acceptance.
- **Keeping a diary:** Writing about your experiences can be a therapeutic way to process and organize your thoughts, helping you acknowledge the truth of what occurred.

The path forward

Accepting the reality of narcissistic parental abuse is not an easy step, but it is a transformative one. It allows survivors to begin separating their identity from the narratives imposed by their abuser. As survivors move through this process, they gain the clarity and strength needed to seek validation, set boundaries, and reclaim their lives. While the journey of recovery may be long, acceptance is the cornerstone that makes every subsequent step possible.

1 Expert therapeutic support – being safe, being seen, being soothed

Many of you will have seen the now famous YouTube video of Dr Tronick's Still Face Experiment demonstrating the importance of 'mirroring' (another of Donald Winnicott's tremendous contributions to the world of child psychology). The short film demonstrates the impact of facial mirroring from a mother to her developing infant, which allows the child to feel seen and heard and to connect with their own emotions. In the video, you can see the warmth, connection, and reassurance reflected in the child's eyes, their demeanour and movement when the mother is attuned to her offspring, as she acknowledges him and follows and mirrors his pointing, smiling, and touch with genuine interest, care, and understanding.

We then see the swift distress the same child falls into when the mother offers back not an empathetic mirror but a blank face, emotionless and disconnected from the child. As the confused and anguished child moves through myriad emotions and techniques to once again find and connect with his caregiver, we see the impact this loss of attunement truly has. It is heartbreaking to watch and difficult to observe. If only that video alone was given to every parent to be before they had a child in their care.

By now, we are clear that a narcissistic parent was unlikely to have empathically mirrored to us as children – in fact, possibly the opposite, unless for manipulative reasons – and so our awareness of misattunement, lack of empathy, and unresponsiveness is all too clear to us. Allow me then to take you one step further in underlining how we must therefore find only safe spaces to which we can now bring our true selves as we seek to heal.

With narcissism now on the lips of the world, many people may feel they have some base level and casual understanding of what it is and how it presents – but sadly, this surface-level colloquialism is fundamentally causing great damage to those seeking to identify and heal from this abuse. Why? Because misunderstanding the depth of abuse and despair narcissism causes means that its true victims are being met by friends, family members, doctors, and even professional therapists who do not truly comprehend the deep, insidious nature of the abuse and therefore struggle to engage effectively with the depth of the behaviours and hopelessness the individuals are describing. This painful misattunement not only leaves the victims feeling alone, further misunderstood, shamed, and growing increasingly desperate but potentially with retriggered of the lack of care and empathy the culprit parent induced in their childhood.

It is therefore absolutely imperative that you only seek healing from those who truly understand this personality disorder, and also that you decide initially only to share your stories and seek validation from those who have experienced true narcissism. When you experience both expertise and validation, the road to recovery opens up like a secret beautiful pathway, that keeps you sane, seen, and surrounded by safety.

While the growth in social media is allowing many to seek information and ideas for recovery, it lacks filters, and so there is a cascade of narcissistic abuse recovery 'experts' offering courses and training and one-to-one coaching for a pretty penny and not all are of the qualifications or have the experience required to ensure safety, let alone healing. With every frontier that opens come opportunists, and sadly the field of narcissism is no exception. Always be sure to ask for qualifications, evidence, and referrals.

Sarah's journey to effective healing

Sarah, a 32-year-old woman, sought therapy to address feelings of anxiety, self-doubt, and a pervasive sense of unworthiness. She had endured years of covert emotional manipulation and neglect from her narcissistic mother, leaving her with complex trauma. However, Sarah struggled to articulate the depth of her pain as much of the abuse was subtle, invisible to others, and often dismissed as 'normal family dynamics'.

Sarah's first therapist, Ben, was kind but not well versed in the dynamics of narcissistic abuse. In their sessions, Ben encouraged Sarah to focus on 'mending' the relationship with her mother. He suggested strategies such as open communication and empathy towards her mother's perspective, framing the conflict as a mutual misunderstanding. When Sarah expressed hesitation and recounted instances of her mother's gaslighting and emotional cruelty, Ben minimized these experiences, labelling them as typical generational conflicts and suggesting her mother had done the best she could.

This approach left Sarah feeling invalidated and even more confused. She began doubting her perception of the abuse and questioning whether her pain was legitimate. After several months, Sarah felt stuck and increasingly anxious, as the therapeutic space seemed to echo the same dismissal she had experienced from her mother.

Realizing she wasn't making progress, Sarah decided to seek another therapist. She found Kitty, a qualified trauma-informed psychotherapist who specialized in narcissistic abuse recovery. From the very first session, Kitty validated Sarah's feelings, acknowledging the insidious nature of her mother's behaviour and how it could deeply impact self-esteem and emotional health.

Kitty avoided pushing reconciliation and instead focused on empowering Sarah to trust her perceptions. She introduced Sarah to concepts such as gaslighting, enmeshment, and emotional invalidation, helping her understand that her experiences were real and not her fault. This validation was a revelation for Sarah, as it gave her permission to set boundaries and prioritize her healing over societal expectations of family loyalty.

With Kitty's guidance, Sarah began unpacking the long-term effects of the abuse. She rebuilt her self-worth, learning to set boundaries and identifying safe and supportive relationships. Therapy became a space where Sarah felt seen and heard for the first time.

Discernment becomes one of the most critical values you must now adopt if you are to seek and engage with the type of healing you need and deserve. Seek support from individuals who are trained, experienced, and attuned to the often mind-bending behaviours of narcissists, all types, especially coverts, and can seek to understand you before they seek to help you.

2 The critical role of validation in recovery

Recovering from narcissistic parental abuse is a deeply personal and often isolating journey. You may find you frequently grapple with feelings of self-doubt, guilt, and confusion due to the covert and insidious nature of the abuse. One of the most critical aspects of recovery is seeking validation from others who have experienced similar dynamics. Connecting with fellow survivors offers an understanding that is often difficult to find elsewhere, providing emotional support, shared insight, and a sense of community.

Validation from fellow survivors is therefore vital in the recovery process, supported by research and expert perspectives. Validation is the acknowledgement and affirmation of your experiences and emotions as legitimate. For survivors of narcissistic parental abuse, seeking validation from other survivors fulfils several key functions.

Narcissistic abuse often isolates victims, not only during childhood but also into adulthood. Narcissistic parents may actively alienate their children from external support systems, leaving survivors with a sense of loneliness and mistrust. Connecting with others who share similar experiences counters this isolation, creating a sense of belonging and understanding.

Gaslighting is a hallmark tactic of narcissistic abuse, leaving you questioning your perceptions and memories. Hearing others describe nearly identical experiences reinforces the reality of the abuse and dismantles internalized doubt. This mutual understanding allows us as survivors to begin to trust our feelings and interpretations, which is essential for healing.

Many survivors internalize responsibility for the abuse, believing they were 'not good enough' or that they somehow provoked their parent's behaviour. Validation from other survivors challenges this narrative by highlighting the patterns of narcissistic abuse and showing that the problem lies with the abuser, not the victim. Survivors in peer groups often exchange coping strategies, from setting boundaries to managing feelings of guilt and grief. Practical advice from others who have walked the same path can accelerate recovery and provide tools tailored to the unique challenges of narcissistic abuse.

Validation is therefore a powerful antidote to the erosion of self-worth caused by narcissistic abuse. Survivors learn to view their experiences through a compassionate lens, replacing self-criticism with self-acceptance. Witnessing others' journeys of healing reinforces the possibility of reclaiming a sense of worth and autonomy. Studies on trauma recovery by K. D. L. Barlow, T. D. R. Pearson, & J. T. T. Moen (2013) and others consistently emphasize the importance of peer support and validation.

In my experience both treating survivors and facilitating groups, I have found validation from fellow survivors has been one of the most transformative steps towards healing. Sharing your story and hearing others recount eerily similar experiences, while sad, provides an unparalleled sense of connection and understanding. Survivors often describe the profound relief that comes with realizing they are not alone – a realization that not only validates their feelings but also helps counteract the self-doubt instilled by years of manipulation and gaslighting. This shared recognition creates a safe space where survivors can begin to trust their perceptions and emotions once again.

Research also supports the importance of shared validation in trauma recovery. A study published in *Psychological Trauma: Theory, Research, Practice, and Policy* highlights how peer support among trauma survivors fosters a sense of belonging and reduces feelings of isolation. This process, often referred to as 'trauma-informed peer support', allows individuals to experience emotional resonance – the feeling of being deeply understood without needing to explain every nuance. For survivors of narcissistic abuse, this shorthand of shared experience alleviates the burden of constantly justifying their pain, which can be a significant barrier to healing.

The neuroscience of trauma also underscores the importance of connection in recovery. When survivors share their stories with others who have endured similar experiences, their brains experience a reduction in stress responses. According to research on interpersonal neurobiology by Dr Daniel Siegel, being understood and validated activates the brain's social engagement system, which can help regulate emotional responses and foster resilience. For those recovering from the deep wounds of narcissistic abuse, this interpersonal connection offers not only emotional solace but also a biological pathway towards healing and growth.

While specific research on narcissistic parental abuse remains limited, broader findings on trauma and abuse survivors can be applicable. Here, just to begin, are three insights you may find interesting.

- **Shared experiences enhance healing:** Research published in the journal *Trauma, Violence, & Abuse* highlights that group-based interventions, such as support groups, foster a sense of community and shared understanding. This reduces feelings of isolation and enhances emotional well-being.
- **Validation reduces distress:** A study in the *Journal of Aggression, Maltreatment & Trauma* found that survivors who received validation from peers experienced lower levels of distress and self-blame compared with those who did not.
- **Narrative sharing builds resilience:** Sharing their story in a supportive environment allows survivors to reframe their experiences, leading to increased resilience and empowerment, as noted in research by the American Psychological Association.

Emma's journey to healing through shared stories

Emma, a 41-year-old graphic designer, struggled with self-doubt, anxiety, and feelings of isolation after years of narcissistic abuse by her father. His behaviour was marked by relentless criticism, gaslighting, aggression, and emotional neglect, leaving Emma unsure whether her memories were valid or if she was simply 'too sensitive', as he often claimed. Despite seeing a therapist who was somewhat helpful, Emma felt there was still a deep need to be understood by someone who truly 'got it'.

While researching what she was experiencing Emma came across a support group for survivors of narcissistic abuse. At first she hesitated to join, worried her story might not be 'bad enough' compared with those of others. But curiosity and a longing for connection compelled her to attend an initial online meeting. During the meeting, members shared their experiences – stories of gaslighting, invalidation, and the lingering effects of narcissistic manipulation. Emma was stunned by how familiar their accounts felt.

One member described the constant self-doubt created by their parent's shifting narratives, and another spoke about struggling to set boundaries as an adult with an engulfing mother. Emma felt tearful – for the first time, she realized she wasn't alone, and her experiences weren't imaginary. When it was Emma's turn to share, she tentatively recounted a story about her father's frequent undermining of her achievements. To her surprise, the group responded with nods, empathetic smiles, and validation. One participant said, 'I've been there – it's so exhausting when they make you feel like nothing you do is ever enough.' Another added, 'That's gaslighting; they condition you to doubt yourself so they can stay in control.'

Hearing these responses was transformative for Emma. Not only did they reassure her that her pain was real, they also gave her a language to describe her experiences. Sharing her story and receiving genuine understanding created a profound sense of trust – both in the group and in herself.

Over time, Emma became a regular participant in the group. She found the 'shorthand' of shared understanding to be incredibly healing. There was no need to explain every nuance or justify her feelings – the group instinctively understood the complexities of her experiences. This sense of belonging and mutual validation helped Emma feel less isolated and more empowered to trust her instincts. Over many months, Emma found a close friendship within the group, allowing her, in moments of panic, upset, or confusion as she worked through the trauma towards recovery, to call her friend late at night or between sessions and feel the support of someone who truly understood. She advocates for many others now and feels this deep validation allowed her increasingly to trust her lived experience, coming into the light of the life she was always meant to live.

Emma's journey illustrates the power of connecting with others who share similar experiences and I encourage you to find the safe spaces to do the same. In my experience, the sharing of stories within a supportive community offers validation that has an exponentially positive effect and allows for the growth of trust in ways traditional therapy alone cannot. Through this connection, Emma found not only a sense of belonging but also the courage to embrace her truth and begin to heal.

3 Somatic healing – attending to trauma in the body

One of the finest books to be published in the last 30 years is *The Body Keeps the Score*. In this seminal work, Dr Bessel van der Kolk emphasizes trauma isn't just a psychological burden – trauma is also stored in the very cells of our bodies, manifesting as tension, chronic stress, and even physical pain. So, while we can cognitively and emotionally address what has happened to us, we can find our body needs attention too.

Over the past decade further research has helped us to understand the link between emotional abuse and physical health problems, including higher rates of chronic illnesses such as heart disease, auto-immune disorders, and gastrointestinal issues. Our body's response to stress is regulated by the hypothalamic-pituitary-adrenal (HPA) axis, which controls the release of cortisol, the stress hormone. In healthy individuals, cortisol levels rise in response to stress and fall once the threat is gone. However, when we have suffered narcissistic abuse, the HPA axis can become dysregulated due to constant psychological stress, leading to chronically elevated cortisol levels within us. Elevated cortisol can suppress our immune system, increase blood pressure, and contribute to the development of various and chronic metabolic conditions.

Autoimmune disorders are another category of physical illnesses linked to narcissistic abuse. Our immune system can become hyperactive and start attacking healthy tissues in response to prolonged stress. This phenomenon, known as autoimmunity, has been observed in victims of emotional abuse. A 2019 study in the journal *Rheumatology* found those with such a history were twice as likely to develop conditions such as rheumatoid arthritis, lupus, and multiple sclerosis compared with those without such a history. Being aware allows us to contemplate whether we need to draw attention here as part of our ongoing healing.

Equally the gut–brain axis, the bidirectional communication pathway between the gastrointestinal tract and the brain, plays a critical role in our overall health. Chronic stress and emotional trauma can disrupt this communication, leading to gastrointestinal disorders. Irritable bowel syndrome (IBS) and other functional gastrointestinal disorders have been strongly linked to emotional abuse. A study by Dr Emeran Mayer published in *Gastroenterology* in 2017 found that individuals who had experienced emotional abuse were significantly more likely to develop IBS. The research highlighted that 'the gut's sensitivity to stress is heightened in individuals with a history of emotional trauma', leading to chronic digestive issues.

Chronic inflammation is another physical manifestation of the stress induced by narcissistic abuse. Inflammation is a natural immune response to injury or infection, but when it becomes chronic, it can contribute to a host of health problems, including heart disease, diabetes, and cancer.

For many of us, escaping the cycle of narcissistic abuse and breaking the trauma bond is the first step towards healing. However, the physical repercussions often require ongoing medical and psychological treatment. Addressing our underlying trauma through therapy, particularly specialist narcissistic recovery work, trauma-focused CBT, and EMDR, can be crucial in alleviating both psychological and physical symptoms. Equally, understanding the need to rebalance your chemicals of cortisol, dopamine, oxytocin, and your hormones overall can help to persuade your body that it is no longer under attack and allow it to return to a calm parasympathetic state.

Anger, injustice, and suppressed rage are often reported by the clients I work with who are recovering from sustained narcissistic abuse. Practices such as somatic scream therapy offer a vital pathway for releasing the suppressed anger and rage that survivors of narcissistic abuse often carry, rooted deeply in the body. Suppressed emotions such as anger often remain trapped within us, compounding feelings of powerlessness and disconnecting us from our bodies. Somatic scream therapy works by accessing these embodied emotions, allowing you as a survivor physically and vocally to express the rage you may have felt unable to articulate or even acknowledge up until now. This intentional release not only alleviates the physiological burden of stored trauma within you, it also fosters a sense of empowerment, helping you reclaim your voice and rebuild a healthier connection with your body. In the following chapter we will meet Helen, who bravely undertook a form of somatic therapy to positive effect. I hope this real-life example will encourage you to consider how your body needs support and healing, too.

Conclusion

Expert support, empathetic validation from other survivors, and specialist somatic work form the cornerstone of recovery from narcissistic parental abuse. These offer a lifeline of understanding, shared experiences, and empowerment that counters the isolation and self-doubt instilled by the abuse. Survivors are reminded that they are not alone, their feelings are valid, and healing is possible. By seeking out supportive professionals and likeminded communities, survivors can reclaim their voices, rebuild their self-worth, and embark on a journey towards resilience and freedom.

10

Utilizing therapeutic practices to heal

'Speak the truth, even if your voice shakes.'

Maggie Kuhn

You are not alone if you have not yet explored therapy and are anxious or confused as to how to start finding and engaging in this level of work, or if you have experienced some level of therapy that you felt just did not engage you or the issues you brought in an impactful way. Psychotherapy, and more importantly healing, is not an exact science – but utilizing therapy to support your discovery and recovery is most certainly a route worth considering.

As with all things in life, the relationship between client and therapist – something we call the therapeutic alliance – is critical. It is also critical for the therapist to have studied, experienced, or practised in the area of narcissistic abuse.

However you currently feel about therapy, there are some wonderful therapeutic techniques, ones I have found hugely supported for my clients in making a breakthrough to their healing. All caveated, of course, with my repeated notion that narcissism is such a specific personality disorder that seeking and finding an expert who really does understand the maze of behaviours, distortions, and abuse these individuals can dispense, and the subsequent impact on those around them, is a critical part of the pathway. To invest in therapy emotionally and financially, only to be met with someone who does not truly appreciate the strengths of trauma bonds or enmeshment, can, in my opinion, leave clients feeling even more isolated and unheard, so research and discernment in finding a good therapist for you are key.

In this chapter I offer you examples of three different techniques used to help three different clients investigate, explore, and express their feelings about abuse and to demonstrate how psychotherapy can support in the discovery of and recovery from narcissistic parents. All have healed and released many decades of pain and difficulty – I hope the breadth of the work will enlighten and encourage you to see that skilful therapy can facilitate healing.

Case study 1

Using Gestalt two-chair work to support a victim of parental narcissistic abuse

The client, Neal, was a 50-year-old man who had been in therapy to address the long-term effects of emotional and psychological abuse by his narcissistic mother. Neal was a successful executive in the outside world, and a husband and father. However, inside he struggled with low self-esteem, self-doubt, and difficulty asserting his needs in relationships. He had never confronted his mother about the abusive dynamics of both violence from his father and neglect by omission and aggression from his mother, alongside his painful unmet childhood needs. Recently, Neal expressed a desire to address these issues directly with his mother but felt paralyzed by fear, guilt, and uncertainty about how to articulate his feelings.

He reminded me of a quote by Shannon L. Alder, 'You're afraid to tell people how you feel because you fear it will destroy them, so you bury it deep inside yourself where it destroys you,' which I shared with him. He agreed that he needed to start by facing what was destroying him inside, to seek healing.

Our agreed weekly therapeutic work grew in strength across a six-month period and after some time, as Christmas approached, Neal's goal focused on helping him to rehearse expressing to his mother his feelings about the abuse and lack of parental care, in order to break the news that he was no longer going to invite her to his house for the festive period. Being a father himself had allowed him to connect with the wise parent within him and while he still struggled to protect himself, he was able to hear the protective father within him who did not want to subject his own sons to his narcissistic mother.

It was important we first empowered Neal to hear his own voice, accept that what he had experienced was real and true and unacceptable, and then explore how he would like to set boundaries and assert his needs. Second, it was also critical to manage his expectations on his mother's ability or willingness to take any responsibility. We worked carefully on building Neal's confidence in his ability to have this difficult conversation long before he tried it in the real world, and one of the best ways to do this was through what we call 'empty chair work'.

Application of Gestalt two-chair work

I introduced Neal to the empty chair technique as a way to practise the conversation he wanted to have with his mother. A chair was placed opposite each other: one representing Neal and the other representing his mother.

I asked Neal to sit in the 'Neal' chair and describe the key points he wanted to communicate to his mother. These included:

- acknowledging the pain caused by the narcissistic abuse
- acknowledging his father's violence and his mother's unwillingness to protect him
- highlighting his mother's failure to provide a safe, loving, and nurturing environment
- expressing the emotional and psychological impact of this neglect
- communicating his need for space, boundaries, and respect going forward.

Figure 10.1 Artistic depiction of Gestalt chair work

In the early weeks, as soon as Neal sat in the chair and we invited his mother (in the imaginary sense) to enter the room and take the other seat, I asked him to describe what she was wearing, how she held her body, and how she looked at him. I observed his body tense and his irritation rise; it was instantaneous. At this point, I simply spent time enquiring what Neal was feeling in his body and asked him to tune into what was happening. As is often the case with adult children of trauma, the body starts to retreat into the memory before any words are even spoken and as trauma-informed therapists, we are trained to slow the process down, remind the client this is not happening now, and allow them to begin to open their window of tolerance by reassuring them they are safe. After a while I asked his mother to leave the room so Neal could recover himself and to reassure him that I could take care of him. It was palpable just how fearful this grown man was of even the imagined presence of his narcissistic mother, and I am sure many of you reading this will be able to relate to that.

Many weeks of work passed and when Neal felt ready we started to get into dialogue with his mother. He began tentatively to express the five key points that he wanted to explain to his mother, to seek her acknowledgement of them. Taking time is imperative in this work, to allow the mind, body, and spirit to remain as regulated as possible while the client begins to hear their own voice, sometimes for the very first time. After several weeks of Neal rehearsing his dialogue towards his mother and his confidence growing in imagining even being in a room with her, I knew it was time for us to move to the next stage.

In the following session, I introduced two chair work and invited Neal to sit in his mother's chair. And I asked him to become his mother – to see him from her vantage point, imagine what she felt in being addressed by him, and then respond to what had been Neal's chair with a response to any of the five areas he had been attempting to talk about. It was helpful for Neil to imagine how his mother may have heard, received, and then responded to his dialogue, but it was equally incredibly helpful to me as his therapist to appreciate the sharpness, intimidation, and unmistakable gaslighting his mother offered in return.

Over the next few weeks we played with the Gestalt two-chair technique back and forth until Neal and I felt certain that his sense of truth, the validation, and his desire to challenge his mother were felt firmly in his bones. All through this process, I reminded him that he did not actually have to follow through with this plan. That it was helpful for his mind, his amygdala, his body, and his brain to hear his true voice finally speaking up for himself, if nothing else.

A month before Christmas, Neal decided it was time to confront his mother in real life. He set a time to go to his mother's house in Southampton, a place which in itself held trauma from the past. Neal had the distinct view he wanted to recover his adapted inner child, whom he felt he may have abandoned at his childhood home, to deliver his truth to his narcissistic mother, to cut ties, and to leave.

The day before his trip, we had a final session. In that session, within five minutes Neil felt nauseous, shaky, irritable, and angry to the point that he had to visit the bathroom, lie down on the couch, prematurely ended the session and took a car home. I watched him deteriorate from a strong, wise, and confident man to the inner child who had experienced so much trauma.

Often when we are working with individuals who have experienced high levels of trauma we will be observing their 'window of tolerance' – how much they are able to work with their material and story before they either risk becoming so hyper-aroused they struggle with anger, tears, or a level of losing control; or in fact the memories and sensations connected with them bring the body into a hypo-arousal state – one where they fall silent, disassociate (lose connection to the story, the therapist, and the room), and feel numb. See Figure 10.2.

Expanding the 'Window of Tolerance'

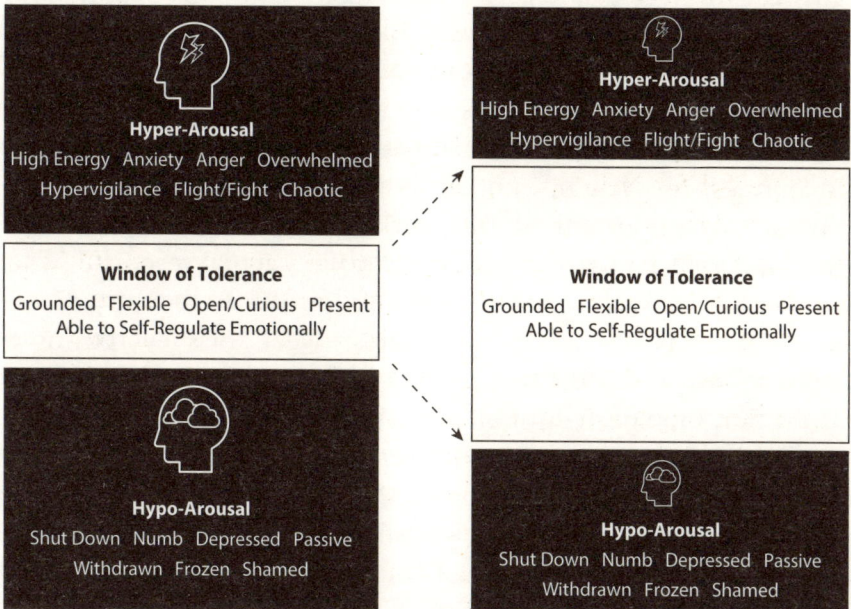

Figure 10.2 The Developing Mind, 3rd ed – 1999

This is a form of fight and flight, the coping mechanism you will already be familiar with. When this happens in this work we consciously acknowledge and respect the tolerance window and know we might be able to work on slowly widening the window at a pace the client can operate with, gradually allowing the body and mind to appreciate they are safe, no longer in the original situation, and can begin to recall or feel both the high and low emotions and 'tolerate' them more and, importantly, 'enough' to understand what was truly happening at the time. It is painstaking work but it can allow clients to know they are able to face their feelings, without being overrun or frightened by them.

We agreed by the end of the session that his wisdom and kindness meant he accepted he was not ready (and may never be ready) to confront his mum in person. It is never in my, or their, interest to suggest or encourage any client to do anything that is not 100 per cent healthy for them. Neal cancelled the time with his mother without explanation and we continued to work together for another five months. Neal was determined to speak up for his inner child, but he and I agreed that it would not be until and if his true self felt ready, safe, protected, and able to regulate his emotions that he would undertake this critical final part in his journey to reclaim his childhood and his true self. We worked on further expanding the window over the following few sessions and widening his ability to tolerate and sit with his feelings of both anger and desolation, and bring care and kindness in a way his mother never had.

What was important in the work – and initially surprising to Neal – was to acknowledge that his mother's actual response (whatever it would be) was very minor in this journey to recovery. Giving her any more power was of no interest; Neal knew everything he needed to know – he did not need to seek validation from her (and this is often unexpected for clients). What was more important was for Neal to hear his own voice deliver the harsh truth to his mother. For the first time, his inner protective part was able to stand up and protect the inner children within his psyche that had grown so scared and adaptive as a result of the abuse he'd grown up with for so many years.

Neal was eventually able and ready to confront his mother and drove down to see her. She predictably denied, disputed, and diminished many of the incidents that Neal brought forward, but because his work had been so deep, careful, and detailed, Neil was no longer wrongfooted by his narcissistic mother's dramatic behaviours. As we had discussed many times, 'You cannot wake a person who is pretending to be asleep.' He had seen all this in our two-chair rehearsals and was able to ignore and let go of her responses and continue to deliver the critical messages that he needed to land in order to facilitate his healing.

Neal no longer has regular contact with his mother. However, in his heart he has left the door open should he wish to make contact with her again, and our joint sense is that his liberation within himself to have that choice is something that's critical for him. As his mother ages we have had to address the notion of her death at some point in his life (something we will cover more generally in the next chapter) and again have undertaken the work to think about what Neal may want or need to do when that time comes.

Conclusion

The two-chair technique provided Neal with a structured and emotionally safe environment to rehearse a very difficult conversation. This process helped him articulate his feelings, anticipate potential challenges, and develop strategies for assertive communication. Neal now presents as a liberated, softer, carefree, humorous, and wise man. The echoes and torments of his past have been released and he has no doubt of his ability to accept the truth of what happened to him and his sister as children: how the duty of care was not performed by either of his parents and how he has done the challenging work to reparent himself and accept the love of his in-laws and older work colleagues as a level of substitute for the love he deserved all along.

The work has been a triumph for Neal and I now see a man liberated to live his life. From initially struggling to stay in the room, never mind finding any words to express to the empty chair, to the real-life ability finally to overcome the abuse, this is what therapy is here to facilitate.

Case study 2

Helping Izzy confront her father using the Karpman Drama Triangle, inner child, and understanding of parentification

Izzy, whom we met earlier in this book, had become a 21-year-old woman, entering therapy again, this time as an adult to address the unresolved feelings of anger, guilt, and confusion she had begun to realize actually stemmed from her relationship with her father, Mike.

Throughout her childhood, Mike emotionally enmeshed Izzy into a surrogate spouse role after abusing his wife and her mother to the point she suffered a breakdown and left. In making Izzy his confidante and emotional support system, and demonstrating signs of emotional incest, Izzy became his 'golden child' and was showered with praise and attention, but was also manipulated into taking on adult responsibilities and prioritizing her father's emotional needs over her own. She was the epitome of a parentified child in a narcissistic family dynamic, taking on roles and responsibilities beyond her years, acting as a caregiver, offering emotional support, and even as a mediator for the parent and others in the family. This happens because the narcissistic parent prioritizes their own needs, requiring the child to fulfil emotional or practical roles that the parent neglects. The child then suppresses their own emotions, needs, and development to focus on meeting the parent's demands to secure validation and attention. As a result, they often struggle with feelings of guilt, anxiety, or inadequacy in adulthood, coupled with a deep-seated drive to please or control others and a loss of connection with their own identity.

This dynamic caused significant strain on Izzy's relationship with her mother, Jenny, whom Mike often painted as the family's villain. Following his divorce from Jenny, Mike remarried. Izzy then found herself in a similar dynamic with her stepmother, Ruth, attacking and ultimately rejecting her due to the enmeshment and triangulation her narcissistic father had constructed as a means to divert and shift blame for the struggles his narcissism was causing in his intimate adult relationships once again. Izzy is beginning to realize and clearly describe that Mike had inappropriately recruited her as his surrogate partner, protector, and aggressor, he was in fact recreating within his new relationship the intimate abuse experienced by his wives and had manipulated Izzy into believing he was once again the victim.

Now an adult, Izzy struggles with confusion and guilt about what really happened, and a growing resentment towards her father, alongside a residual difficulty with forming healthy personal relationships, especially with older women. Interestingly, she is now herself being accused of entitlement, perfectionism, and even narcissism and yet she feels deep down this is not her true self but something developed in her late teenage years. Izzy shared the pain of being made to feel responsible for her father's emotional well-being and of her realization that the attention she received as the golden child was manipulative rather than nurturing. She wondered how these experiences were impacting her adult relationships, making her hypervigilant and fearful of abandonment and loss of control.

She was unsure what she wanted to do to resolve this dynamic, or how to separate from her father's ongoing desired closeness as she moved further into her adult life, but she sensed her anger and the burden of responsibility had fed into her long-running and chronic anxiety, something she remained heavily medicated for. Difficult work.

I observed early on in our sessions that triangulation was always present in the stories Izzy retold (as is frequently the case in narcissistic situations), so I started by inviting Izzy to explore something we call the Karpman Drama Triangle (see figure 10.3). The Karpman Drama Triangle is a psychological model that illustrates dysfunctional interactions in relationships, often involving three roles: the Victim, the Persecutor, and the Rescuer. These roles are interconnected and perpetuate cycles of conflict and dependency. The Victim feels helpless and seeks support but resists solutions, the Persecutor criticizes or blames, and the Rescuer intervenes to 'save' the Victim, often ignoring their own needs. While these roles provide temporary emotional payoffs, they hinder genuine problem-solving and healthy communication. Breaking free from the triangle involves taking responsibility,

Karpman Drama Triangle

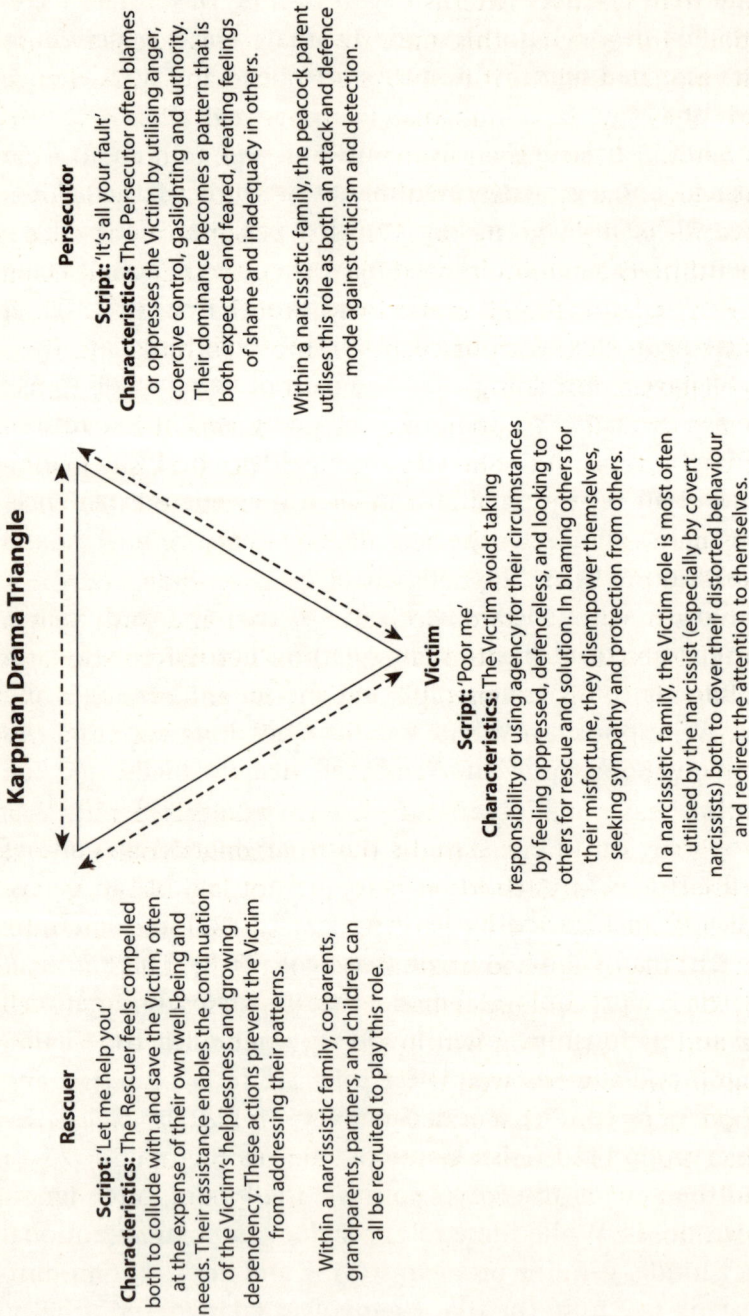

Rescuer

Script: 'Let me help you'

Characteristics: The Rescuer feels compelled both to collude with and save the Victim, often at the expense of their own well-being and needs. Their assistance enables the continuation of the Victim's helplessness and growing dependency. These actions prevent the Victim from addressing their patterns.

Within a narcissistic family, co-parents, grandparents, partners, and children can all be recruited to play this role.

Persecutor

Script: 'It's all your fault'

Characteristics: The Persecutor often blames or oppresses the Victim by utilising anger, coercive control, gaslighting and authority. Their dominance becomes a pattern that is both expected and feared, creating feelings of shame and inadequacy in others.

Within a narcissistic family, the peacock parent utilises this role as both an attack and defence mode against criticism and detection.

Victim

Script: 'Poor me'

Characteristics: The Victim avoids taking responsibility or using agency for their circumstances by feeling oppressed, defenceless, and looking to others for rescue and solution. In blaming others for their misfortune, they disempower themselves, seeking sympathy and protection from others.

In a narcissistic family, the Victim role is most often utilised by the narcissist (especially by covert narcissists) both to cover their distorted behaviour and redirect the attention to themselves.

Figure 10.3 The Karpman Drama Triangle
Source: Stephen B. Karpman, M.D.

fostering empowerment, and engaging in honest, constructive dialogue rather than reactive patterns.

In initially introducing this idea to Izzy I was keen to check whether it resonated, given it is always central to any work that the client leads the way. Izzy immediately recognized what was being shown to her and I knew then we had some work to do. It can take time, gentleness, and empathy to allow a client to start to see what might have really been going on. While it is tempting at once to start dismantling the manipulative dynamics of the Karpman Drama Triangle in any relationship, it is also important that we start to build an alternative paradigm for our clients to move towards and this is what we collaborated in doing.

It was also critical to support Izzy in processing her regret and guilt over past interactions. She was able to notice how she believed her father and allowed him often to take the victim role, so widely favoured by narcissists, while she became the rescuer for him. And she also appreciated the times she had been aggressive, rude, and threatening as the persecutor towards both her mother and Ruth, leaving them trying to rescue the entire family while her narcissistic father remained happily in his favoured place of victim and everyone oscillated around him in the chaos he created to distract everyone from his calculated behaviour.

I spent time reassuring Izzy that the healthy adults in her life, Ruth especially, who was less tangled in the Halston family dynamic, would have appreciated the distortions at play and not laid blame at Izzy's door, knowing she was a child, and a manipulated and enmeshed one. Given the dialogue I had had with all the family, I had no doubt Ruth and some of the nannies had sought to rescue Izzy, but the narcissism and the distortion within the house and indeed the wider Halston family were overpowering for them all.

The good news was that seeing this clear breakthrough point of what had truly happened started to open up the opportunity to release and empower Izzy to reclaim her autonomy and establish healthier boundaries.

Inner child connection

The next part of our work was to help and guide Izzy to connect to her true inner child. Given she had been parentified and made a surrogate spouse from as young as five, Izzy had never truly experienced the liberation, freedom, and playfulness within herself of the child she never knew during her actual childhood. Using Russian dolls (Figure 10.4), we explored the inner parts of herself.

We explored the playful, the reckless, the liberated, the unencumbered, and the innocent child – the parts that had never had the true opportunity to run free. Izzy initially struggled, seeing the work as pointless and confusing given these inner parts were so foreign to her. Her place of comfort was being an adult child, a parentified child, a child that had been given adult responsibility before she was even in double digits. While this brought frustration, our therapeutic alliance held strong and it was only when her defences softened and she dropped into great sadness and grief for the little girls that she had never had a chance to explore or to be that she began to hear the small voices and hope for the young parts within her.

Utilizing Matryoshkas to Identify the Inner Parts

Figure 10.4 Inner Parts

For some weeks I simply prescribed that she went to play with, and talk to, the little children within her – literally playing on a swing, buying her inner little girl sweets, and even reading her stories. Over time, once her sadness had stabilized, her anger began to emerge. Anger at her father for manipulating her in this way. Anger at her mother for not being more present and available to her to guide her. Anger with Mike's family for not stepping in, noticing, and protecting her when he began to manipulate her. Over time, her guilt at the way she had treated Ruth and some of the nannies whom she now understood were trying to help her emerged as she realized the distortions her father portrayed were lies to avoid accountability for his narcissistic behaviour.

There was work to do to grieve the childhood that she had lost. There was work to do in noticing her co-dependency with her father. There was work to do in noticing her enablement and insistence on leadership around other people. She grew to understand that her need to control people and things was an antidote to her baseline of anxiety and a coping mechanism to control most things, in the way she felt she had needed to as a child.

As the weeks went by, Izzy began to process guilt and regret. She expressed deep remorse over how her alignment with Mike strained and then broke her relationship with her mother and stepmother. She tearfully acknowledged moments when she had dismissed or judged them based on Mike's narrative and at times, she confessed, she even verbally attacked and bullied them, realizing she had been made an enabler but had enjoyed that at the time as it came with privileges and reward. Working together to help her see the innocence of her young self and her need for survival with the only parent in the house, she was able to consider forgiveness of self as well as an appropriate response to her father.

At this point in her therapy, I was able to introduce 'two-chair' work – where I invited Izzy to imagine her father Mike in the empty chair and tentatively to tell him how she truly felt. Initially she found it awkward but after a few minutes, the feelings began to flow. Finally, she was able to express, in the safety of the empty chair, how his narcissism had deeply affected her childhood.

Figure 10.5 Artistic Depiction of Gestalt chair work

Over time Izzy was able to hear herself say:

> 'I was a child, and it was not my role to meet your emotional needs.'
> 'The attention I received came with strings attached; I wasn't free to be myself.'
> 'I can now see you painted Mum and Ruth as the enemy to justify your struggles with intimacy within yourself.'
> 'Suki and I were robbed of a mother twice because you put yourself and your inability to admit you needed help before everyone else. We all suffered because of you.'

As the therapist I was able to support Izzy in:

- validating her younger self's actions as a product of manipulation rather than malice
- identifying opportunities to grieve and repair her relationships with Jenny and Ruth if she chose to
- letting go of the unrealistic expectation that she could have 'fixed' her father or the family dynamic as a child
- addressing the learned narcissistic traits that subsequently emerged.

By the end of the sessions, Izzy:

- felt more prepared to confront her father with clarity and emotional strength
- understood how her childhood role as rescuer had shaped her adult patterns and recognized the need to break free from that role
- began to forgive herself for past decisions, acknowledging them as survival strategies under difficult circumstances
- started to notice how her learned narcissistic behaviour was not her own and could be addressed.

There is a way to go in her healing work – 21 years of deep narcissistic abuse takes patience, kindness, bravery, and commitment to heal – but thank goodness Izzy sought therapy when she did, offering herself the opportunity to work on healing before she embarks on a serious relationship or becomes a parent herself. In allowing herself the opportunity to be clear eyed about what a healthy pathway ahead may look like, she opens up the possibility to halt the destruction narcissism has brought to her life so far and move towards a healthy and unenmeshed self.

Case study 3

Using alchemical processing and somatic fire to express pain from narcissistic abuse

Helen had struggled with both a narcissistic mother and father throughout her childhood years. Despite being highly academic and musical, she had been blamed, chastised, ridiculed, ostracized, isolated, and threatened on a regular basis by both her mother and her father. While her mother took the more grandiose and overt narcissistic route, parading her daughter's academic and musical achievements, she criticized, scolded, belittled, and frightened her behind closed doors, controlling her through lack of money, food, basic care, or even transport to school leaving her trapped at home in her teenage years. Her father displayed covert narcissistic tendencies, presenting himself as a meek, charming introvert while at the same time enabling and at times encouraging her mother. He confused Helen further by doubling down on her mother's accusations, forming a dual narcissistic shield. As Helen reached her teenage years and tried to bargain, plea, or argue to have her voice heard or herself noticed, she would sometimes lie, steal, or not come home as a way to survive or to demonstrate her desperation. As a result, her parents accused her of being too much, overly dramatic, and difficult. She felt frightened, dismissed, and ridiculed most of the time.

At the age of 20, Helen had taken the decision to cut herself off completely from her parents. Rather than her parents becoming concerned or enquiring as to what they could do to remedy the situation or check on the welfare of their young daughter, they instead took the aggressive approach of what we might now consider malignant narcissists. They set about screenshotting any messages Helen had sent in desperation and circulating them to wider members of the family, claiming she was 'troubled'.

To justify and excuse further why it was their daughter no longer spoke to them, Helen's parents recreated stories where they positioned themselves as victims, and as confused, desolate, and sad that they had no contact with their daughter – when in private they hadn't made a single attempt to reach her by phone, text, or email. When her grandfather attempted to question her mother about her treatment of Helen during this time, he was dismissed himself, a dismissal that lasted until he died.

Helen was left in a position of great isolation and fear, believing that she did not matter, and never had. The pain and the anger were deep. When she first attended therapy, Helen's sessions risked overrunning week after week as a never-ending stream of consciousness, bile, desolation, and angry tears flooded the room. My sense was to look towards what we call the 'alchemical process' as a pathway to reaching her and inviting her to undertake the tender work of healing her pain.

The alchemical process draws from ancient alchemy, which describes transformation through stages such as nigredo (decomposition), albeido (purification), citrinitas (gaining insight), and rubedo (realisation). In trauma therapy, these stages symbolize the inner journey of confronting pain, disintegration, and renewal. *Nigredo*, for instance, corresponds to the initial acknowledgement of trauma, where the client faces the 'dark night of the soul'. This can feel chaotic and painful, but it is necessary for transformation and forms part of the acceptance we have already discussed. Gradually, *calcinatio* represents the process of burning away old patterns and beliefs, as part of finding the true self, reducing the client to their essence. Each stage invites the client to embrace and work through their emotional struggles rather than avoid them.

ALCHEMICAL TRANSFORMATION PROCESS MODEL

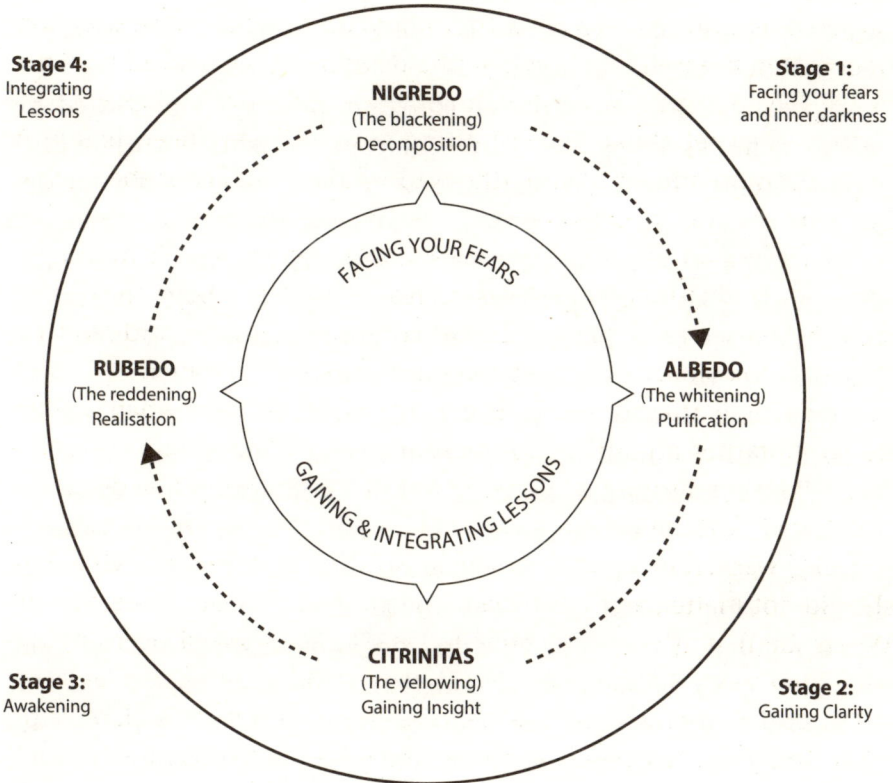

Figure 10.6 The alchemical process

Source: CCPE Diploma course Alchemy lectures

While purely symbolic, the visual references allow us to imagine where we are in the healing process and what might be required at each stage – allowing individuals to connect to and engage with the different types of emotional responses as the process of healing is undertaken. The classical elements – fire, earth, water, and air – are central to this transformative process, representing different psychological energies. Fire corresponds to *calcinatio*, symbolizing the purifying heat of anger, passion, or determination needed to confront trauma. Earth, tied to grounding and *coagulatio* (solidification), helps clients find stability and rebuild a secure sense of self. Water is linked to *solutio* (dissolution), representing emotional release, fluidity, and the cleansing tears of grief. Air, associated with *sublimatio* (rising), supports mental clarity, insight, and the capacity to see beyond the pain. These elements reflect the cyclical nature of healing, as clients move between grounding, emotional release, and rising above their challenges.

Ultimately, the culmination of this process, represented by *rubedo*, signifies integration and wholeness. Clients emerge with a renewed sense of self, having transformed their wounds into wisdom. By consciously engaging with each stage and element, therapists help trauma clients navigate their inner landscape, encouraging deep healing and lasting change. The alchemical approach, though symbolic, can be a powerful way to contextualize and guide the complexities of psychological transformation.

Helen was displaying 'waterlogged' levels of emotion, and her overthinking and high anxiety indicated a high use of air that caused her to spiral into despair at times. While I could sense her inner fire and anger, it wasn't being overtly expressed. I knew that in order to activate her anger safely, I would need to ensure there was enough earthly matter around her to contain the fire; in other words, so she could regulate. I aimed at teaching her how to do that before our somatic work commenced. Although initially a struggle, I was able to model techniques for her and consistently hold her therapeutically when she became overwhelmed. Slowly, she was able to utilize regulation and grounding techniques and together we expanded her window of tolerance for experiencing feelings, while staying present and in control. When she was ready, we then moved to the next stage – meeting her inner child.

As we started to journey slowly into her experience further, I saw the fear, confusion, and disbelief of her inner child at the abandonment she had suffered. In other moments I noticed her need to be reassured that I truly understood the depths of the pain and abuse that she had suffered. She tested me with questions around my understanding of the insidious nature of this type of abuse so often hidden, excused, and masqueraded by skilful narcissists like her parents. Alongside this dynamic was a younger sibling who was the apple of her parents' eyes, and the juxtaposition Helen felt between the treatment of her younger brother and herself made her deep sense of unworthiness and faultiness even more rigid. We spent many months painstakingly sifting through the debris of what had happened and how she felt, discriminating between the true and the false stories that underpinned this upbringing coloured by gaslighting.

There came a moment in the therapy where Helen was both needing and ready to express her suppressed anger and felt that we could find a way to bring it out of the cellular level of her body. At the start of the session, I handed her a pair of boxing gloves, took off my shoes, and put on a matching set of pads. I asked her to consider what she would most like to say to either of her parents and then as she landed those sentences, she needed to land a punch on my pads. Although she found this awkward to start with, and was rather tender in her punches, I encouraged her slowly to find more and more courage, fire, and weight to put into the punches until she was punching hard and fast while she told my pads exactly how she felt and allowed her body to express somatically what she needed to say.

After only 15 minutes, Helen was sweating and exhausted and asked to stop. We sat quietly looking at each other. And when I asked her how she felt, she simply said, 'Relieved.' We undertook this exercise in two more sessions intermittently over the following few months, just to dig a little deeper and be sure that we were excavating the inner buried anger that Helen had carried for so many years.

Now that she was in touch with her healthy fire, I was able to restart the journey of her alchemical process – finding our way to transform the narcissistic abuse she had so chronically suffered into delicate, precious, and lifelong learnings. It was important that Helen could take this understanding and some supporting techniques with her as treasure in her pocket as she travelled forward in life, clear on the true story of herself, free from the suppressed anger of the abuse, and clear in the truth of who she was and what had happened to her.

In summary

While everyone's experience of therapy, the therapeutic alliance, and the mode of therapy they choose to work with will of course differ, it's important to say again that finding the right therapist, who is truly able to understand narcissistic abuse, is essential – a therapist who has a collection of methods they can offer you so that you can decide which suit and which do not. This really can allow you to work through the process in the right way for you.

Therapeutic modalities can seem confusing from the outside, but the way I look at it, a psychotherapist is like a doctor's bag. I have many remedies, medications, and abilities to offer you pathways to healing within my 'bag' and some may work for you and some may not. But we keep reaching into that bag to find the right 'medicine' for healing until we hit the spot. And it is your responsibility, with love and tenderness, to give feedback to us as therapists: what's working, what's chiming, what's resonating, and what's not. The strength of the therapeutic alliance is in your being brave enough to tell the truth, being brutally honest, and to discover feedback between us is perfectly safe and okay (in a way it was not with your narcissistic parent) – in order for you to receive the love and healing that you deserve.

As you can see, these three examples used different methods depending on the character, the story, the relationship, and the ability of the client to withstand certain amounts of memory, to trust the therapist, and to process trauma carefully. As therapists we have a duty of care to make that call based on our lived experience of you as our client. Our job is to take care of you, to hold you, and only to move you at the pace at which you are comfortable. Any good therapist will want nothing more than to hold you tenderly while you undertake this very precious work. In fact, it is our honour and privilege to do so.

11

The demise and death of a narcissistic parent

'Grieving the impossible while grieving the past.'

John Perry Barlow famously said, 'Groundless hope, like unconditional love, is the only kind worth having.' For me and the many clients I work with in this narcissistic realm, this sentiment seems to epitomize the very essence of what a full-hearted person experiences when faced with a narcissistic parent.

We are taught from an early age never to give up hope, and certainly as therapists sometimes holding hope for our clients is all we can do as they work through their difficulties and struggles while they are in our care. So to face the idea directly that we must give up hope that our parent, or someone who is meant to love us, is either unwilling or unable to change feels challenging and even abhorrent. On one hand we may ask ourselves, 'Who am I to give up on any fellow human being, especially one who is my parent?' But equally, who are we to think we should or could change anyone on this planet? Even that belief to some ironic extent has a sliver of narcissism within it. And yet, the clock tautology continues to audibly tick.

After all, time is all we have and so, in the end, there will undoubtedly come a time when our parent becomes frail, old, or ill, and at some point passes away. This very notion can be so overwhelming for many children of narcissistic parents that it creates a drive to remain in contact and suffer the parent, despite the growing awareness or long-held belief that their behaviour and treatment of their children is no longer acceptable. For others who have successfully placed firm boundaries or even cut all contact, it can be the first time they are given pause for thought or have a moment of reconsideration, or most certainly a wobble. And yet for others, if they were truly honest, it offers a genuine sense of relief.

215

The impending mortality of this key figure in your life can stir up a complex and often contradictory mix of emotions. It's not just the grief of anticipating their death that surfaces, but also grief for the childhood you didn't have. The safety, love, and validation that might have shaped you differently. This kind of grief is layered: it's mourning for the parent you needed but never had, the version of them you might have wished for in your most vulnerable moments; and knowing the stark truth that all they should have been and at times said they were was not actually a truth or your reality. In your adult life and understanding you now have the ability to accept that distortion, the deep incongruence of the public persona versus the private pain of a narcissistic parent, and yet you still seek from them an understanding or an explanation that only they could ever satisfy. It can feel like grieving all at once a loss you've been carrying for your entire life, now brought sharply into focus by your parent's decline.

At the same time, their mortality forces you to confront the reality of their absence, both the one you already feel and the one that is coming. Even when the relationship has been deeply harmful, the finality of death can provoke an unexpected sense of loss. It may not be the parent themselves you mourn but the irrevocable loss of any possibility for repair, understanding, or change. This tension – the grief for what was and what will never be – can feel overwhelming, leaving you caught between anger, sorrow, guilt, and a yearning for closure that might never come. It's important to recognize that these feelings are valid and human, even if they seem contradictory or confusing.

This can also be the point in life when the outside world begins to weigh heavy. Those with no or little experience in this space may suggest it's for the best for you to forgive and forget, often encouraging you to consider such poorly formed opinions as 'You only have one set of parents' and 'Time is running out.' Others may attempt to shame or school you with reminders that 'They are frail, old, from a different generation, softened, physically impaired' – and a challenge of 'What threat to you are they now?' Many people don't understand that the children of narcissistic parents experience complex PTSD symptoms such as shaking, freezing, dissociation, and physical fear even at the sound of the parent's voice, at seeing their name light up their phone, never mind the reality of a physical encounter with them – so such attempts to help may in fact hurt and hinder them further. One of the greatest woundings in my experience in this space is the unwillingness or inability for people truly to see and believe the reality of your experience as a victim of a narcissist.

Equally, you may even have always held a quiet but hopeful inward wish to reconcile. Finally to hear them acknowledge their behaviour, and maybe even to hope for an apology.

In becoming aware of their impending death, you too might also sense you have something you and your true inner child still wish to communicate – whether that be a tender wound or a suppressed rage. What we do know in life is that imminent endings often provoke a sense of urgency and of 'now or never' that can tempt or persuade us to lower our defences, and so I think it's an appropriate juncture to discuss this.

When the narcissistic parent becomes ill

When a narcissistic parent falls ill, the adult child may experience a profound sense of dissonance. On one hand, there is the natural human response to illness or suffering – concern, empathy, and a desire to provide care. You would most probably willingly provide it for an old lady next door who you barely know, so it would seem incomprehensible not to provide it to your own parent, right? On the other hand, the history of manipulation and emotional abuse will have created conflicting feelings and by now you may have formed healthy boundaries or even distance that has served you well. Yet the adult child may struggle with guilt over not feeling more compassionate or may feel trapped between their own needs and the demands of their now unwell parent.

The onset of illness can often lead to a role reversal, where the recovering adult child becomes the caregiver. This shift can be particularly distressing when the adult child finds themselves in a position where they are forced to confront unresolved issues and conflicts while simultaneously managing the demands of caregiving.

Genie: the boomerang effect

Genie, an only child, had long suffered at the hands of her cold, cruel, and narcissistic mother. Growing up in a single-parent household, Genie had little choice but to conform, swerve, and cope with the callous behaviour of her mother. Her mother classically projected all her dark and difficult material onto Genie and later seemed to inject many beliefs and distorted views into her only child. Genie had finally moved away from her mother through a relationship but had sadly run straight into the arms of a narcissistic and abusive man. Over time she had eventually escaped him and set up a simple but peaceful home, away from her mother, putting in a healthy boundary with only occasional calls or visits. Life began to feel better, if a little lonely.

It was only when Genie's mother started to be regularly admitted to hospital that Genie again started to feel the weight and the pull of her mother's demands and would struggle when well-meaning nurses commented on how much they knew Genie loved her mother and must be worried about her. Given her inner feelings about her mother, guilt and shame surrounded Genie; when she was expected to look after her mother on her return from hospital, or to drop everything each time she had an episode, Genie understandably did not want to. That said, during one session a few weeks later, when I asked her how she might feel when her mother finally passed away, tears leaked from the corners of her eyes and she said she dreaded it and was not sure she could cope. And right there, she offered me the true insight into the tussle we have when dealing with the fallout of a narcissistic upbringing. While the day-to-day boundary had supported Genie's stabilization, the trauma bond still had tendrils attached – an underlying belief planted by her mother that Genie could not ultimately cope alone.

So, our work moved on to how together we could uncover the true parts of Genie that would cope just fine with or without her mum. These parental bonds are deep, long, and complex. Illness and impending demise can dysregulate some of the most stoic individuals. The psychological separation between child and parent as we enter adulthood is key to the healthy work we must undertake in reaching self-actualization – and living a confident life with or without our parents.

Here are some other unexpected consequences when a narcissistic parent becomes ill.

Exacerbation of existing trauma

Illness can exacerbate existing trauma and unresolved issues from the past. The adult child may find that the stress of caregiving brings up old wounds and triggers. Memories of abuse or neglect may resurface, intensifying emotional responses and making it harder to cope with the situation. Whether you needed to distance from engulfment or enmeshment and now feel yourself pulled back in, or experience a silent resentment that you are being asked to give the caregiving you were never offered – the situation is fraught with challenge.

Conflicted feelings and guilt

Feelings of guilt are common in these circumstances. As an adult child you might grapple with a sense of obligation to care for your parent despite a lack of genuine desire to do so. You may also struggle with guilt over your negative feelings towards the parent or the frustration of seeing your parent's vulnerabilities, especially when bystanders or well-meaning relatives who have not lived behind the closed doors as you have expect you to be a doting child. This is natural and I encourage you gently to observe these feelings but not allow them to sway you.

Challenges in setting boundaries

Setting boundaries can be particularly difficult when dealing with a narcissistic parent who is ill. Your parent's demands might become more intense, and as a kind adult you may struggle to maintain limits without feeling overwhelmed or excessively pressured. Navigating these boundaries requires a delicate balance between self-care and caregiving responsibilities.

There can be added difficulty when you have siblings who hold differing views and experiences of your parent, depending on the position they played or had bestowed upon them – bringing further pressure and guilt into your sense of responsibility. Remember, this is your life, your experience, and your feelings. You are able to own them and only you know what you experienced then and how you feel now. Trust in yourself and be mindful of any ongoing enabling or gaslighting in play.

So where is the hidden treasure?

If we are to hold some notion that every opportunity may offer some hidden treasure, what might it be in the circumstances that your narcissistic parent falls ill or is aging?

From a psychotherapeutic perspective, this process can provide an opportunity to explore unresolved dynamics and reframe your relationship with the parent and yourself. Reconciliation, whether merely in the physical realm of visiting them at home or in hospital just once, or in a deeper, more emotional sense via more regular conversation, in this context is less about condoning past harm and more about seeking closure, understanding, or the release of emotional burdens. For some, making contact may offer a chance to voice experiences, assert boundaries in a final way, or witness the parent's humanity in their final vulnerability. This act can sometimes aid in the healing of old wounds by fostering a sense of agency and completeness in you as the survivor, regardless of the parent's response.

However, the risks inherent in reconnecting with a narcissistic parent should not be underestimated. Narcissistic individuals often struggle to acknowledge their impact on others, and old age or illness may amplify manipulative tendencies as they seek to regain control or attention. This can reopen psychological wounds, destabilize hard-won boundaries, and potentially reverse personal progress. It is crucial to assess whether the desire to reconnect arises from authentic emotional readiness or lingering guilt, societal expectations, or internalized familial obligations. The therapeutic frame emphasizes self-compassion and discernment in such decisions, recognizing that reconciliation is a deeply personal process that must honour your mental and emotional well-being above external pressures.

The case for contact

For the child victim of a narcissistic parent, saying what needs to be said before the parent dies can offer profound psychological benefits. This act can serve as a powerful reclaiming of voice and agency in a relationship that may have been dominated by silencing or invalidation. Speaking your truth, whether it is to confront your parent, share feelings of pain, or even acknowledge complexities in the relationship, can be cathartic. It allows you to release emotional burdens you may have carried for years, creating space for healing and self-acceptance. This expression can also provide a sense of closure, reducing the likelihood of unresolved feelings festering into regret or guilt after your parent's death. Even if your parent cannot or does not respond in a validating way, the act of articulating these emotions can affirm your reality and experiences, fostering a deeper connection to your sense of worth and emotional resilience.

The case against contact

The case against speaking one's truth to a narcissistic parent before they die rests on the inherent risks of further emotional harm and the potential futility of seeking resolution. Narcissistic individuals often lack the capacity for genuine empathy or accountability and their response – whether dismissive, defensive, or manipulative – can retraumatize you as a child. In such cases, attempting to communicate deeply held feelings may reinforce your sense of invisibility or rejection, potentially undoing hard-won progress in healing. Additionally, the emotional intensity of such interactions, compounded by the parent's vulnerability or impending death, can trigger feelings of guilt or self-doubt in you, especially if your parent weaponizes their condition to elicit pity or compliance.

Moreover, you may inadvertently place expectations on the encounter – hoping for acknowledgement, an apology, or a moment of clarity that your narcissistic parent may never be able to provide. When these expectations go unmet, you risk further disillusionment and emotional pain. Psychotherapeutically, it is often emphasized that healing does not depend on external validation but on internal work. For some, choosing not to engage and instead processing unresolved emotions in therapy or through personal reflection can be a more empowering and self-protective path. Silence, in this context, can be an act of self-preservation, safeguarding your boundaries and emotional well-being.

Only you can enquire within yourself as to what might be for you in the specific circumstances you find yourself in. What is critical to remember, whether you decide to engage or not, is what you feel and what you want to say that might need to be expressed. It is about being seen and heard by the inner, younger child who suffered and by the now outward adult child who coped. What the narcissistic parent does or does not do with the challenge is in large part immaterial and this is the work you might want to bring to therapy. Some healthy two-chair work, where you imagine placing your parent in the chair while you rehearse talking to them, supported, and guided by your therapist, can provide an informative warm-up should you decide it's time, just like Izzy and Neal.

The death of a narcissistic parent

Losing any parent can be a challenging life experience for most people. Losing an estranged parent can be an emotionally complex and deeply layered experience for children of narcissists. The grief that accompanies such a loss often defies conventional expectations of mourning. When the relationship was one of estrangement, unresolved feelings such as sadness, anger, regret, or even relief may surface, making it challenging to process the loss.

For many, the grief stems not just from the loss of the parent but also from mourning what could have been. This experience may bring forward lingering questions about the relationship and 'what ifs' regarding missed opportunities or unresolved conversations. The death of a narcissistic parent can also reopen old wounds, forcing you to confront painful memories or emotions you thought you had already worked through. Even if the relationship was fraught with pain or disappointment, it's not uncommon to feel shock, emptiness, or sorrow upon learning of their passing.

If you find yourself experiencing a mix of emotions, it's important to remember that all your feelings are valid, even if they seem contradictory. Grieving an estranged parent doesn't follow a linear path or adhere to the typical stages of grief. Simply acknowledging the complexity of your emotions can provide relief, as can giving yourself permission to grieve in your own way – free from societal expectations or timelines. Just as validating the lived experience of having a narcissistic parent is crucial, so is recognizing the emotional nuances of their death.

Talking to others who have experienced similar losses or seeking support from a therapist can be invaluable. These avenues can help you navigate the labyrinth of emotions that accompanies this type of loss.

Grieving a parent you were estranged from shares similarities with grieving a parent you actively disliked or even hated. The loss of an abusive parent, in particular, is uniquely complicated and often isolating. This form of grief defies conventional mourning as it encompasses a web of intense, conflicting emotions that can be hard to understand, let alone articulate to others.

No matter the nature of your relationship, the loss of a narcissistic parent is a deeply personal journey. Embrace the complexity of your feelings, seek support where needed, and allow yourself the time and space to heal.

Here are some unique phenomena people may encounter:

1 **Grieving the absence of a 'good' parent:** Often, there's a grief not for your abusive parent themselves but for the loving parent you wished you'd had. This is sometimes referred to as 'ambiguous loss', where you mourn not the reality of the person but the hope, dream, or fantasy of who they could have been. For some, it's the grief of never experiencing unconditional love or support from a parent figure.

2 **Conflicted emotions and 'disenfranchised grief':** The emotions surrounding an abusive parent's death can range from anger and relief to sadness and guilt. Society often expects people to mourn a parent's death, but grieving the loss of an abusive parent doesn't follow the typical script. This can lead to 'disenfranchised grief', where you feel as though you don't have permission to feel sad or even relieved, or as if your grief is somehow 'invalid' or 'wrong'.

3 **Revisiting trauma and reopened wounds:** The loss can stir up unresolved trauma. In many cases, the death of an abusive parent reawakens painful memories or feelings that may have been buried. This is sometimes accompanied by flashbacks or intrusive thoughts as your mind revisits traumatic experiences. The death may force a reckoning with the abuse in a new way – knowing that they are now beyond confrontation or accountability.

4 **Guilt and relief in combination:** It's common to feel relief when an abuser passes away because the threat they posed – whether physical, emotional, or psychological – feels definitively over. But this relief can be accompanied by guilt or shame, as if feeling relieved about their death somehow reflects poorly on you. There might also be guilt for not having 'reconciled' before they passed, even though reconciliation was never truly possible or healthy.

5 **Loss of chance for closure:** Losing an abusive parent can feel like losing the possibility of true closure. Survivors may have held onto

a faint hope that, someday, their parent would apologize or show remorse. When they die, the chance for that acknowledgement is gone, which can feel like a final, painful reminder that certain things will remain forever unresolved.

6 **Confusion over self-identity and self-worth:** The death of an abusive parent can lead to a deep questioning of self-identity. A parent's abusive behaviour may have contributed to feelings of unworthiness, guilt, or shame since childhood. Their passing can lead to a re-examination of how much of your self-view was shaped by the abuse and what it means to redefine yourself beyond that relationship. It is why the identity theft and true self work in Chapters 7 and 8 are so critical as part of your recovery.

7 **Isolation and lack of empathy from others:** Mourning an abusive parent can be a lonely experience. Those around you may not understand why you're grieving or may believe that you should be able simply to 'move on'. Some may even expect you to feel only relief, creating an emotional isolation where you feel unable to talk openly about your true feelings.

8 **The pressure of societal expectations:** Society often reveres the bond between parent and child and assumes that familial love is unconditional. There can be social pressure to 'forgive and forget' or to honour a parent simply because of their role. This expectation can be hard to bear, and it can prevent you from processing your grief in an authentic way that truly honours your experience. In fact, I would go so far as to say that while I am a strong advocate for seeking forgiveness because it can offer healing, you should stand firm in the knowledge that it is perfectly okay not to forgive if that better honors your experience of the abuse. It is your choice and your choice alone to decide that which is forgivable and that which can no longer be.

9 **Redefining 'family' and healing without reconciliation:** The death of an abusive parent may force a revaluation of what family means. With this revaluation, there is often a new focus on chosen family or supportive relationships outside the biological family. Healing may now need to happen without the prospect of reconciliation, which can feel liberating or saddening depending on your circumstances.

10 **Acceptance and self-compassion:** The journey of grieving an abusive parent often includes learning to extend compassion to yourself. Many people who have experienced abuse carry an inner critic, often fuelled by the abusive parent's words or actions. Grieving in these circumstances involves, perhaps more than anything, releasing the hold that this relationship has over your self-worth and moving towards accepting that survival itself is an act of strength.

Ultimately, grieving an abusive parent can be a path of healing in unexpected ways. Processing this type of loss is deeply personal and whatever feelings come up – anger, sorrow, resentment, relief – are valid. Allowing space for these emotions, possibly with the support of a therapist or support group, can help in moving through grief towards healing and acceptance.

Saying goodbye to the peacock

Endings are important in life and the tradition of funerals, no matter your beliefs, will hold emotions, rituals, and societal behaviours which will bring forth an often urgent and public decision for those who are children of these parental peacocks.

Whether you attend the final farewell is always going to be a decision only you can make, and I hope there are people around you who will support whichever decision you choose. Your inner wisdom will know and there should be no judgement or need for justification. Here are the stories of two people who kindly contributed their experiences.

Priti: choosing absence for self-preservation

Priti was estranged from her father, a man whose narcissistic tendencies had dominated her childhood. He had belittled her achievements, ignored her emotional needs, and used manipulation to control her even into adulthood. While her family had been sympathetic to her experience, tradition and family pride had meant that there was an expectation for her to attend his funeral when the time came. When he passed away, Priti was faced with the decision of whether to attend his funeral, with 48 hours to decide. While she felt the draw of respect, culture, and judgement, she was also too far into her therapeutic work to consider abandoning herself lightly for others. After much reflection and consultation with her therapist, she chose not to go.

For Priti, the funeral represented not a moment of healing but a potential reopening of wounds. Many family members had long excused or minimized her father's behaviour, even some of her siblings, and she knew the event would most likely be filled with narratives that celebrated him while dismissing the harm he had caused. Instead of attending, Priti held her own private ritual to honour her journey. She lit a candle, wrote a letter expressing the pain and anger she had carried, and then burned it as an act of release of both her feelings and her father. By choosing absence, Priti was able to prioritize her mental health and affirm the boundaries she had worked so hard to establish. Though her decision was met with criticism and disdain by some family members, Priti found peace in staying true to herself.

Julian: attending for closure

Julian had a complicated relationship with his mother, who was emotionally abusive and narcissistic. She had a knack for making every situation about her, often at Julian's expense, and their dynamic left him feeling invisible and invalidated for much of his life – something that had affected his romantic relationships and even his relationship with his children at times. Despite their estrangement, Julian decided to attend her funeral when she passed, driven by a need to confront his emotions and seek closure.

At the funeral, Julian took a close friend with whom he had fully shared his experiences and they sat together in quiet reflection. He didn't speak during the service or engage with relatives who glorified his mother's memory. Instead, after the formalities, he visited her grave alone and spoke aloud the words he had long held back. He acknowledged the pain she had caused, the love he wished she could have given, and the resilience he had built despite her. Though the funeral did not provide resolution in the traditional sense, it offered Julian a sense of finality. He left feeling more grounded in his identity and more committed to his healing journey.

Both choices – whether to attend or abstain – reflect a deep engagement with personal needs and boundaries. Each path offers its own challenges and opportunities for growth, demonstrating that there is no single 'right' way to navigate the complexities of a parent's death.

Reclaiming the self after the goodbye

The aftermath of the death of a narcissistic parent can evoke a complex array of emotions. While there may be relief or freedom from a burdensome relationship, there can also be profound sadness, guilt, and confusion. The adult child might feel conflicted between mourning the loss and celebrating their newfound freedom from the long toxic relationship.

The process of grieving a narcissistic parent can be complicated by the nature of the relationship. The adult child might struggle with acknowledging and processing their grief as their relationship with the parent was fraught with emotional conflict. They may also face challenges in finding closure, given that narcissistic parents often leave their children with unresolved issues and unmet needs.

The death of a narcissistic parent can prompt an adult child to confront their sense of identity and self-worth. The parent's influence might have been so pervasive that the adult child has difficulty separating their identity from the expectations and demands imposed by the parent. This period can be a time of re-evaluating your sense of self and working towards self-discovery and healing.

Family dynamics and inheritance issues

Other challenges may arise, such as conflicts over inheritance and family dynamics. The narcissistic parent may have left behind a legacy of unresolved family disputes or financial complications. Navigating these issues can add stress and complexity to an already difficult emotional period. I have worked with individuals who, as the lost or scapegoated child, have been left out of the will or even been left an abusive letter from the parent. Equally, I have worked with many who have been gifted a sum of money and whose decision to accept this gift against the backdrop of the abuse inflicted churned up complex emotions.

My perspective on complicated or conflicted legacies is similar to that of when a client asks me what to do with their expensive engagement ring after a painful pre-marital breakup, and I often offer this thought: Sell the bauble and invest the money in something you will love in the way they should have loved you. Put right a little of what they did wrong and be proud of yourself for knowing better and doing it differently.

Setting boundaries and prioritizing self-care

Establishing and maintaining boundaries, both during the parent's illness and after their death, is crucial. Prioritizing self-care and acknowledging your needs and limits can help you as the adult child navigate the emotional complexities of the situation. Don't allow well-meaning relatives – or even those now feeling guilt that they stood by while you were abused – impact or advise you. With your true self now in place and your experience of the parent validated by yourself and witnessed by those who love you, protect your space by ensuring opinions can be offered by invitation only.

Processing and releasing guilt

It is important for the adult child to address and process feelings of guilt and responsibility. Recognizing that your feelings are valid and working through them can help in moving towards a healthier emotional state. Guilt is one of the most common emotions my clients express to me, fundamentally because you are registering a normalized response to a loved one dying and struggling to find the expected feelings of sadness and longing. But once again, remember, this was not your lived experience, and so with grace and elegance you can respect your truth by accepting your grief may look and feel different from that of those who had a different, more loving upbringing.

Seeking professional support

I've said it many times in this book – therapy and counselling can be invaluable in navigating the emotional challenges associated with an ill or deceased narcissistic parent. A mental health professional can provide support in processing feelings of guilt, grief, and confusion, and help the adult child develop strategies for self-care and healing. However, I say with my whole heart, please ensure you land in the safe hands of someone who has studied narcissism well. Working with a well-meaning therapist who does not understand the growing knowledge of this personality disorder and its impact can expose you to being misunderstood or misheard and I can tell you from experience that once you find someone who utterly understands, magic and healing can happen.

Conclusion

Whether your narcissistic parent is unwell or has passed away, there is often a sense of mourning not only the person but also the potential relationship that never was. With an estranged parent, you might grieve for the lost opportunities to connect, wondering if things could have been different, and of course the never-ending questions of 'why?' – which I hope you feel you now have a greater understanding of, from the early chapters. When it's a parent you disliked or even hated, the grief might stem from knowing the opportunity for closure is lost – knowing that any chance to confront them, forgive them, or gain a sense of justice is now gone.

Both types of grief can also bring deep feelings of resentment, disappointment, and unresolved anger to the surface. Losing a parent with whom you had a strained relationship can lead to a surge of old wounds and memories, as well as a sense of unfinished business. For some, these emotions can feel like a weight that the person leaves behind, complicating the path to healing. Both types of loss can also lead to a re-examination of self – questioning how their role in your life shaped you and to what extent you carry that influence forward.

Additionally, guilt might come from feeling relieved at their passing, or from the guilt of never having mended the relationship. There may also be a sense of shame in mourning someone you weren't close to or actively disliked, and society can sometimes reinforce this with a 'good riddance' attitude that may not reflect the whole reality of the emotional experience.

Ultimately, both types of grief require a way to process feelings without judgement. Losing any parent, regardless of the quality of the relationship, can have a profound emotional impact because it touches on the core of identity, family, and the formative years of your life.

I encourage you to embrace the life you now have ahead of you, with freedom and kindness and the inner knowledge that you survived. Don't allow historical abuse or cruelty to assume any more space or take up room in your life, your home, or your mind. It is over and you are free to live your life authentically without their shadow anymore. Be sad for the love you didn't receive, but be sure to know you deserved every ounce of it; they just didn't have it to give. Actively seek parental-type figures in your wider life who may now offer it with the generosity you've only dreamt of. You can put my name down on your list, for a start.

12

Freedom and fortitude

Our deepest fear is not that we are inadequate.
Our deepest fear is that we are powerful beyond measure.
It is our light, not our darkness
That most frightens us.
We ask ourselves
Who am I to be brilliant, gorgeous, talented, fabulous?
Actually, who are you not to be?
You are a child of God.
Your playing small
Does not serve the world.
There's nothing enlightened about shrinking
So that other people won't feel insecure around you.
We are all meant to shine,
As children do.
We were born to make manifest
The glory of God that is within us.
It's not just in some of us;
It's in everyone.
And as we let our own light shine,
We unconsciously give other people permission to do the same.
As we're liberated from our own fear,
Our presence automatically liberates others.

Marianne Williamson, from A Return to Love

Now that we are conscious of the levers in play and indeed our power to redirect our lives, there comes a moment, whether that be a crisis point, a crescendo in the level or frequency of episodes, or even an ultimatum from a loved one, when we may decide it is time finally to break the cycle we have felt forced to participate in often for many decades.

This bid for freedom may happen overnight, when your heart can truly take no more, or indeed you may have been preparing for this moment for months or even years – but you feel the call of the wild so clearly that you know it is time to make the break.

There is a persistent rumour that we may pass through this life-time only once and if that is the case, surely it is right and fair that we choose to live our lives in the best way we see fit. Accepting your inner adult self, you are at liberty to choose what, when, how, and why, and to bring fortitude and hard-won boundaries into practice to ensure you are free to live the life you deserve.

The freedom that comes with stepping away from the control, manipulation, and emotional drain of a narcissistic parent is profound. It is not just a relief from the constant tug-of-war for validation or the weight of their expectations – it is an open door to a life you were always meant to live. As a survivor, you now have something truly precious: time, energy, and the ability to direct your thoughts towards creating a future on your terms. This is your opportunity to reconnect with your soul's purpose and embrace the unique gifts you were born to share with the world.

Imagine the hours you once spent walking on eggshells, analysing their moods, or working out how to appease them. These are now yours to fill with dreams, aspirations, and actions that align with your truth. What will you do with this one wild and precious life? This is your moment to take a leap of faith into the life you've always envisioned but perhaps felt was out of reach. With the mental clarity and emotional space you now have, you can uncover what truly sets your soul on fire. Perhaps there's a creative passion that has always been calling to you – a song unsung, a story unwritten, a vision unexplored. Or maybe your heart longs to connect with others in a way that uplifts and heals, turning your experiences into a source of inspiration for those who walk similar paths.

Whatever it may be, know that you already possess the fortitude to pursue it. Surviving and healing from narcissistic abuse has cultivated within you a resilience that is nothing short of remarkable. You've already proven you can endure, adapt, and overcome. Now it's time to use that strength not just to survive but to thrive.

This journey now is about rediscovering your authentic self – the one untainted by the expectations and criticisms of a parent who could never truly see you for who you were and are. Spend time with yourself in reflection, in nature, or in activities that bring you joy. What values truly matter to you? What sparks a sense of wonder, fulfilment, or peace? Listen closely because your soul already knows the answers. It is guiding you towards the path you were always meant to walk.

Action is the bridge between dreams and reality, so take those first steps boldly. Sign up for that class, write that book, start that project, or travel to that place you've always longed to see. Let go of the fear that held you captive for so long. You are not confined by the narrative someone else imposed on you. You are free to author your own story, and it begins with the realization that your life is yours alone.

As you step forward, you'll find that freedom isn't just about what you leave behind – it's about what you gain. You gain a sense of purpose, a wellspring of creativity, and a deep connection to yourself. You are here for a reason. Embrace it. This is your one wild and precious life – live it fully, unapologetically, and with the courage of someone who knows the true meaning of liberation.

Letting go of responsibility

Letting go of the sense of responsibility for the emotions of a narcissistic parent (NP) is an act of self-liberation. It's like taking a deep, unburdened breath for the first time in years, realizing that the air has always been there, ready to fill your lungs with clarity and strength. This process is neither instant nor easy, given it may illuminate the co-dependency in play that will need care and attention, but it is absolutely worth it. Freeing yourself from this emotional tether doesn't mean abandoning compassion or respect, it means rediscovering where your responsibility ends and their choices begin. It's about reclaiming your emotional real estate and planting seeds of joy where guilt and obligation once grew.

Many of us who have grown up with a narcissistic parent have internalized the unspoken rule: their feelings matter more than ours. Narcissistic parents often weave intricate emotional narratives, positioning themselves as the perpetual victims or misunderstood heroes of their stories. As children, we're drawn into these stories, learning to anticipate their needs, smooth over their disappointments, and absorb their emotional outbursts as if it's our duty. But here's the liberating truth: it is not.

A parent's emotions are not your responsibility. Say it aloud. Write it down. Scribble it on a sticky note and slap it on your mirror if you have to. This isn't a declaration of selfishness, it's a statement of fact. When you let go of this false responsibility, you're not abandoning your parent or being cruel, you're simply stepping out of a role you

233

were never meant to play. The pleasure of relinquishing this burden can feel like stepping offstage after playing a role you were cast in without auditioning. It's exhilarating and slightly unnerving, but mostly, it's liberating. You may feel lighter, as though you've dropped an invisible backpack crammed with rocks. With time, you'll notice small joys creeping in: the delight of spending time with friends without guilt; the ease of saying 'no' without explaining; and the simple relief of not walking on eggshells every time you answer your phone. These are the pleasures of emotional autonomy.

Imagine what it's like to sip a morning coffee, not dreading a guilt-laden text or phone call. Picture the freedom of making choices based on your desires, not on how your parent might react. The colour of your days begins to change, like a washed-out photograph gradually regaining its vibrancy. The world feels bigger, more inviting. You're no longer a supporting character in someone else's drama, you're the star of your own story.

Resisting the pull back into old dynamics, though, can be challenging. Narcissistic parents are often skilled manipulators, deploying guilt, charm, or even outright rage to reel you back in. They might say things such as, 'After everything I've done for you,' or 'I guess I'm just a terrible parent.' These are baited hooks designed to tug at your well-worn sense of responsibility. But you don't have to take the bait. Building boundaries as we have discussed is your shield against manipulation. Think of boundaries as the locks on the doors to your mental and emotional house. Not everyone gets a key, and that's okay. Saying, 'I can't talk right now,' or 'I don't agree with that,' might feel foreign at first, like wearing a new pair of shoes. But with practice, it becomes second nature, and it's astonishing how empowering it can be to realize that you're allowed to enforce those boundaries without guilt.

Is change truly possible? Neuroscience offers us hope

With our advances in neuroscience and the wonderful job of Dr Joe Dispenza, we now have a greater understanding of the plasticity in the brain and with it the knowledge that we have the ability (to some degree) to rewire our brain. In a therapeutic sense we call it 'walking the cornfield'.

Imagine a dense cornfield that has no pathway. If we usually walk to work for example along the pavement but one day choose to change our route and cross a cornfield, we might have a very different experience. If we push through and walk from one end of the field to the other, initially it will be a rather arduous and tough task. Pushing aside the corn, finding stability underfoot, and avoiding too many scratches or even field rodents will all be part of the journey. This may bring you to regret taking a new path or indeed wondering whether you're doing the right thing. However, when you look back along your path you forged on day one, you may just about be able to make out the line you took across the field. Imagine, then, taking that path each day going forward for several weeks. In a short while that pathway becomes more defined as we approach it every day and a little more familiar. After we form a habit walking that way, the path would become clear and easy, and even identifiable from the air.

We have the power to find new pathways, but we have to start somewhere and know it will feel unfamiliar and even a little uncomfortable in the beginning. Expecting and tolerating that discomfort for a while is completely normal and in time the discomfort will disappear as your new pathway in this narcissistic family becomes your new normal.

Humour can be an unexpected ally in this journey. Narcissistic parents often take themselves very seriously, creating a heavy, oppressive atmosphere. By finding humour in the absurdity of some situations, you can lighten your emotional load. Imagine responding to a guilt trip with a light-hearted, 'Wow, you're really going for an Oscar with that performance!' (Even if you only say it in your head.) Humour doesn't diminish the seriousness of your boundaries, it reinforces your sense of control over your emotions.

Surrounding yourself with supportive people can make a world of difference. Whether it's friends, a therapist, or a support group, having allies who validate your experiences and encourage your growth is invaluable. These relationships remind you what healthy interactions look and feel like, making the contrast with toxic dynamics even clearer.

You may occasionally stumble. You might answer a manipulative phone call or fall into an old habit of over-explaining yourself. That's okay. Growth isn't linear, it's a messy, beautiful spiral. Each time you catch yourself and gently guide your actions back in line with your newfound freedom, you're reinforcing your progress. Celebrate these moments as victories because they are.

As you continue this journey, you might notice unexpected benefits. You'll start to recognize and appreciate your worth regardless of your parent's approval. You'll feel less anxious and more at peace. Your other relationships might even improve as you bring your healthier, more authentic self into them. Letting go of this misplaced responsibility doesn't just free you from your parent's grip, it frees you fully to live your own life.

Ultimately, the choice to let go of this responsibility is an act of love – love for yourself. It's a declaration that your feelings, your dreams, and your well-being matter. And they do. By releasing the weight of someone else's emotions, you're not only giving yourself permission to thrive, you're also demonstrating for others that it's okay to put themselves first. In this way, your courage becomes a ripple of change, inspiring those around you.

So, take the first step. Whether it's a boundary you've been hesitant to enforce or a guilt trip you've been silently enduring, choose one small action to reclaim your emotional freedom. And then another. You don't have to have all the answers right away. Just start. The path to liberation is built one brave moment at a time.

Breaking the generational patterns

Given you now appreciate the wonderful saying 'It ran in my family, until it ran into me,' you are now able to observe the NPD at play, appreciate how it has affected you and other members of your family, as well as the way the family dynamic has evolved, and through self-awareness and determination you can be sure to steer your own life and family in a different direction and will have achieved something that many generations before you have never mastered. The tribute to your suffering and the acknowledgement of all you have endured can be honoured in your developing and nurturing a family of your own which no longer holds the heartbreak and distortions of that which you endured under the fear or control of a narcissistic parent.

Managing the enablers

Dealing with enablers in a narcissistic family can feel like walking through a maze filled with emotional landmines. These individuals, often well meaning but misguided, may function as the narcissist's allies, urging you to re-engage, take sides, or 'keep the peace' for the sake of the family. Their attempts can be subtle – a quiet comment here, a guilt-laden question there – or overt, such as outright accusations of being ungrateful or unforgiving. Navigating these dynamics requires clarity, compassion, and an unwavering commitment to your freedom.

Enablers often act from a place of fear or denial. They may not fully grasp the damage caused by the narcissist's behaviour or may feel more comfortable maintaining the status quo. To confront the dysfunction would mean facing their own pain or complicity, which can be terrifying. In their minds, it's easier to pressure you into compliance than to challenge the narcissist or question the family's unhealthy dynamics. Recognizing this doesn't excuse their behaviour, but it can help you see their actions for what they are: a reflection of their own struggles, not a measure of your worth or the validity of your choices.

When enablers try to persuade you to re-engage, it's essential to ground yourself in your truth. Remember why you chose to distance yourself from the narcissist in the first place. You made this decision not out of spite or selfishness but to protect your well-being and reclaim your life. Let that truth be your anchor. You're not responsible for convincing the enabler to see things your way. Your only responsibility is to stay aligned with your boundaries and values. It's okay to acknowledge the enabler's perspective without letting it derail you. For instance, you might say, 'I understand that you want the family to get along, and I wish that were possible too. But I need to prioritize my mental health and emotional safety.' Statements such as these validate their feelings while reaffirming your stance. You're not attacking them, nor are you capitulating. You're simply stating your truth with calm confidence.

Handling enablers also requires accepting that you cannot control their journey. Some may eventually come to understand your perspective, while others may remain entrenched in denial or loyalty to the narcissist. It's not your job to open their eyes. Your job is to walk your path with integrity, trusting that clarity and healing will come to those who seek it in their own time.

Amidst the challenges, there is hope. By standing firm in your decisions, you model the courage and self-respect that enablers might one day find inspiring. You show them that it's possible to break free from toxic patterns, even if they're not ready to do so themselves. Your strength becomes a quiet beacon, a reminder that freedom and peace are within reach for anyone willing to pursue them.

Above all, remember that your journey is your own. It's not selfish to prioritize your well-being, it's necessary. The enablers may struggle to understand your choices, but that's okay. Their confusion doesn't diminish your clarity. You're choosing freedom, healing, and a life unshackled by the weight of dysfunction. Stay true to that choice and trust that in doing so, you're creating a brighter, healthier future – not just for yourself but for anyone brave enough to follow your example.

Transcending the abuse

Recovering from narcissistic abuse, particularly when it stems from a parent, is an arduous and deeply personal journey given it involves grappling with the betrayal, confusion, and shattering of the trust and bond that a parent–child relationship is supposed to embody. During this process, it is natural and even necessary to acknowledge the role of victimhood – to validate the pain, acknowledge the abuse, and seek to understand its impact. However, remaining entrenched in a victim mindset can hinder the healing process and limit the freedom we aspire to achieve.

Let me be clear. Viewing oneself as a victim serves an important purpose in the initial stages of recovery. It helps to name the injustice, establish boundaries, and gain clarity on the dynamics of the abuse. This perspective is often a critical step in reclaiming power and self-worth, especially for those who have endured gaslighting, manipulation, or emotional neglect. Embracing the idea that you were wronged allows you to validate your feelings and lay the groundwork for healing. However, as you grow stronger and begin to reconnect with your true self, holding onto the label of 'victim' can become a barrier rather than a bridge.

One reason to shun the sense of perpetual victimhood is that it anchors you to the past. Defining your identity solely through the lens of what happened to you gives undue power to the abuser and the trauma. It is crucial to remember that while the abuse is part of your story, it is not the entirety of it. To move forward, it is helpful to frame the experience as something you endured and overcame, not as something that continues to dictate your life and self-concept.

Moreover, adopting a mindset beyond victimhood empowers you to focus on your growth rather than your wounds. This shift enables you to embrace agency, responsibility, and the ability to shape your present and future. For instance, rather than dwelling on how the abuse limited you, you can explore how it shaped your resilience, empathy, or capacity for understanding. While this perspective doesn't diminish the harm done, it allows you to redefine the narrative of your life in terms of strength and recovery rather than pain and loss.

This transition also creates space to consider drawing a line under your experience as something that happened rather than something that defines you, fostering a sense of liberation. It allows you to step into the role of the survivor, a person who has faced adversity and emerged stronger. Survivorship is an active, for-ward-moving identity, contrasting with the passive connotations of victimhood. It shifts the focus from what was done to you to what you are doing now.

Finally, this mindset helps you reconnect with joy, purpose, and authenticity. When you stop viewing yourself through the lens of the abuse (and you must take as much time as you need in that feeling), you reclaim the freedom to explore who you are beyond that experi-ence. This includes your passions, relationships, and dreams, which are not defined by what happened to you but by the person you choose to reclaim and become.

The reality of voluntary adult orphans

Many of you may choose to find a healthy way to navigate some level of relationship with the narcissist in your life, with regular bound-aried contact, or an occasional deep dive with the support of your loved ones, therapists, and validating friends – but for some this can be an impossible task, certainly initially. So I wanted to honour those of you who have either lost contact or have no contact with their narcissist parent or choose to sever the ties that bind.

The term 'voluntary orphaning yourself' is often used to describe those who, as adults, choose to sever ties with their parents. For some adult children, the only path to reclaiming their sense of self and well-being is to take the drastic step of going no-contact. However, becoming an 'adult orphan' in this context is never an easy choice and carries its own complex layers of grief, loss, and stigma.

Breaking ties with a parent is not a decision made lightly. Society holds strong expectations about familial bonds, often promoting the idea that parents deserve unconditional respect and loyalty. For many, the choice to sever contact with a parent can feel counterintuitive and deeply painful. It is essential to educate others about the desperation and emotional toll that led someone to this point. No one opts for estrangement on a whim; it is often the result of years of trying to salvage the relationship, enduring cycles of abuse, and realizing that maintaining the connection is causing more harm than good.

When an adult child makes this decision, they are not just walking away from a toxic relationship – they are also confronting the loss of the parent they wish they had. This grief can be complicated because it is not simply about mourning the parent's absence but also the hope and potential for a healthier relationship that will never materialize. Grieving this loss is a necessary part of the healing process. It involves acknowledging the reality of the situation and allowing oneself to feel the sadness, anger, and betrayal that come with it.

It's also important to recognize that this path is not for everyone. Some adult children of narcissistic parents choose to maintain a relationship, whether for cultural, emotional, or personal reasons. They may find ways to set boundaries, minimize contact, or reframe their expectations to manage the relationship on their terms. This approach is equally valid and should not be judged or diminished. Everyone's circumstances and capacities for navigating these complex dynamics are different – there is no one-size-fits-all solution.

For those who do choose to step away, becoming an adult orphan can be a pathway to freedom and self-discovery. By removing the source of constant emotional harm, they can focus on rebuilding their lives, cultivating healthier relationships, and reconnecting with their authentic selves. It is not an easy road, but for some it is the critical step needed to break free from a cycle of pain and create a life that prioritizes their mental and emotional health. Studies indicate that estrangement can lead to significant relief and improved mental health, as individuals remove themselves from ongoing toxic dynamics and emotional manipulation. The reduction in stress and anxiety levels is a common benefit, allowing for the development of healthier self-esteem and greater personal autonomy.

However, the decision to break away also brings its own set of challenges, including feelings of guilt, societal stigma, and the loss of extended family connections. Estranged adults may experience a grieving process for the relationship they wish they had, and they often require strong social support and therapeutic intervention to navigate these emotions. Despite these difficulties, many find that the overall outcome is positive, with enhanced emotional well-being and the opportunity to build a life free from the harmful influence of their abusive parent.

Supporting someone who has made this choice means offering understanding rather than judgement. It requires acknowledging the courage it takes to make such a decision and the strength needed to navigate the accompanying grief. By educating others about the complexities of this experience, we can foster greater compassion and reduce the stigma surrounding estrangement.

Ultimately, whether one chooses to cut ties or stay connected, the goal is the same: to find a path forward that honours one's well-being and authenticity. The journey is deeply personal, and both choices deserve respect and support.

Self-reparenting

Self-reparenting is a therapeutic process through which you can nurture and heal your inner child by providing yourself with the care, validation, and support you may not have received from your parents but you know you would provide for others. This involves developing self-compassion, setting healthy boundaries, and engaging in self-care practices that promote emotional well-being. Techniques such as inner-child work, where you begin to visualize and communicate with your younger self, can help address your unmet needs and unresolved trauma. By cultivating a nurturing internal dialogue and practising self-compassion, you can reframe negative beliefs and foster a sense of security and self-worth. Self-reparenting empowers you to break free from past conditioning, build resilience, and create a more fulfilling and balanced emotional life. It starts by you talking to yourself as you would a young child who is wounded – gentle enquiry, regular check-ins – putting your hand on your heartspace and simply asking, 'How are you doing?' and listening hard for the true answer.

Finding qualities of a good parent in others

In addition to self-reparenting, I encourage you to seek out and cultivate relationships with individuals who embody the qualities of a good parent. This could include friends, mentors, therapists, or supportive community members who provide empathy, encouragement, and stability. Such relationships offer opportunities for you to experience unconditional positive regard, constructive feedback, and a sense of belonging. By surrounding yourself with nurturing and trustworthy individuals, you can create a support network that helps to fill the gaps left by your parental figures. These relationships can provide new models of healthy interaction, enabling you to internalize positive relational patterns and further your emotional growth and healing. Engaging with these supportive figures can help reframe past experiences and contribute to a more positive self-concept and outlook on your life.

Awareness of others less healed

One of the other challenges you will undoubtedly face comes from family members or other survivors who hold a different strategy or belief system to you. They may question your methods, behaviours, and beliefs and equally feel intimidated by your ability to hold your own in a way they may never feel able to accomplish. They may also be recruited into the flying monkey position, used as go-betweens and influencers on behalf of the narcissist parent, or indeed, while fully seeing the situation for what it is, are so terrified, bullied or simply fed up with the antics of the NP that they simply want you to 'do your bit' to keep the peace for the wider family.

Life is full of moments, incidents, and of course eventualities which each time can pose the question of whether, and to what level, you want to, need to, or should engage or re-engage with the NP. Existential moments such as illness, accidents, aging, and impending death can truly bring into focus the question and pull of conversation and contact. Each time, the allure of the peacock feather, symbolizing hopes of repair, acknowledgement, apology, even love and care before the moment is no longer available, will brush against your heart. Only you can make that decision based on what you need and how you can cope. Each and every person will need to manage it differently, but always remember you are free to make your own choice.

Equally, moments of happiness, such as the birth of a child, a new home, a promotion at work, your own children's triumphs and special days, will naturally be a time for you still to hold that hope that 'if only we were in a normal family' things could be so different. To your child, grandma or grandad (or auntie or uncle) might seem perfectly wonderful, but you hold the parental position and will decide what you genuinely think is best for your family.

Siblings especially can find it difficult to adhere to your boundaries and you may come under pressure to 'give everyone a good family Christmas' or 'call mum on her birthday' when you know deep down that the risk of further damage to you is enough to justify maintaining your boundary and protection.

Research such as that by Katherine A. Lammers (2014) indicates that narcissistic parents often use money and inheritance as tools of manipulation to maintain control over their adult children. By leveraging financial dependency and the promise or threat of inheritance, these parents create an environment where their children feel obligated to comply with their demands all through their lives, even long after they are married or parents themselves. Studies have shown that narcissistic parents frequently use economic means to exert power and manipulate relationships. For instance, they might offer financial support conditionally (such as to pay for their grandchildren's schooling), reinforcing compliance and punishing any perceived defiance. This financial manipulation can lead to a profound sense of obligation and guilt in adult children, making it difficult once again for them to establish independence and boundaries. Furthermore, the unpredictability of inheritance promises keeps the children in a state of anxiety and dependence, ensuring the narcissistic parent's influence remains intact.

As narcissistic parents age and face illness, their manipulation tactics often intensify and they may use their health and impending mortality as additional leverage. They might exaggerate their medical needs or play the victim to elicit sympathy and ensure their children's constant attention and care. This behaviour is rooted in their need for control and validation, which does not diminish with age. Research such as that by M. L. Roberts and P. J. Trull (2003) suggests that personality disorders, including narcissism, are resistant to change over time, with less than 10 per cent of individuals showing significant improvement in their traits as they age. Consequently, the likelihood of a narcissistic parent changing their manipulative behaviour in old age is remarkably low. Instead, these parents may become more entrenched in their patterns, continuing to exploit their vulnerabilities and health conditions to manipulate their adult children until the end of their lives.

Sometimes writing can be a softer landing place if you do feel the desire or need to acknowledge the NP in some way, like feeding a lion from a distance, and, again, there is no right or wrong here but only options as you begin to live your life, free of the ties that bound you to unhappiness and despair.

A word on forgiveness

From an incredibly young age we are taught to learn to forgive, that to carry anger is poisoning us. We are told that blood is thicker than water and therefore we must find a way to forgive and to be the bigger person. People around you, from well-meaning friends to other members of your family, possibly even siblings, may appeal to you to 'bury the hatchet' when parents start to age, or become ill or infirm, and when our sense of guilt and even shame can cause us to question whether we are being too harsh, selfish, or even stubborn. This may especially be the case when your distance from the NP has meant you no longer suffer in the way you did in the past and the distance has improved your sense of self.

Sadly, so often, the moment you are once again in close proximity, the NP will revert to their old ways of behaving and before long you are having to reinstate the boundary and repeat the painful process of distancing.

I would like to offer you an alternative perspective. If we are to appreciate and accept we are made up of many parts, sub-personalities if you like (including our inner child, our critical parent, our naughty, or ambitious, or fearful or aggressive selves, for example), there are multiple feelings, perspectives, and outlooks all at play, sometimes in harmony but other times conflicting within. This idea is an element of the incredible work of Dr Richard Schwartz (1995), referred to as Internal Family Systems, in which he identified we have many 'parts' in trauma, called 'protector parts', which are activated when under stress:

- manager parts (the bossy or organized parts that like to take control)
- firefighter parts (the parts that get you out of actual or perceived trouble or danger)
- exiled parts (the parts we find uncomfortable, foreign, or were shamed).

INTERNAL FAMILY SYSTEMS™

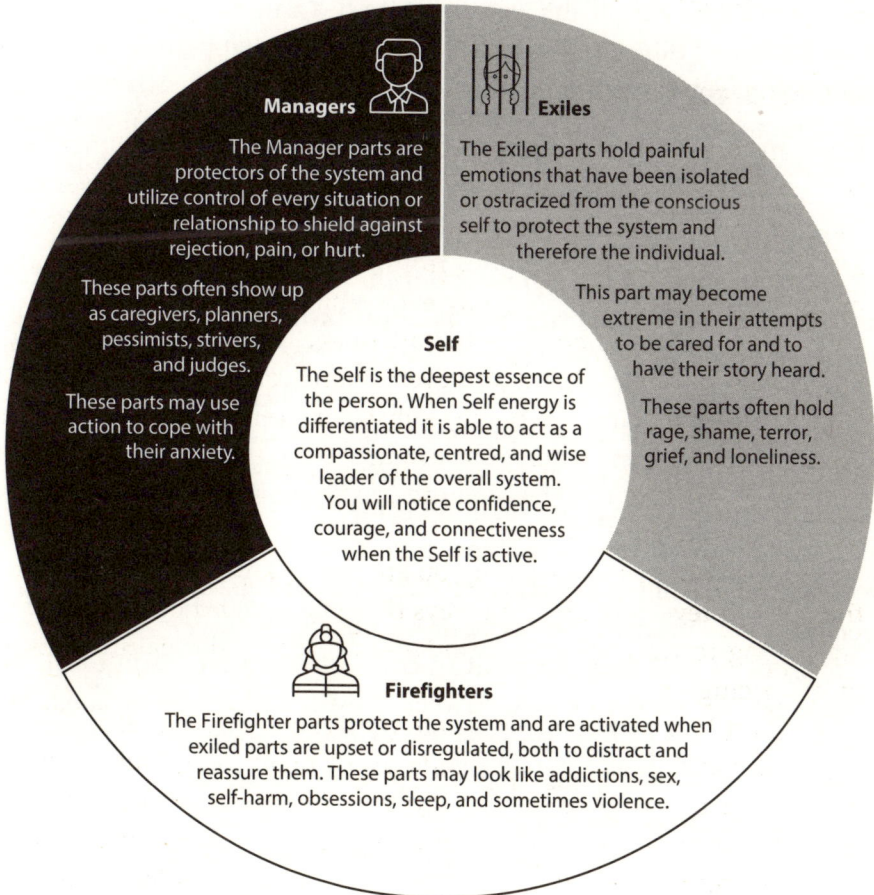

Managers

The Manager parts are protectors of the system and utilize control of every situation or relationship to shield against rejection, pain, or hurt.

These parts often show up as caregivers, planners, pessimists, strivers, and judges.

These parts may use action to cope with their anxiety.

Exiles

The Exiled parts hold painful emotions that have been isolated or ostracized from the conscious self to protect the system and therefore the individual.

This part may become extreme in their attempts to be cared for and to have their story heard.

These parts often hold rage, shame, terror, grief, and loneliness.

Self

The Self is the deepest essence of the person. When Self energy is differentiated it is able to act as a compassionate, centred, and wise leader of the overall system. You will notice confidence, courage, and connectiveness when the Self is active.

Firefighters

The Firefighter parts protect the system and are activated when exiled parts are upset or disregulated, both to distract and reassure them. These parts may look like addictions, sex, self-harm, obsessions, sleep, and sometimes violence.

Figure 12.1 Internal Family Systems

Source: Richard C. Schwartz, PhD
Internal Family Systems™ and IFS™ are trademarks of the IFS Institute and used here with permission.

Dr Schwartz's framework offered us the idea that we need to manage these parts in order to become conscious of what we are thinking or feeling and utilize that to our advantage. Getting the parts into dialogue and at times negotiation with each other can allow you to have smoother internal dialogue and to get ahead of the limbic knee-jerk reactions from each part, instead creating a more co-ordinated response. We saw this at work in Izzy's case study when she accessed the different parts of herself. Her parentified child part was used to being in charge and getting her own way, yet there was an inner child mourning her mother, and firefighter parts causing arguments with females towards whom she was diverting her anger at her parents. All these parts had differing feelings about what was happening and what to do about it. In getting her parts into dialogue with each other she was able to see what was truly happening and to utilize all her parts to make better sense of the truth and offer her choice in how she responded going forward.

With this in mind, then, there will be a number of parts that are very certain they are not happy about the way they have been treated and they are relying on the overall adult protector parts to stand up for them and ensure they are now looked after. If the adult protector part within you too easily rolls over and accepts poor treatment once again, imagine how your unhappy inner child or exiled parts will want to react. This is when you risk starting your own journey of cognitive dissonance! So, tune in, and decide.

If we simply forgive time and time again, despite how we truly feel, we are in some way betraying ourselves and abandoning the very person we are meant to love the most: ourselves.

Each of us will find our limit to coping with a NP – some will be able to see the parent every day/week/month and ignore or laugh off the constant complaints, suggestions, rudeness, appeals, guilt trips, or pleas, but some people may have decided to cut off all together. If we were then to break the boundary for fear of abandoning this parent, we are in fact simply abandoning ourselves and in doing so we can undo all the work of protecting ourselves and finding clarity over what is okay for us.

Black-and-white thinking, as we have already discussed, is not necessarily helpful and indeed there is no template to follow – you will know what you need to be true to yourself. But fundamentally, if you know in your heart, and have witnessed your NP being able to behave in front of others in a way that is acceptable, then you must accept they have control over the way they behave towards you and, therefore, they are choosing to mistreat you, still.

So, choice is once again residing in your hands. You and you alone can decide whether forgiveness is something you wish to consider, or revisit from time to time, even in the final days or weeks of their life. But remember, you are the prize and you deserve to be treated with kindness, and love is critical.

Parents who seem to find their way to putting us down, questioning our decisions, parading us around like prized possessions, or those who are to be observed and obeyed, have no jurisdiction over how you respond, react, or indeed behave. From the time you reach the age of 18 they have no legal power over you and now the power is purely in your hands.

Return to love

As you close this chapter and this book and step into the next phase of your life, remember that reclaiming your power and establishing healthy boundaries is not only an act of self-love but also a declaration of your inherent worth. Your narcissistic parent, much like a peacock, may have dazzled and distracted with grand displays, seeking to overshadow your light, but now it is time for you to shine, not in their reflected glory but in the brilliance of your true self.

Embrace the courage and resilience you have cultivated through this journey. Know that your worth is not dependent on their validation, and your strength lies in your ability to set boundaries that honour your needs and aspirations.

As you navigate this path, hold steadfast to the knowledge that you deserve peace, respect, and a life free from manipulation. May this be the beginning of a future where your true voice is heard, your boundaries respected, and your spirit unburdened. Stand tall, as you were always meant to, and let your true colours illuminate the world.

I wish you the utmost fortitude in your brave and ongoing discovery and I send you my heartfelt love in your healing and lasting recovery.

Go well.

Further materials and resources

Key contributors

Over the last 30 years, many contributors have significantly shaped how we comprehend, identify and address narcissistic behaviour. Here's an overview of some of the most influential figures and their key contributions.

W. Keith Campbell

W. Keith Campbell is a leading researcher in the study of narcissism and has collaborated extensively with Jean Twenge. His work focuses on the psychological mechanisms underlying narcissistic traits and their consequences. Campbell's research contributes to a deeper understanding of the personality disorder and its impacts on interpersonal relationships and social behaviour.

Significant contributions

Campbell co-authored *The Narcissism Epidemic* (2010), which examines how narcissistic behaviour is influenced by social and cultural factors and discusses its broader implications for society.

Narcissism and Social Media: A Review and Future Directions (2014) explores the relationship between narcissism and social media use, suggesting that platforms such as Facebook and Instagram may exacerbate narcissistic traits.

The Relationship Between Narcissism and Self-Esteem: A Meta-Analysis (2007) provides insight into how narcissistic self-views are linked to broader self-esteem issues.

Prof. Sam Vaknin

Sam Vaknin is a prominent figure in the field of narcissism, primarily known for his extensive writing and expertise on Narcissistic Personality Disorder. His work is particularly noted for its detailed and sometimes provocative exploration of narcissism from both a clinical and a personal perspective.

Significant contributions

Vaknin's book *Malignant Self-Love: Narcissism Revisited* (1999) remains a seminal text in the study of narcissism. Although published just before the turn of the millennium, its influence persisted into the 2000s due to its comprehensive examination of narcissistic traits and behaviours.

Vaknin's approach is unique in that it combines personal anecdotes with clinical observations, offering a first-person perspective on the disorder. His writing often critiques mainstream psychological approaches and provides a provocative analysis of narcissism's impact on relationships and society.

Narcissism: A Disorder of the Self (2006) expands on Vaknin's previous analyses, offering a deeper exploration of the disorder and its effects on individuals and those around them.

Vaknin's contributions are often discussed in the context of debates about the clinical accuracy and ethical considerations of his approaches, particularly his self-identification as a narcissist and his critiques of other psychological perspectives.

Dr Ramani Durvasula

Dr Ramani Durvasula is a clinical psychologist and professor known for her work on Narcissistic Personality Disorder and her efforts to make this topic accessible to a broader audience. Her contributions are particularly valuable in both academic and popular settings, bridging the divide between clinical research and practical advice.

Significant contributions

Dr Durvasula's book *Should I Stay or Should I Go? Surviving a Relationship with a Narcissist* (2015) provides a practical guide for individuals dealing with narcissistic partners. It combines clinical insights with actionable advice, making it a valuable resource for those affected by narcissism in personal relationships.

Dr Durvasula's work also emphasizes the importance of understanding narcissism in various contexts, including its impact on family dynamics and professional environments. Her approach is rooted in both empirical research and real-world experience, providing a well-rounded perspective on managing narcissistic behaviour.

Her *It's Not You: Identifying and Healing from Narcissistic People* (2024), offers targeted advice developed through years of clinical experience and research. The book aims to help readers recognize narcissistic behaviours, resist gaslighting, break trauma bonds, establish healthy boundaries and recover their sense of self after enduring invalidation. By shifting the focus from self-blame, Dr Durvasula empowers individuals to become the solution in their healing journey.

Jean Twenge

Jean Twenge is a prominent psychologist known for her extensive research on narcissism, particularly within generational cohorts. Her influential book *Generation Me: Why Today's Young Americans Are More Confident, Assertive, Entitled – and More Miserable Than Ever Before* (2006) explores the rise in narcissistic traits in younger generations. Twenge's work is pivotal in understanding how cultural and societal changes contribute to increased narcissism, especially among Millennials and Gen Z.

Significant contributions
Twenge's research often relies on large-scale surveys and psychological assessments. Her findings suggest that contemporary generations exhibit higher levels of narcissistic traits compared with previous ones, largely due to societal shifts towards individualism and self-esteem-focused parenting.

Christopher J. Graver

Christopher J. Graver is known for his work on the clinical aspects of narcissism and how it manifests in therapeutic settings. His research focuses on effective methods for treating NPD and understanding its nuances in clinical practice.

Significant contributions
Graver's contributions are valuable for professionals seeking to identify and manage narcissistic traits in therapeutic contexts.

The Clinical Characteristics of Narcissistic Personality Disorder: Insights from Recent Research (2012) offers an updated overview of clinical features and treatment strategies for NPD.

Treatment Approaches for Narcissistic Personality Disorder (2017) is a review of therapeutic techniques and their efficacy in treating individuals with high levels of narcissism.

Eli J. Finkel

Eli J. Finkel's work focuses on the broader implications of narcissism in personal relationships and social contexts. His research often explores how narcissism affects romantic relationships, marriage and interpersonal dynamics.

Significant contributions

Finkel's work provides a comprehensive look at how narcissistic traits impact not only individuals but also their relationships with others.

Narcissism and Relationship Quality: Insights from Recent Studies (2013) examines how narcissistic traits influence the quality and stability of personal relationships.

The Impact of Narcissism on Marital Satisfaction: A Longitudinal Study (2015) explores how narcissistic behaviours affect marital satisfaction over time.

Emily L. P. Brown

Emily L. P. Brown's research delves into the societal and cultural factors that influence narcissism. Her work often intersects with issues of identity, culture and social media, providing a contextual understanding of how narcissism develops and manifests in twenty-first-century society.

Significant contributions

Brown's contributions are essential for understanding the interplay between narcissism and modern cultural trends.

Cultural Influences on Narcissism: A Review and Analysis (2018) investigates how cultural values and norms contribute to the prevalence of narcissistic traits.

Social Media and Narcissistic Behaviour: An Analysis of Online Self-Presentation (2020) explores the relationship between social media use and the development of narcissistic behaviours.

Melanie Joy

Melanie Joy's research focuses on the psychological and emotional aspects of narcissism in the context of relationships and personal identity. Her work often intersects with broader psychological concepts and provides insight into managing and understanding narcissistic behaviours.

Significant contributions

Joy's contributions, particularly *Understanding Narcissistic Dynamics in Personal Relationships* (2014), provide a detailed examination of how narcissistic traits affect personal and professional relationships.

Managing Narcissistic Behaviour: Strategies and Techniques (2019) offers practical advice for managing interactions with narcissistic individuals.

Robert C. Cramer

Robert C. Cramer's research focuses on the evolutionary and biological underpinnings of narcissistic behaviour. His work seeks to understand the genetic and neurobiological factors that contribute to narcissistic traits.

Significant contributions

Cramer's research is crucial for exploring the biological aspects of narcissism and its implications for treatment and understanding.

The Genetic Basis of Narcissistic Traits: A Review of Recent Findings (2020) examines the role of genetics in the development of narcissistic traits.

Neurobiological Correlates of Narcissistic Personality Disorder (2022) explores how brain structure and function relate to narcissistic behaviours.

John D. Mayer

John D. Mayer is known for his work on emotional intelligence and its relationship to narcissism. His research explores how emotional intelligence can influence and mitigate narcissistic behaviours. Mayer's work is important for developing strategies to manage narcissism and enhance emotional awareness.

Significant contributions

Emotional Intelligence and Narcissism: An Analysis of Their Relationship (2016) investigates how emotional intelligence affects narcissistic traits and behaviours.

Improving Emotional Intelligence to Manage Narcissistic Traits (2019) offers insights into how enhancing emotional intelligence can address and reduce narcissistic tendencies.

Conclusion

The study of narcissism has evolved significantly over the past two decades, thanks to the contributions of these influential researchers. Their work has advanced our understanding of narcissism from various perspectives: cultural, clinical, relational and biological. Each has provided valuable insights into how narcissism manifests itself, its impact on individuals and society, and effective strategies for managing and mitigating its effects.

Further reading on narcissism

It's Not You – Dr Ramani Durvasula (2024)
Malignant Self-Love Revisited – Prof. Sam Vaknin (2003)
You're Not the Problem – Helen Villiers and Katie McKenna (2024)
Raised by Narcissists – Dr Sarah Davies (2024)
Adult Children of Emotionally Immature Parents – Lindsay C. Gibson PsyD (2015)
Silently Seduced: When Parents Make Their Children Partners – Kenneth M. Adams PhD (2011)
Will I Ever Be Good Enough? Healing the Daughters of Narcissistic Mothers – Karyl McBride (2008)
Understanding Parental Alienation: Learning to Cope, Helping to Heal – Karen Woodhall and Nick Woodhall (2017)

The Covert Passive-Aggressive Narcissist: Recognizing the Traits and Finding Healing After Hidden Emotional and Psychological Abuse – Debbie Mirza (2017)

Rethinking Narcissism: The Secret to Recognizing and Coping with Narcissists – Craig Malkin (2015)

The New Science of Narcissism: Understanding One of the Greatest Psychological Challenges of Our Time—and What You Can Do About It – Keith W. Campbell and Carolyn Crist (2020)

Further reading on reclaiming the self

The Untethered Soul: The Journey Beyond Yourself – Michael A. Singer (2007)
Internal Family Systems – Richard C. Schwartz (1997)
No Bad Parts – Richard C. Schwartz (2021)
The Drama of the Gifted Child – Alice Miller (1979)
Codependent No More – Melody Beattie (1986)
Attached – Amir Levine and Rachel Heller (2010)
A Game Free Life – Stephen B. Karpman, MD (2014)
The Body Keeps the Score – Bessel van der Kolk, MD (2014)

Further reading on therapeutic techniques discussed

Dr Tronicks Still Face Experiment: https://www.youtube.com/watch?v=f1Jw0-LExyc

Empty chair and two-chair Gestalt technique: https://www.mental-health.com/library/gestalt-therapy-the-empty-chair-technique

The Karpman Drama Triangle: https://karpmandramatriangle.com/

Internal Family Systems framework: https://ifs-institute.com/resources/articles/internal-family-systems-model-outline

Alchemical process of transformation – citing Nigel Hamilton: https://www.ingrid-dengg.at/sites/ingrid-dengg.at/files/attachments/alchemy.pdf

True and False Self – Winnicott Theory: https://www.youtube.com/watch?v=A02Ucd6monY

Family constellations framework: https://www.hellinger.com/en/family-constellation/

Window of tolerance: https://drdansiegel.com/

Neuroplasticity: https://drjoedispenza.com/dr-joes-blog/evolve-your-brain

Glossary of narcissistic abuse terms (DARVO/enablers/trauma bond, etc.): https://mynara.app/glossary

Top podcasts on narcissism and recovery

Narcissist Apocalypse: Patterns of Abuse

Description: This podcast features survivor stories, providing insights into various forms of narcissistic abuse and offering support to those affected.

Platform: Available on Spotify and Apple Podcasts.

Link: Narcissist Apocalypse on Spotify – https://open.spotify.com/show/3MYWa9mrMlN3FSTLiFkK7F

In Sight – Exposing Narcissism

Description: Hosted by Katie McKenna and Helen Villiers, this podcast delves into topics related to narcissism, parentification and emotional abuse, aiming to empower listeners through psychoeducation.

Platform: Available on Apple Podcasts.

Link: In Sight – Exposing Narcissism on Apple Podcasts – https://podcasts.apple.com/us/podcast/in-sight-exposing-narcissism/id1613030538

Trauma & Narcissism Redefined

Description: This podcast explores the intricacies of trauma and narcissism, offering insights into the narcissistic abuse cycle and strategies for healing.

Platform: Available on Spotify.

Link: Trauma & Narcissism Redefined on Spotify – https://open.spotify.com/show/6nVRF6t2Eg4XlQHkYjMlWU

Waking Up to Narcissism

Description: Hosted by Tony Overbay, LMFT, this podcast helps individuals recognize and navigate narcissistic traits in their relationships and within themselves, focusing on emotional immaturity and personal growth.

Platform: Available on Apple Podcasts and Spotify.

Link: Waking Up to Narcissism on Apple Podcasts – https://podcasts.apple.com/us/podcast/waking-up-to-narcissism/id1582045099

The Covert Narcissism Podcast

Description: This podcast focuses on understanding covert narcissism, offering support and insights for those affected by covert narcissistic individuals.

Platform: Available on Apple Podcasts and Spotify.

Link: The Covert Narcissism Podcast on Apple Podcasts – https://podcasts.apple.com/us/podcast/the-covert-narcissism-podcast/id1566895530

Navigating Narcissism with Dr Ramani

Description: Hosted by Dr Ramani Durvasula, a renowned clinical psychologist, this podcast delves into the complexities of narcissistic relationships and offers guidance on navigating them.

Platform: Available on Apple Podcasts and Spotify.

Link: Navigating Narcissism on Apple Podcasts – https://podcasts.apple.com/us/podcast/navigating-narcissism-with-dr-ramani/id1629909313

The Narcissistic Abuse & Trauma Recovery Podcast

Description: This podcast provides insights and strategies for recovering from narcissistic abuse and trauma, aiming to empower survivors on their healing journey.

Platform: Available on Apple Podcasts and Spotify.

Link: The Narcissistic Abuse & Trauma Recovery Podcast on Apple Podcasts – https://podcasts.apple.com/us/podcast/welcome-to-the-narcissistic-abuse-trauma-recovery-podcast/id1527479270?i=1000487939888

The Narcissist in Your Life Podcast

Description: Hosted by Linda Martinez-Lewi, PhD, this podcast explores the intricacies of narcissistic personality disorder and offers guidance for those dealing with narcissists in their lives.

Platform: Available on Apple Podcasts and Spotify.

Link: The Narcissist in Your Life Podcast on Apple Podcasts – https://podcasts.apple.com/us/podcast/the-narcissist-in-your-life-podcast/id1278783469

Top YouTube channels for narcissism recovery

Dr Ramani – Hosted by clinical psychologist Dr Ramani Durvasula, this channel provides in-depth discussions on narcissistic personality disorder and strategies for healing. https://www.youtube.com/doctorramani

Surviving Narcissism – Led by Dr Les Carter, this channel helps viewers understand narcissism and establish healthy boundaries in relationships. https://www.youtube.com/c/SurvivingNarcissism

Inner Integration – Hosted by Meredith Miller, this channel focuses on healing from narcissistic abuse with practical recovery tools. https://www.youtube.com/c/InnerIntegration

Narcissistic Abuse Healing – This covers narcissistic tactics, terminology and the effects of abuse to support survivors on their healing journey. https://www.youtube.com/channel/UCI6yC6no7mJxOjqt43KYhHA

The School of Life – While not exclusively about narcissism, this channel explores psychology and relationships to help people navigate toxic dynamics. https://www.youtube.com/c/theschooloflifetv

Sam Vaknin – A professor of psychology and the author of *Malignant Self-Love*, Sam Vaknin's channel offers deep insights into narcissism from an academic and experiential perspective. https://www.youtube.com/c/samvaknin

Jerry Wise Relationship Systems – Jerry Wise, a self-differentiation expert and relationship coach, provides guidance on breaking free from narcissistic abuse patterns. https://www.youtube.com/c/JerryWiseRelationshipSystems

Jill Wise (The Enlightened Target) – Jill Wise shares personal experiences and professional insights on healing from narcissistic abuse. https://www.youtube.com/c/TheEnlightenedTarget

Jim Brillon – This therapist shares insights on narcissistic relationships and how to recover from emotional abuse. https://www.youtube.com/@JimBrillon

Emily Gibson & Co – This channel offers a mix of personal stories, psychological insights and practical recovery strategies for those affected by narcissistic abuse. https://www.youtube.com/@emilygibsonandco

Charliechalk12 on TikTok – This brainspotting therapist and narcissistic abuse survivor is the most pioneering and refreshing new contributor in this space. Worth a follow. https://www.tiktok.com/@charliechalk12

Karenwoodhall.blog – Karen Woodhall's blog is a vital resource for raising awareness about the harmful effects of parental alienation on children. Worth subscribing. https://karenwoodall.blog/

Scholarly articles on narcissism

These papers provide a comprehensive overview of various aspects of Narcissistic Personality Disorder, including its diagnosis, clinical challenges, underlying dimensions and treatment approaches.

'Pathological Narcissism and Narcissistic Personality Disorder'

Authors: Aaron L. Pincus and Mark R. Lukowitsky

Journal: Annual Review of Clinical Psychology, 2010

Summary: This paper provides a comprehensive review of pathological narcissism, discussing its manifestations, assessment methods and implications for NPD diagnosis. https://scholar.google.com/citations?hl=en&user=yo7DcKMyMoUC&utm_source=chatgpt.com

'Narcissistic Personality Disorder: Diagnostic and Clinical Challenges'

Authors: Eve Caligor, Kenneth N. Levy and Frank E. Yeomans

Journal: American Journal of Psychiatry, 2015

Summary: The authors explore the complexities in diagnosing NPD, highlighting the challenges clinicians face and proposing strategies for effective assessment. https://scholar.google.com/citations?hl=en&user=YistH8oAAAAJ&utm_source=chatgpt.com

'Narcissistic Grandiosity and Narcissistic Vulnerability'

Authors: Aaron L. Pincus and Michael J. Roche

Book: The Handbook of Narcissism and Narcissistic Personality Disorder, 2011

Summary: This chapter delves into the dual dimensions of narcissism – grandiosity and vulnerability – and their relevance to NPD. https://scholar.google.com/citations?hl=en&user=sDEzcb-wAAAAJ&utm_source=chatgpt.com

'Distinguishing Between Grandiose Narcissism, Vulnerable Narcissism, and Narcissistic Personality Disorder'

Authors: Brandon Weiss, Aidan G. C. Wright and Aaron L. Pincus

Journal: Clinical Psychology Review, 2019

Summary: The study differentiates between the subtypes of narcissism and discusses their unique clinical presentations and implications for NPD. https://scholar.google.com/citations?hl=en&user=U9hrWm0AAAAJ&utm_source=chatgpt.com

'A Comparison of the Criterion Validity of Popular Measures of Narcissism and Narcissistic Personality Disorder Via the Use of Expert Ratings'

Authors: Joshua D. Miller, Lauren R. Few and W. Keith Campbell

Journal: Psychological Assessment, 2010

Summary: This research evaluates the effectiveness of various narcissism assessment tools in accurately diagnosing NPD. https://scholar.google.com/citations?hl=en&user=aYorz5IAAAA-J&utm_source=chatgpt.com

'A Historical Review of Narcissism and Narcissistic Personality'

Authors: Kenneth N. Levy, William D. Ellison and Joseph S. Reynoso

Book: The Handbook of Narcissism and Narcissistic Personality Disorder, 2011

Summary: This chapter offers a comprehensive historical overview of the concept of narcissism and the evolution of NPD as a clinical diagnosis. https://scholar.google.com/citations?hl=en&user=6WGVJIUAAAAJ&utm_source=chatgpt.com

Narcissistic recovery support groups

Recovering from relationships with narcissists can be challenging, but numerous support groups are available both in-person and online to assist individuals on this journey. Below is a curated list of notable support groups in the UK, the US and globally, categorized by in-person and online options.

United Kingdom

In-person support groups:

- **London Narcissistic Trauma & Abuse Survivor Support Group:** A group offering a safe space for survivors to share experiences and support each other in healing from narcissistic abuse. https://www.meetup.com/topics/narcissism-survivor/gb/?utm_source=chatgpt.com

Online support groups:

- **Victims of Narcissistic Abuse (MyNARA) Support Group:** A Facebook community providing support and resources for

individuals affected by narcissistic abuse. https://www.facebook.com/groups/1173575726175953/?utm_source=chatgpt.com
- **MyNARA App:** A professionally guided domestic abuse recovery app designed for those in relationships with narcissists, offering resources and support for recovery. https://mynara.app/?utm_source=chatgpt.com

United States

In-person support groups:

- **Survivors of Narcissistic Abuse & Codependency Support Group:** A group providing a platform for individuals to share their experiences and support each other in overcoming narcissistic abuse and co-dependency. https://www.meetup.com/find/?source=GROUPS&keywords=Survivors%20of%20Narcissistic%20Abuse%20%26%20Codependency%20Support%20Group&distance=twentyFiveMiles
- **Reclaim Your Life After Narcissistic Abuse:** Focused on helping individuals reclaim their lives post-abuse, a group offering support and resources for healing. https://www.meetup.com/find/?source=GROUPS&keywords=Reclaim%20Your%20Life%20After%20Narcissistic%20Abuse&distance=twentyFiveMiles

Online support groups:

- **Survivors of Narcissistic Abuse – Recovery and Support Group:** An online community where survivors can connect, share their stories and support each other through the recovery process. https://www.meetup.com/find/?source=GROUPS&keywords=Survivors%20of%20Narcissistic%20Abuse%20%E2%80%93%20Recovery%20and%20Support%20Group&distance=twentyFiveMiles

Global

Online support groups:

- **Narcissism Survivor Groups on Meetup:** Meetup hosts various groups worldwide dedicated to supporting survivors of narcissistic abuse. Members can find both in-person and online meetings tailored to their needs. https://www.meetup.com/find/?source=GROUPS&keywords=Narcissism%20Survivor

• **Overcoming Narcissism: The Narcissistic Abuse Conference:** An annual conference that brings together experts and survivors globally to share insights, strategies and support for overcoming narcissistic abuse. https://www.overcomingnarcissism.com/?utm_source=chatgpt.com

When seeking support, it's essential to find a group that resonates with your personal experiences and comfort level. Whether you prefer in-person interactions or the flexibility of online communities, these groups offer various resources to aid in your recovery journey.

Index

criticism
  and early narcissistic wounding 32
cultural factors
  and causes of narcissism 36
  and causes of NPD 15

DARVO (Deny, Attack, Reverse Victim
  and Offender) 19–20, 27
daughters
  and emotional incest 120, 122–6
  and narcissistic fathers 72–3, 120,
    122–6, 127–8
  and narcissistic mothers 69–70
  and psychosexual enmeshment
    127–8
death of narcissistic parent 222–5
depressive disorders
  and children of narcissistic parenting
    113, 125
  mistaken for NPD 12
developmental theories in childhood
  30–2
diagnosis of NPD 10–13
*Diagnostic and Statistical Manual of
  Mental Disorders* (DSM-III) (American
  Psychiatric Association) 3, 4, 5
dialectical behaviour therapy (DBT) 179
Dickinson, Emily 155
divorce 57
  and parental alienation 132–4
dopamine receptor genes 14
Drama of the Gifted Child, The (Miller)
  23–4

early narcissistic wounding 32–5
EMDR therapy 179
emotional exploitation
  and breaking trauma bonds 168
  and narcissistic parenting 23, 61
emotional incest
  description of 119
  fathers and daughters 122–6
  mothers and sons 126–7
  and single parents 128–9
  therapeutic options for 138
emotional suppression 125–6
empathy
  and death of narcissistic parent 224
  and narcissistic parenting 22, 60

enablers
  case study for 100–5
  management of 236–8
  in narcissistic parenting 64–5
enmeshment
  description of 119
  and golden child 121–2
  in narcissistic parent–child
    relationships 120–2, 124
  and new partners 129–32
  psychosexual enmeshment 127–8
  therapeutic options for 138
epigenetics
  and causes of NPD 15
eye movement desensitization and
  reprocessing (EMDR) 117

false self
  as coping mechanism 148–9
  description of 143, 144–5
  in families 149–50
  and golden child 147
  as survival tool 159
families *see also* children
  adapted self in 149–50
  case study for 75–111
  enablers in narcissistic parenting 64–5
  false self in 149–50
  golden child in 61–2
  impact of narcissism on 18–22
  impact of narcissistic parenting 58–61,
    65–8
  lost child in 63–4
  non-narcissistic co-parent in 65
  scapegoated child in 62–3
  survival tools 158–61
  therapeutic options for 116–17,
    138–40
  true self in 146–8, 149–50, 152
  varieties of 57–8
family therapy 117
fear
  as trauma bond creation 163
flying monkeys 21, 87–90, 91–4, 100–2
forgiveness 244–7
Freud, Sigmund 3, 30, 37, 124

Gardner, Richard A. 134
gaslighting 19, 20, 61, 162, 167–8, 188

About the author

Kathleen Saxton is a fully qualified and accredited psychotherapist and a registered member of both the UKCP and BACP. She initially trained in Psychotherapy and Counselling at Regent's University and did a further four years of study in Integrative and Humanistic Psychotherapy at the renowned CCPE in London.

She has undertaken additional training in Trauma, Complex Trauma, Anxiety, Narcissism, Couples Work, Hoarding, ADHD, Sexual Abuse, Borderline Personality Disorder and Suicide in recent years, offering Trauma Informed Therapy as a specialism.

For the last 10 years Kathleen has practiced at The Grove, The Priory and, in 2016, she co-founded her own clinical practice called Psyched Ventures in London.

Kathleen is a Board Trustee of the NSPCC, a registered pcyscho-therapist with the British Association for Performing Arts Medicine, a Fellow of the Marketing Society, a columnist for Stylist and a regular contributor for the Speakers for Schools.

Kathleen lives and practices in both London and New York.

RAISING READERS
Books Build Bright Futures

Dear Reader,

We'd love your attention for one more page to tell you about the crisis in children's reading, and what we can all do.

Studies have shown that reading for fun is the **single biggest predictor of a child's future success** – more than family circumstance, parents' educational background or income. It improves academic results, mental health, wealth, communication skills and ambition.

The number of children reading for fun is in rapid decline. Young people have a lot of competition for their time, and a worryingly high number do not have a single book at home.

Our business works extensively with schools, libraries and literacy charities, but here are some ways we can all raise more readers:

- Reading to children for just 10 minutes a day makes a difference
- Don't give up if your children aren't regular readers – there will be books for them!
- Visit bookshops and libraries to get recommendations
- Encourage them to listen to audiobooks
- Support school libraries
- Give books as gifts

Thank you for reading.
www.JoinRaisingReaders.com